THE COOKBOOK TO SERVE 2, 6 OR 24

America's Best Restaurant Recipes

Also by Barbara Kraus

The Cookbook of the United Nations
Calories and Carbohydrates

THE COOKBOOK TO SERVE 2, 6 OR 24

America's Best
Restaurant Recipes

Compiled and Tested by

BARBARA KRAUS

QUADRANGLE/ **NYT**
The New York Times Book Co.

Library of Congress Catalog Card Number: 72-90450
International Standard Book Number: 0-8129-0317-X

Design by Anita Duncan

I dedicate this book to the 3,700,000 men and women who prepare and serve almost 55 billion meals a year in the 335,300 restaurants of America. Their labors in the difficult art of food preparation and service require the utmost talent, dedication, patience—and endurance.

Barbara Kraus

Acknowledgments

Without the cooperation of the chefs, managers and owners, and others intimately involved with the creation and recording of these sought-after recipes, there would be no book. I am deeply grateful to them.

I also express my thanks to the following, whose efforts were essential to the publication of this book: Carol Barnett, Murray Cohen, Anita Duncan, Susan Friedland, Barbara Le Bow, Betty Ann and Richard Ottinger, Carrie Pavelle, Ilene Slater, Sheila Tunney and Alfred Wasserstrom.

And I am especially indebted to Tina Cassel for her enormous contribution in the exhaustive testing of these recipes, over and over and then over once again.

A Note from the Author to her Editor

I don't know if Herbert Nagourney [president of Quadrangle/The New York Times Book Co.] has told you how he came to sign me up for this cookbook. Some while back—however long it has been since Tricia Nixon and Ed Cox's wedding—I suggested to him that what was sorely needed in this proliferating cookbook market was a book that gave a recipe with its conversions to smaller and larger sizes. Herb's answer was extremely straightforward: "Who do you think buys our books—idiots? Any of our readers can multiply by two or divide by three."

I tried to explain that recipes just don't work that way. *Usually* but not always, you *can* multiply or divide by two successfully, but beyond that— watch out. It may not work.

I posed certain problems. What if a girl wants to make a special dinner for her new boy friend. She has a favorite Boeuf Bourguignonne recipe but it serves eight. Is she going to make it for eight and eat Boeuf Bourguignonne for the rest of the week? Or should she quarter the recipe and hope for the best? Suppose she's having an after-theater party for 20. Can she triple her favorite recipe?

But Herb wasn't interested. And then, there was the White House Wedding Cake catastrophe. In June 1971, the White House released to the public a recipe for a scaled-down version of Tricia's wedding cake—a "lemon-flavored pound cake" made by the White House pastry chef.

The huge cake's formidable proportions had been reduced, by ordinary division, to a family-size recipe so that just-plain-folks all around the country could enjoy a piece of Tricia's cake.

What happened was disaster.

One food reporter tested the recipe for her paper's readers and discovered that batter overflowed the pan and made utter havoc of the oven. The cake was mush on the outside and soup on the inside. Parts of the 12-by-12-inch layer burned before the suggested 45-minute cooking time was over.

Cooks and housewives all over the country who tried the cake had the same results. They ended up with a flat, gooey-looking mess that made them wonder about the White House kitchen, and caused them some concern for the welfare of the wedding guests, as well as the state of their ovens.

The White House pastry chef—more than a little discomfited by the furor his recipe was causing—issued a series of official revisions of the original recipe.

Nothing worked. There was just no saving that recipe in any of its reduced versions. The same intrepid food tester's last attempt is immortalized in this decription: "It shook like jelly but tasted like a very soft French lemon soufflé when it emerged from the oven into the light."

Newspapers had a grand time with the plight of the poor pastry chef. When I went in to see Herb, news clips in hand, he had of course already seen the stories and simply said, "You're on. Give us a cookbook."

In writing any cookbook, the author must sense what is known and what is foreign to the reader. There is no way to know the various kitchen backgrounds and expertise of the cooks who are going to use this first-of-a-kind cookbook.

Therefore, I want to reassure our readers that none of the recipes selected from restaurants are very difficult. A few recipes are tricky but helpful hints accompany those. Some take longer than others, and this is clearly stated in the preparation times, but above all, these dishes really are fun to cook and deliciously different to taste.

The recipes that were chosen are considered by me and many other food lovers to be the finest rendition or innovation of an already popular dish, or an entirely new creation. These specialties are not necessarily on the restaurants' menus now or served every day. In a very few cases the recipes are from restaurants no longer in business, but they are well-remembered culinary achievements and are included.

Barbara

Please Do Not Skip

This section includes several important things you will need to know to make the best use of this book.

Instructions for cooking the different quantities are coded by symbols and italics. The small quantity is identified by a bullet (●), the middle quantity by a triangle (▲), and the largest quantity by a square (■). Variations in utensils, ingredients, timing, and temperature for the different quantities appear in italics, preceded by one of the symbols. In the few cases where there are variations in technique, they are simply preceded by the symbol for that quantity. If you are preparing a recipe to serve six, follow the triangle throughout the recipe.

Preparation time includes cooking but not chilling or marination times. If these are significant, they appear in parentheses so the cook will not be misled. It is assumed that the cook will take advantage of available cooking and marination times within the recipe to dice, chop, prepare a sauce, etc.

Freezing time indicates an average safe period for these foods. In actuality, if your freezer is zero degrees or below, many will keep for a longer time.

Reheating time specified in "Special Notes" at the end of each recipe is based on food which is at room temperature.

Yields which are not in cup or other specific measurements, and are given only in terms of portions, have been liberally interpreted. They are large-size servings and you need not fear an extra guest. In the case of the 2–3, it means a very generous two servings or an adequate three servings. As to the conversion of the 9-inch pie to the smaller two 5-inch pies, don't be fooled by the arithmetic; they are not at all equal in quantity. A 5-inch pie is shallow and provides only 2 servings.

Utensil symbols: a fork ⎮ , spoon ⎮ , and/or knife ⎮ are indicated for each recipe to help in the selection of a buffet menu, where the only resting place for the plate may be the guest's lap.

$\boxed{S}$ the stop sign illustrates the last step in the recipe where you can best or only freeze. If the entire dish can be frozen successfully that is noted under "Special Notes" following each recipe. Food should be frozen at room temperature, not while hot.

It was sometimes difficult to decide whether to place a recipe in the appetizer, salad or entrée section, each of which might be fitting. A traditional entrée is easily made into a surprise first-course simply by serving smaller portions or by making half the recipe. You can generally multiply or divide a recipe by two (with a few special exceptions such as soufflés and breads). Why won't this work for larger multiples? The reasons are elementary to a physicist but a little more difficult for us to comprehend. They go something like this.

The internal temperature of your filled cooking vessel depends upon the total volume of food and upon the rate of cooling due to heat radiating away from the exposed free surface—that part of the preparation not in direct contact with the cooking vessel.

As the amount of food to be cooked increases, the area of the cooking vessel in contact with it will generally increase proportionately. But the free surface area generally doesn't increase in the same proportion. Therefore, the balance achieved between the heat flowing in and the heat radiating away will not be the same as in the smaller vessel. Hence, cooking times and temperatures have to be adjusted.

In the larger quantity recipes, there is a longer cooking time and more liquid evaporation. A concentration of salt or other ingredients may occur— another reason why things go awry when you simply multiply a basic recipe.

If all three quantities for a recipe are not given, this is why: If the recipe was a lot of work and/or could not be made without a significant investment in many ingredients, only a small amount of which would be used in the small-size conversion, I concluded that it was better to make a larger quantity and freeze the rest. It was the choice made in very few cases, but the recipes were good and to omit them for the sake of conformity was senseless.

There are other reasons for not making all sizes, as in recipes with sour cream sauces, which are often impossible to handle in large quantities. In other cases the utensils necessary are not usual household equipment and would require too large a financial investment for the cook. In still other recipes, the difficulty in preparing large quantities of ingredients which easily discolor, such as some fruits, made their conversion impossible aesthetically.

Equipment

Stove: All recipes were tested on a landlord-owned gas stove. No restaurant equipment was used.

Utensils: small bowl = 1 quart
              medium bowl = 1½ quarts
              large bowl = 2½ or 3½ quarts

Shallow baking dishes: These are heatproof glass vessels that are designed to be used in oven cooking.

Dutch oven: Directions to use this utensil signal you to get out a high-sided heavy pan with a cover if you do not have a Dutch oven. This type of pan is also necessary for deep frying, to prevent the fat from splattering.

Ingredients

Beef or chicken broth: You can use canned broths in place of homemade stocks, but do not substitute bouillon cubes or powder or canned consommé.

Beef tenderloin: This is generally regarded as the tenderest meat and requires less cooking time than the less expensive but still desirable cuts, eye round or top round. If you make substitutions, allow for a longer cooking time.

Butter: The recipes were tested with sweet (unsalted) butter used by many restaurants. Although there should be no trouble substituting lightly salted butter, if you are in doubt, reduce the salt initially and adjust the seasoning toward the end of the preparation.

Cream: The recipes were tested and written as they were given by the restaurants, but you can easily substitute half-and-half for cream, as in the cold soups.

Curry and other strong spices: The dishes were tasted upon completion of the recipes, and the spices and condiments reflect this procedure. If a dish is left to stand or is reheated, there may be a change in either the consistency or the pungency of some ingredient.

Egg: U.S. Graded "Large" eggs should be used. To get half an egg—break and lightly beat one egg, measure and use half.

Lemon juice: Unless fresh juice is specified, reconstituted lemon juice will do.

Seasonings: When a recipe calls for ¼–½ teaspoon, it means you should try the lower amount to make certain you don't overseason. You can build to the higher amount slowly, tasting as you go. This designation (¼–½) is only used where there is a strong taste, such as with curry or garlic.

Be sure to adjust the seasonings after you refrigerate or freeze. Temperature has an effect on taste.

Sugar: Use granulated sugar unless other is specified.

Whipped cream: The exciting differences one finds in many restaurant recipes is in the use of small amounts of varied sauces, and the same applies to the use of tiny amounts of whipped cream. You won't be able to whip ⅛ cup; you must whip at least ¼ cup in a measuring cup or other narrow bowl. You can always use the remainder for coffee or toppings.

Contents

Poultry

Meat

Vegetables, Grains and Potatoes

Salads and Relishes

Breads and Muffins

Desserts

Cakes, Pies and Cookies

Miscellaneous

THE COOKBOOK TO SERVE 2, 6 OR 24

America's Best Restaurant Recipes

APPETIZERS

Cheese Puffs

Ingredients

2-3

SAUCE

1½ Tbs butter
2 Tbs finely chopped
  onion
1½ Tbs flour
¾ cup milk
⅛ tsp salt
  pinch of freshly ground
  white pepper
1 tsp dry mustard
1 tsp water
1½ Tbs prepared mustard
1 Tb honey

PUFFS

⅓ cup water
2½ Tbs butter
⅛ tsp salt
⅓ cup flour
1 egg
2½ Tbs freshly grated Swiss
  cheese
1 tsp dry mustard
  pinch of cayenne pepper
  dash–⅛ tsp Worcester-
  shire sauce
  vegetable oil for deep
  frying

SAUCE

4 Tbs butter
¼ cup finely chopped onion
¼ cup flour
2 cups milk
¼ tsp salt
⅛ tsp freshly ground white
  pepper
1 Tb dry mustard
2 tsps water
⅓ cup prepared mustard
3 Tbs honey

PUFFS

1 cup water
8 Tbs (1 stick) butter
1 tsp salt
1 cup flour
3 eggs
½ cup freshly grated Swiss
  cheese (about 2 ozs)
1 Tb dry mustard
  pinch of cayenne pepper
¼ tsp Worcestershire
  sauce
  vegetable oil for deep
  frying

6-8

FRONTIER HOUSE, 460 Center Street, Lewiston, New York

2

Instructions

1) To make sauce: melt butter in a 1-quart saucepan.
2) Add onion; cook until tender.
3) Stir in flour and blend with a wire whisk until smooth. Cook 1 minute.
4) Add milk and cook, stirring constantly, until mixture thickens and comes to a boil. Remove from heat.
5) Add salt and pepper.
6) In a small dish mix dry mustard and water.
7) Add prepared mustard and honey to dry mustard; blend well.
8) Stir mustard mixture into sauce; blend well. Reserve.
9) For the puffs: heat water, butter and salt to the boiling point in a heavy
   ● *1 quart saucepan,* ▲ *1½-quart saucepan.*
10) Add flour all at once, beating vigorously with a wooden spoon.
11) Cook over a low heat, beating constantly, until mixture pulls away from the sides of the pan and forms a ball in the center.
12) Transfer paste to a medium bowl and add eggs, one at a time, beating well with an electric mixer after each addition. Mixture should be stiff and glossy.
13) Stir in cheese, dry mustard, cayenne and Worcestershire sauce.
14) Heat 2 inches of oil in a heavy saucepan or deep fryer to 375 degrees.
15) Drop 1 heaping teaspoon of the batter into the hot fat to make each puff. Fry 5 or 6 at a time until golden brown, about 2 to 3 minutes.
16) Cut one in half to see that it is cooked through completely. If not, lower heat slightly.
17) Drain puffs on paper towels.
18) Reheat mustard sauce over low heat, stirring occasionally. Serve puffs with hot mustard sauce.

preparation time: ● 45 minutes; ▲ 1½ hours
yield: ● 18 1-inch puffs; ▲ 40 1-inch puffs

Special Notes
- Puffs and sauce, separately packed, will freeze very well for 2 to 3 months. Thaw puffs, and warm uncovered on a tray in a preheated 350-degree oven for 5 minutes or until crisp.
- Puffs can be refrigerated and then reheated as above, but they will not be as crisp.
- Sauce will keep well refrigerated for about 1 week and would also be good served with meats and poultry.

Cheese Spread

Ingredients

4	Tbs butter, softened
8	ozs soft American cheese spread
¼	cup Worcestershire sauce
2	Tbs prepared English mustard
½	tsp garlic powder
	up to ⅛ teaspoon Tabasco
1½	Tbs kirsch

medium

large

1	cup butter (2 sticks) softened
2	lbs soft American cheese spread
1	cup Worcestershire sauce
½	cup prepared English mustard
1	tsp garlic powder
¼ – ½	tsp Tabasco
6	Tbs kirsch

✳ ROAST BEEF ROOM at the HOTEL ROOSEVELT, 45 East 45th St., New York, New York

Instructions

1) Cream butter with a wooden spoon until light in a ▲ *medium bowl* ■ *large bowl.*
2) Gradually add cheese spread, beating with a wooden spoon to blend well.
3) Slowly beat in Worcestershire sauce, mustard, garlic powder, Tabasco and kirsch.
4) Pack into crocks and chill 2 hours.
5) Serve with crackers or chips.

   preparation time (excluding chilling period): ▲ 20 minutes; ■ 30 minutes

   yield: ▲ 1½ cups; ■ 6 cups

Special Notes
- Spread will keep in refrigerator 1 to 2 weeks.
- Spread freezes very well, and will defrost in about 1 hour, if frozen in ½- to 1-cup quantities.
- Do not beat butter or cheese mixture with an electric beater or it will curdle.

Homus Tahini

Ingredients

medium

- ¾ cup dried chick-peas
- ½ tsp baking soda
- 2 garlic cloves
- 1 tsp salt
- ⅓ cup lemon juice
- ⅓ cup tahini (sesame paste)
- 1½ tsps olive oil
- 2 Tbs chopped parsley
- paprika

large

- 2 cups dried chick-peas
- 1½ tsps baking soda
- 5 garlic cloves
- 1½ Tbs salt
- 1 cup lemon juice
- 1 cup tahini (sesame paste)
- 2 Tbs olive oil
- ¼ cup chopped parsley
- paprika

MIDDLE EAST RESTAURANT, 126 Chestnut Street, Philadelphia, Pennsylvania

Instructions

1) Soak chick-peas overnight with water to cover and baking soda in a ▲ *medium bowl,* ■ *large bowl.* Add more water if it is absorbed.
2) Drain and rinse well. Place chick-peas in a ▲ *3-quart saucepan,* ■ *8-quart Dutch oven* with water to cover and simmer 1 to 1½ hours or until tender. Add more water if necessary. Drain.
3) Put chick-peas through a food mill into a ▲ *medium bowl* ■ *large bowl.*
4) In a mortar, crush garlic with salt until smooth paste is formed.
5) Beat lemon juice, tahini and garlic paste into pureed chick-peas and blend well.
6) Stir in olive oil.
7) Chill mixture thoroughly.
8) Garnish with parsley and paprika before serving as a dip, preferably with Middle Eastern bread.

    preparation time: ▲ 2 hours;   ■ 2½ hours
    yield: ▲ 1½ cups;   ■ 6 cups

Special Notes
- Tahini can be purchased in Middle Eastern grocery stores.
- If you don't have time to soak chick-peas overnight, cover with water in a saucepan, bring to a boil, cover and let stand 1 hour. Then cook as directed.
- Chick-peas are much easier to force through the food mill when hot.
- Homus Tahini keeps refrigerated 1 to 2 weeks.
- Canned chick peas are not a satisfactory substitute for the dried and soaked ones.

Mushrooms à la Grecque

Ingredients

¼	cup olive oil
¼	cup chopped onions
6	bay leaves
1	tsp curry powder
½	cup white vinegar
1	tsp sugar
⅛–¼	tsp salt
⅛	tsp freshly ground black pepper
½	lb medium mushrooms, stems removed

¾	cup olive oil
¾	cup chopped onions
12	bay leaves
1	Tb curry powder
1½	cups white vinegar
1	Tb sugar
¾–1	tsp salt
¼	tsp freshly ground black pepper
1½	lbs medium mushrooms, stems removed

3	cups olive oil
3	cups chopped onions
36	bay leaves
¼	cup curry powder
6	cups white vinegar
¼	cup sugar
1–1½	Tbs salt
1	tsp freshly ground black pepper
6	lbs medium mushrooms, stems removed

Instructions

1) Heat oil over low heat in ● *an 8-inch skillet,* ▲ *a 12-inch skillet,* ■ *an 8-quart Dutch oven.*
2) Add onions and bay leaves; cook until onions are soft.
3) Add curry powder and blend well.
4) Add vinegar, sugar, salt and pepper to taste; add the mushrooms.
5) Cover skillet and simmer over low heat ● ▲ *15 minutes,* ■ *20 minutes.*
6) Remove from heat and let cool.
7) Into a ● *small bowl,* ▲ *medium bowl,* ■ *large bowl,* pour the mushrooms with their liquid and refrigerate, covered, for 24 hours before serving.

preparation time: ● 30 minutes; ▲ 45 minutes; ■ 1¼ hours

Special Notes
- Mushrooms can be preserved. After step 5, pour hot mixture into hot sterilized jars. Use a 1-quart jar for 6; 4 1-quart jars or 8 2-pint jars for 24. Seal immediately and let cool. Mushrooms should keep indefinitely.
- Mushrooms will keep in the refrigerator for several weeks.

Oeufs Farcis Chimay

Ingredients

2   hard-boiled eggs, halved lengthwise
2   Tbs butter
2   shallots, chopped
¼   cup finely chopped mushrooms
3   Tbs light cream
1   Tb dry white wine
    pinch of salt and freshly ground white pepper

SAUCE
1   Tb butter
1   Tb flour
½   cup milk
6   Tbs freshly grated Swiss cheese
    pinch of salt and freshly ground white pepper
1   egg yolk

6   hard-boiled eggs, halved lengthwise
4   Tbs butter
6   shallots, chopped
¼   lb mushrooms, finely chopped
½   cup light cream
¼   cup dry white wine
¼   tsp salt
⅛   tsp freshly ground white pepper

6

SAUCE
2   Tbs butter
2   Tbs flour
1   cup milk
¾   cup freshly grated Swiss cheese (about 3 ozs)
¼   tsp salt
⅛   tsp freshly ground white pepper
1   egg yolk

24 hard-boiled eggs, halved lengthwise
1   lb butter
24 shallots, chopped
1   lb mushrooms, finely chopped
2   cups light cream
1   cup dry white wine
1   tsp salt
½   tsp freshly grated white pepper

SAUCE
8   Tbs (1 stick) butter
½   cup flour
4   cups milk
3   cups freshly grated Swiss cheese (about 12 ozs)
½   tsp salt
½   tsp freshly ground white pepper
4   egg yolks

※ L'ORANGERIE RESTAURANT, 419 O'Farrell Street, San Francisco, California

10

Instructions

1) Carefully remove yolks from egg halves, keeping whites intact. Press yolks through a sieve. Set aside both yolks and whites.
2) Melt butter over moderate heat in ● *an 8-inch skillet,* ▲ ■ *a 10-inch skillet.*
3) Add shallots; cook until tender.
4) Add mushrooms; cook 1 minute.
5) Stir in cream and white wine. Simmer until liquid is considerably reduced and mixture thickens. Cool.
6) Stir in sieved egg yolks to make a smooth paste.
7) Season with salt and pepper.
8) Fill the egg white cavities with the yolk mixture.
9) Preheat oven to 450 degrees.
10) To make cheese sauce: melt butter over moderate heat in a ● ▲ *1-quart saucepan,* ■ *3-quart saucepan.*
11) Stir in flour with a wire whisk and blend well. Cook 1 minute.
12) Gradually add milk and cook, stirring constantly, until thickened and mixture comes to a boil.
13) Stir in ⅓ of the cheese and cook until melted.
14) Season with salt and pepper to taste.
15) In a small bowl, beat egg yolk well.
16) Stir a little of the hot sauce into egg yolk and blend well.
17) Gradually return egg yolk mixture to saucepan, beating constantly until blended.
18) Pour half the cheese sauce onto the bottom of ● *2 small au gratin dishes,* ▲ *a 2-quart baking dish,* ■ *2 3-quart baking dishes.*
19) Arrange stuffed egg halves in baking dish.
20) Pour remaining sauce over top. Sprinkle with remaining cheese.
21) Bake in the preheated oven ● *5 to 10 minutes,* ▲ *10 to 15 minutes,* ■ *15 to 20 minutes* or until top is golden and heated through.

preparation time ● 45 minutes; ▲ 1½ hours; ■ 2½ hours

Special Notes
- Stuffed eggs, without the sauce, are good as cold hors d'oeuvres.
- The Oeufs Farcis can be made ahead and baked just before serving.
- If you have succeeded only some of the time in peeling hard-boiled eggs, try this: make sure there are no cracks in your eggs. Let eggs stand at room temperature for 12 hours. Pierce the top (large end) of the egg with a thumb tack or pin. Place eggs in a saucepan with 70-degree water to cover. Bring to a rolling boil, turn off heat, cover and let stand 15 minutes. Drain eggs, run cold water over them immediately, for at least 5 minutes. Crack on all sides and roll in hands. Starting at the top, peel eggs by working your fingernail under the membrane.

Scotch Eggs

Ingredients

2

½ lb ground lean beef
⅛ tsp minced garlic
   pinch of dry mustard
¼ tsp salt
⅛ tsp freshly ground black pepper
1 Tb chopped onion
2 hard-boiled eggs, peeled
¼ cup flour
¼–½ cup dry bread crumbs
1 egg
   vegetable oil for deep frying

6

1½ lbs ground lean beef
½ tsp minced garlic
¼ tsp dry mustard
1 tsp salt
¼ tsp freshly ground black pepper
¼ cup chopped onion
6 hard-boiled eggs, peeled
6–8 Tbs flour
½–1 cup dry bread crumbs
2 eggs
   vegetable oil for deep frying

24

6 lbs ground lean beef
1 Tb minced garlic
1 tsp dry mustard
4 tsps salt
1 tsp freshly ground black pepper
1 cup chopped onion
24 hard-boiled eggs, peeled
1 cup flour
4 cups dry bread crumbs
5 eggs
   vegetable oil for deep frying

※ THE QUORUM, Grant at Colfax, Denver, Colorado

Instructions

1) Combine and blend well the ground beef, garlic, mustard, salt, pepper and onion in a ● *small bowl,* ▲ *medium bowl,* ■ *large bowl or pot.*
2) Divide mixture evenly into ● *2 parts,* ▲ *6 parts,* ■ *24 parts.*
3) Flatten each part into a circle about ¼ inch thick.
4) Place a hard-boiled egg in the center of each meat circle, wrap meat around egg and seal edges so egg is totally enclosed.
5) Place flour and bread crumbs on separate pieces of wax paper.
6) Beat eggs in a dish.
7) Roll meat-covered eggs first in flour to coat well, then in beaten eggs, and finally in crumbs.
8) Heat 2 inches of oil in a heavy saucepan or deep fryer to 350 degrees.
9) Fry 3 to 4 eggs at a time until golden, about 4 to 5 minutes.
10) Drain on paper towels.
11) Cool. Serve at room temperature.

preparation time: ● 30 minutes; ▲ 45 minutes; ■ 2 hours
yield: ● ▲ ■ 1 egg per portion

Special Notes

• See Notes for Oeufs Farcis (page 11) on preparing and peeling hard-boiled eggs.
• Scotch eggs can be stored in refrigerator for at least 1 week, and eaten cold; however, the crust will be less crisp.
• Eggs can be stored in refrigerator after step 7 and fried when ready to serve.
• Also, try serving these eggs sliced on crackers—they are pretty as well as tasty.

Escalloped Oysters

Ingredients

2

1	8-oz can whole oysters
2	Tbs butter
1	Tb finely chopped shallots
2	tsps flour
¼	cup light cream
1	egg yolk
¼	cup dry white wine
½	tsp Worcestershire sauce
½	tsp chopped chives
	pinch of MSG (optional)
1	tsp lemon juice
	dash of Tabasco
2	Tbs saltine cracker crumbs
⅛	tsp paprika
2	slices white toast, crusts removed

6

3	8-oz cans whole oysters
6	Tbs butter
¼	cup finely chopped shallots
2	Tbs flour
¾	cup light cream
3	egg yolks
¾	cup dry white wine
1½	tsps Worcestershire sauce
1½	tsps chopped chives
⅛	tsp MSG (optional)
1	Tb lemon juice
⅛	tsp Tabasco
6	Tbs saltine cracker crumbs
¼	tsp paprika
6	slices white toast, crusts removed

24

12	8-oz cans whole oysters
1½	cups (3 sticks) butter
1	cup finely chopped shallots
½	cup flour
3	cups light cream
12	egg yolks
3	cups dry white wine
2	Tbs Worcestershire sauce
2	Tbs chopped chives
½	tsp MSG (optional)
¼	cup lemon juice
½	tsp Tabasco
1½	cups saltine cracker crumbs
2	tsps paprika
24	slices white toast, crusts removed

❄ THE GOLDEN LAMB INN, 27 South Broadway, Lebanon, Ohio

14

Instructions

1) Preheat oven to 400 degrees.
2) Drain oysters and reserve ● ¼ *cup liquid,* ▲ ¾ *cup liquid,* ■ *3 cups liquid.*
3) Melt half the butter in a ● ▲ *10-inch skillet,* ■ *8-quart Dutch oven,* and add shallots. Cook until golden.
4) Add flour and stir with a wire whisk to blend well.
5) Gradually add oyster liquid and cream and stir until smooth and thickened.
6) In a ● ▲ *small bowl,* ■ *large bowl,* combine egg yolks, wine, Worcestershire, chives, optional MSG, lemon juice and Tabasco and blend well.
7) Add slowly to cream mixture and blend well.
8) Stir in oysters. Remove from heat.
9) Pour mixture into ● *2 5-inch au gratin dishes,* ▲ *a 1½-quart casserole,* ■ *2 3-quart shallow baking dishes.*
10) Sprinkle cracker crumbs over top.
11) Sprinkle paprika over crumbs, then dot top with remaining butter.
12) Bake in the preheated oven ● *10 to 15 minutes,* ▲ *15 to 20 minutes,* ■ *20 to 25 minutes,* or until mixture is golden brown and bubbly.
13) Cut toast into triangles. Serve oysters on toast points as a first course.

preparation time: ● 30 minutes; ▲ 1 hour; ■ 1½ hours

Special Notes
- If made in advance, dish can be warmed in a preheated 300-degree oven for about 15 minutes.
- If you freeze this dish, the sauce and taste will stay intact, but the oysters will lose their firmness.

Oysters Savannah

Ingredients

2 medium-thick bacon slices, chopped
4 Tbs chopped green pepper
1 Tb chopped pimiento
⅛ tsp salt (optional)
⅛ tsp MSG (optional)
⅛ tsp paprika
pinch of freshly ground black pepper
6 large oysters on the half shell

5½ medium-thick bacon slices, chopped
1 medium green pepper, chopped
2 Tbs chopped pimiento
¼ tsp salt (optional)
¼ tsp MSG (optional)
¼ tsp paprika
⅛ tsp freshly ground black pepper
12 large oysters on the half shell

❄ THE PIRATES' HOUSE, 20 East Broad Street, Savannah, Georgia

Instructions

1) Combine bacon, green pepper, pimiento, optional salt and MSG, paprika and pepper in a ● *small bowl,* ▲ *medium bowl.*
2) Cover each oyster completely with the bacon mixture, using 1 heaping tablespoon for each.
3) Place oysters in ● *1 9-inch pie plate,* ▲ *2 9-inch pie plates.*
4) Place 1 pan at a time under a preheated broiler for 4 to 5 minutes or until bacon is brown and crisp and oysters are curled at edges. Serve immediately.

preparation time: ● 20 minutes; ▲ 30 minutes

Special Notes
● Prepared oysters will keep in the refrigerator 2 to 3 days and can be warmed by placing in a preheated 300-degree oven for 10 minutes.
● If you place the oysters on a bed of rock salt in the pan before broiling, they will keep hot much longer—very useful for a buffet.

Scallops in Green Sauce

Ingredients

½   lb bay scallops
2   Tbs lime juice
½   tsp salt
½   tsp MSG (optional)
½   cup cold water
¾   cup watercress leaves (about ½ bunch)
½   cup parsley leaves (about ½ bunch)
6   Tbs cider vinegar
⅛   tsp garlic powder
⅛   tsp MSG (optional)
⅛   tsp salt
    pinch of freshly ground black pepper
1   Tb light cream

1½   lbs bay scallops
6   Tbs lime juice
1½   tsps salt
1   tsp MSG (optional)
1½   cups cold water
2¼   cups watercress leaves (about 1½ bunches)
1½   cups parsley leaves (about 1½ bunches)
1   cup plus 2 Tbs cider vinegar
½   tsp garlic powder
½   tsp MSG (optional)
¼–½   tsp salt
⅛   tsp freshly ground black pepper
3   Tbs light cream

6

✳ LA GUARDIA TERRACE, La Guardia Airport, Flushing, New York

18

Instructions

1) Rinse scallops in cold water and place in a ● *small bowl,* ▲ *medium bowl.*
2) Add lime juice, salt, optional ● *½ teaspoon MSG,* ▲ *1 teaspoon MSG,* and water.
3) Chill 4 hours.
4) In the container of a blender combine ● all, ▲ ⅓ of the watercress, parsley, vinegar, garlic powder, and remaining optional MSG.
5) Blend at medium speed until pureed; transfer puree to a ● *small bowl,* ▲ *medium bowl.*
6) ▲ Continue pureeing the remaining ingredients in the blender, ⅓ at a time.
7) Season with salt and pepper.
8) Stir in cream and blend well.
9) Drain scallops and dry with paper towels.
10) Stir gently into green sauce.

preparation time (including marination): ● 4½ hours; ▲ 4¾ hours

Special Note
● Leftover scallops in green sauce will remain firm in the refrigerator only 2 days.

Shrimp Remoulade

2

¾ tsp dry mustard
¾ tsp prepared brown mustard
1½ tsps paprika
1½ tsps prepared horse-radish
⅓ cup olive oil
1 Tb chopped parsley
3 Tbs finely chopped green pepper
2 Tbs finely chopped celery
1 small dill pickle, finely chopped
1 scallion, finely chopped
2 Tbs tarragon vinegar
½ tsp Worcestershire sauce
¼ tsp Tabasco
¼ tsp salt
¼ tsp sugar
½ lb cleaned small or medium shrimp, cooked

6

2 tsps dry mustard
2 tsps prepared brown mustard
4½ tsps paprika
4½ tsps prepared horse-radish
1 cup olive oil
¼ cup chopped parsley
½ cup finely chopped green pepper
6 Tbs finely chopped celery
3 small dill pickles, finely chopped
3 scallions, finely chopped
6 Tbs tarragon vinegar
1½ tsps Worcestershire sauce
¾ tsp Tabasco
¾ tsp salt
¾ tsp sugar
1½ lbs cleaned small or medium shrimp, cooked

24

2 Tbs + 2 tsps dry mustard
2 Tbs + 2 tsps brown mustard
6 Tbs paprika
6 Tbs prepared horse-radish
4 cups olive oil
1 cup chopped parsley
2 cups finely chopped green pepper
1½ cups finely chopped celery
12 small dill pickles, finely chopped
1 cup finely chopped scallions
1½ cups tarragon vinegar
2 Tbs Worcestershire sauce
1 Tb Tabasco
1 Tb salt
1 Tb sugar
6 lbs cleaned small or medium shrimp, cooked

❊ CARIBBEAN ROOM at the PONTCHARTRAIN HOTEL, 2031 St. Charles Avenue, New Orleans, Louisiana

Instructions

1) Combine mustards, paprika and horseradish in a ● *small bowl,*
   ▲ *medium bowl,* ■ *large bowl or pot.*
2) Blend well with a wire whisk. Gradually add oil, beating constantly with
   the whisk until mixture is thick.
3) Stir in parsley, green pepper, celery, pickles, scallions, vinegar, Worcestershire sauce, Tabasco, salt and sugar; blend.
4) Stir in shrimp and mix to coat well.
5) Let marinate in refrigerator, covered, for 1 day.

   preparation time: ● 20 minutes; ▲ 45 minutes; ■ 1½ hours

Special Note
● Shrimp Remoulade will keep one week in refrigerator. The sauce alone
  will keep for weeks. Use as you would a vinaigrette: on eggs or asparagus;
  on crabmeat; or fill an avocado half with the Shrimp Remoulade and
  serve as a luncheon entrée, as is often done at the Caribbean Room.

Scampi Raimondo

Ingredients

2-3

1	Tb olive oil
½	lb cleaned fresh medium shrimp
2	ozs prosciutto, thinly sliced
2	ozs mozzarella chesse
½	cup brown gravy
1–1½	anchovy fillets, minced
½	tsp capers, rinsed and drained
½	small garlic clove, minced
1	tsp chopped parsley
	pinch of freshly ground black pepper

6

3	Tbs olive oil
1½	lbs cleaned fresh medium shrimp
5	ozs prosciutto, thinly sliced
4	ozs mozzarella cheese
1½	cups brown gravy
2–3	anchovy fillets, minced
1	tsp capers, rinsed and drained
1	large garlic clove, minced
1	Tb chopped parsley
¼	tsp freshly ground black pepper

24

¾	cup olive oil
6	lbs cleaned fresh medium shrimp
1	lb 4 ozs prosciutto, thinly sliced
1	lb mozzarella cheese
8	cups brown gravy
10–12	anchovies, minced
4	tsps capers, rinsed and drained
4	large garlic cloves, minced
¼	cup chopped parsley
½	tsp freshly ground black pepper

✻ GIAMBELLI'S 50TH RESTAURANT, 46 East 50th Street, New York, New York

Instructions

1) In a ● ▲ *10-inch skillet,* ■ *12-inch skillet* heat ● *1 tablespoon oil,* ▲ *3 tablespoons oil,* ■ *¼ cup oil.*
2) ● ▲ *Add shrimp* and cook, stirring constantly, until shrimp curl and are lightly browned. ■ *Add ¼ of shrimp* at a time, using more oil as needed, and proceed as above.
3) Preheat oven to 350 degrees.
4) Wrap a strip of prosciutto around each shrimp.
5) Arrange the shrimp in a single layer in a ● *9-inch square pan,* ▲ *3-quart shallow baking dish,* ■ *4 3-quart shallow baking dishes.*
6) Slice cheese ¼ inch thick and cut into 1-inch squares.
7) Place 1 cheese square over each shrimp. ☒S☒
8) Bake in the preheated oven 10 to 15 minutes or until cheese is melted.
9) Meanwhile, prepare sauce: combine brown gravy, anchovies, capers, garlic, parsley, and pepper in a ● ▲ *1-quart saucepan,* ■ *3-quart saucepan.* Cook over low heat until heated through.
10) Serve shrimp hot with anchovy-garlic sauce.

preparation time: ● 35 minutes; ▲ 1 hour; ■ 2½ hours

Special Notes
- To save time, you can assemble the scampi ahead, refrigerate and bake at the last minute while heating the sauce.
- Baked Scampi Raimondo will freeze for 1 to 2 months, but sauce should be frozen separately.

Pickled Shrimp

Ingredients

2

3	Tbs white vinegar
½	cup water
1	Tb oil
¾–1	tsp seafood seasoning
1	Tb sugar
2	dozen hot, cooked, medium shrimp

6

6	Tbs white vinegar
1	cup water
2	Tbs oil
1½–2	tsps seafood seasoning
2	Tbs sugar
6	dozen hot, cooked, medium shrimp

24

1½	cups white vinegar
1	qt water
½	cup oil
6–8	tsps seafood seasoning
½	cup sugar
24	dozen hot, cooked, medium shrimp

❊ LE FLEUR'S, Highway 55 North, Jackson, Mississippi

Instructions

1) In a ● *1-quart saucepan,* ▲ *1½-quart saucepan,* ■ *2-quart sauce-pan* combine vinegar, water, oil, seafood seasoning and sugar; bring to a boil and remove from heat.
2) Place shrimp in a ● *small bowl,* ▲ *medium bowl,* ■ *large bowl or pot;* pour hot marinade over.
3) Cover bowl with aluminum foil and let cool to room temperature.
4) Chill in refrigerator overnight. Serve as an hors d'oeuvre or as a first course on lettuce leaves with a garnish of hard-boiled eggs and small pickles.

   preparation time: ● 20 minutes; ▲ 30 minutes; ■ 1 hour

Special Notes
- Seafood seasoning is available in many fish markets. It is not the same as crab or shrimp boil or mixed pickling spices and cannot be substituted. It contains celery salt, pepper, mustard, pimiento, cloves, laurel leaves, mace, cardamom, ginger, cassia and paprika.
- Marinated shrimp will keep 1 week.
- Marinade can be reused by bringing it to a boil and pouring over cooked shrimp. In between times, always keep refrigerated.

Baked Cherrystones

2-3

2	Tbs butter, softened
2	Tbs vegetable shortening
1	small garlic clove, minced
1	Tb chopped parsley
¾	tsp Worcestershire sauce
⅛	tsp salt
¼	tsp paprika
1½	Tbs anisette liqueur
1½	Tbs gin
2½	Tbs cracker meal
12	cherrystone clams on the half shell
2–3	lemon wedges

6	Tbs butter, softened
6	Tbs vegetable shortening
2	medium garlic cloves, minced
4	Tbs chopped parsley
1	Tb Worcestershire sauce
½	tsp salt
1	tsp paprika
4½	Tbs anisette liqueur
4½	Tbs gin
6	Tbs cracker meal
36	cherrystone clams on the half shell
6–8	lemon wedges

6-8

The former JOHNSON'S HUMMOCKS, Providence, Rhode Island

Instructions

1) Preheat oven to 400 degrees.
2) In a small bowl, beat butter and shortening until creamy.
3) Add garlic, parsley, Worcestershire sauce, salt, paprika, anisette, gin and cracker meal.
4) Spoon about 1 teaspoon of dressing on each clam and spread evenly.
5) Place clams on a baking sheet; bake in the preheated oven until golden brown and edges of clams curl, about 8 to 10 minutes.
6) Garnish with lemon wedges.

preparation time: ● 30 minutes; ▲ 45 minutes
yield: ● ▲ 4 to 6 clams per portion

Special Notes
- Clam topping can be made several days ahead and refrigerated.
- Baked clams can be frozen for 2 to 3 months; thaw and reheat uncovered in a preheated 300-degree oven for 5 to 10 minutes.

Crab Rangoon

Ingredients

6

¼	lb cream cheese, softened
¼	lb cooked crabmeat
1	egg yolk
¼	tsp salt
⅛	tsp freshly ground white pepper
30	wonton skins
1	egg, beaten

SAUCE

½	cup vegetable oil
¼	cup ketchup
3	Tbs white vinegar
3	Tbs honey
1	Tb lemon juice
1	Tb soy sauce
1	tsp Worcestershire sauce
½	tsp salt
1	medium onion, grated vegetable oil for deep frying

12

½	lb cream cheese, softened
½	lb cooked crabmeat
1	egg yolk
½	tsp salt
¼	tsp freshly ground white pepper
60	wonton skins
1	egg, beaten

SAUCE

1	cup vegetable oil
½	cup ketchup
6	Tbs white vinegar
6	Tbs honey
2	Tbs lemon juice
2	Tbs soy sauce
2	tsps Worcestershire sauce
1	tsp salt
1	large onion, grated vegetable oil for deep frying

24

1	lb cream cheese, softened
1	lb cooked crabmeat
4	egg yolks
1	tsp salt
¼	tsp freshly ground white pepper
120	wonton skins
2	eggs, beaten

SAUCE

2	cups vegetable oil
1	cup ketchup
¾	cup white vinegar
¾	cup honey
¼	cup lemon juice
¼	cup soy sauce
4	tsps Worcestershire sauce
2	tsps salt
2	large onions, grated vegetable oil for deep frying

❄ DOBBS HOUSES LUAU   3135 Poplar Avenue, Memphis, Tennessee

Instructions

1) Beat cream cheese until smooth in a ● *small bowl,* ▲ *medium bowl,* ■ *large bowl.*
2) Stir in crabmeat, egg yolks, salt and white pepper.
3) Place the wonton wrapper with a corner pointing towards you on the table.
4) Put 1 teaspoon of the filling in center of bottom half of the wrapper.
5) Moisten lower 2 edges with the beaten egg.
6) Bring top point of wrapper down to bottom point and seal edges to form a triangle.
7) Brush a little egg on the front of the triangle's right corner and on the underside or back of the left corner.
8) With a twisting action, bring the two moistened surfaces together and pinch to seal.
9) To make dipping sauce: combine oil, ketchup, vinegar, honey, lemon juice, soy sauce, Worcestershire sauce and salt in a ● *small bowl,* ▲ *medium bowl,* ■ *large bowl.*
10) Add grated onion and blend well.
11) Heat 2 inches of oil in a heavy saucepan or deep fryer to 370 degrees.
12) Fry 5 or 6 wontons at a time until golden, 1 or 2 minutes.
13) Drain on paper towels and serve warm with sauce.

preparation time: ● 1½ hours; ▲ 2½ hours; ■ 3½ hours
yield: 5 per portion; ● 30 Crab Rangoons; ▲ 60 Crab Rangoons; ■ 120 Crab Rangoons

Special Notes
- Test temperature of oil with 1 wonton. If it browns too quickly, reduce heat slightly.
- Crab Rangoon freezes excellently, but keep the sauce in the refrigerator. To reheat, place wontons on a cookie sheet in a preheated 400-degree oven for 5 minutes or until crisp.

Tiki-Tiki Chicken

Ingredients

2-3

½ lb boned and skinned chicken breasts, cut in 1-inch pieces
1 Tb hoisin sauce
1 Tb gin
1 Tb ketchup
1½ tsps peanut oil
½ tsp salt
3 scallions, cut in 1-inch pieces
vegetable oil for deep frying

1½ lbs boned and skinned chicken breasts, cut in 1-inch pieces
3 Tbs hoisin sauce
3 Tbs gin
3 Tbs ketchup
4½ Tbs peanut oil
½ tsp salt
12 scallions, cut in 1-inch pieces
vegetable oil for deep frying

6-8

❄ THE ISLANDER, 385 North La Cienega Boulevard, Los Angeles, California

Instructions

1) Place chicken pieces in a   ●*medium bowl,* ▲ *large bowl.*
2) Add hoisin sauce, gin, ketchup, oil and salt; toss to coat pieces well.
3) Let marinate at room temperature for 2 hours.
4) Cut ● *16 6-inch squares* ▲ *52 6-inch squares* of heavy-duty aluminum foil.
5) Place 2 pieces of chicken with its marinade and 2 pieces of scallion in center of each square.
6) Fold square in half. ·
7) Bring the 2 opposite open ends together to the center and slip one end into the other making a packet.
8) Fold open end twice to seal.
9) Heat 2 inches of oil in a heavy saucepan or deep fryer to 375 degrees.
10) Fry 4 to 5 packets at a time for 3 minutes.
11) Drain packets. Serve hot.

preparation time (including 2-hour marination): ● 3 hours; ▲ 4½ hours

yield: ● 16 packets; ▲ 52 packets

Special Notes
- Hoisin sauce is a sweet bean sauce available in oriental markets.
- Packets can be fried in advance, kept in refrigerator and heated for 10 minutes in an oven that has been preheated to 350 degrees.
- Fried packets can be frozen for 2 months. Thaw; reheat as directed above.

Brandied Liver Pâté

Ingredients

¼ cup rendered chicken fat
¼ lb bacon, diced
¼ lb smoked ham, cubed
1 large onion, chopped
¼ lb mushrooms, chopped
¾ lb chicken livers
¼ cup brandy
2 Tbs dry sherry
⅛ tsp salt
⅛ tsp freshly ground black pepper

medium

large

½ cup rendered chicken fat
10 ozs bacon, diced
10 ozs smoked ham, cubed
2 large onions, chopped
¾ lb mushrooms, chopped
2 lbs chicken livers
10 Tbs brandy
5 Tbs dry sherry
¼ tsp salt
¼ tsp freshly ground black pepper

✳ IVANHOE RESTAURANT, 3000 North Clark Street, Chicago, Illinois

Instructions

1) Melt chicken fat over moderate heat in a ▲ *12-inch skillet,* ■ *6-quart Dutch oven.*
2) Add diced bacon; cook 5 minutes.
3) Add ham, onions and mushrooms; cook until vegetables are tender.
4) Stir in chicken livers; cook 10 to 15 minutes or until livers are brown outside and slightly pink within.
5) Stir in brandy, sherry, salt and pepper; cook 2 minutes longer.
6) Put mixture through a meat grinder to make a paste.
7) Pack pâté into crocks or a bowl and chill overnight. Serve as a spread with crackers.

preparation time: ▲ 45 minutes; ■ 1½ hours
yield: ▲ 3 cups; ■ 6 cups

Special Note
• This is a valuable spread to have on hand for guests: freeze in small crocks or ½-cup soufflé dishes. Defrosting takes about 1 hour in this size. In the refrigerator, pâté will keep only 3 or 4 days.

Pâté Maison

Ingredients

PARISIAN SPICE

¼	cup salt	⅛	tsp ground nutmeg
1½	tsps ground cinnamon	¾	tsp crumbled bay leaf
¾	tsp ground mace	¾	tsp dried rosemary
½	tsp paprika	¾	tsp dried basil
½	tsp ground cloves	¾	tsp dried thyme
¼	tsp freshly ground white pepper		
⅛	tsp ground allspice		

3   Tbs rendered chicken fat
1   cup chopped onions
½   lb chicken livers
1½   cups diced cooked meat (any combination of chicken, beef, pork, turkey, etc.)
12   Tbs (1½ sticks) butter, softened
½   cup rendered chicken fat, at room temperature
3   Tbs Cognac
1–1½ Tbs Parisian spice (see recipe)

M

6   Tbs rendered chicken fat
2   cups chopped onions
1   lb chicken livers
3   cups diced cooked meat (any combination of chicken, beef, pork, turkey, etc.)
1½   cups (3 sticks) butter, softened
1   cup rendered chicken fat, at room temperature
6   Tbs Cognac
2–2½ Tbs Parisian spice (see recipe)

❆ THE BAKERY RESTAURANT, 2218 North Lincoln Avenue, Chicago, Illinois

Instructions

1) To make Parisian spice: combine salt, cinnamon, mace, paprika, cloves, pepper, allspice and nutmeg in a small bowl.
2) Chop crumbled bay leaf, rosemary, basil, and thyme with a food chopper until it is very fine, almost ground.
3) Combine spices in bowl; blend well. Store in a covered jar and use as needed.
4) Melt the ▲ *3 tablespoons chicken fat,* ■ *6 tablespoons chicken fat* in a 10-inch skillet over moderate heat.
5) Add onion and cook until tender.
6) Add chicken livers; sauté, stirring occasionally, until brown on the outside and slightly pink within, about 8 to 10 minutes. Let mixture cool slightly.
7) Put chicken liver mixture and cooked meat through the fine blade of a food grinder; place mixture in a ▲ *medium bowl,* ■ *large bowl.*
8) Add butter and remaining chicken fat.
9) Beat with an electric mixer until mixture is light.
10) Add Cognac and Parisian spice; blend well.
11) Pack mixture into a soufflé dish or individual crocks. Chill 3 to 4 hours before serving. Serve with crusty French bread and baby gherkins.

   preparation time: ▲ 1½ hours; ■ 2 hours
   yield: ▲ 3½ cups; ■ 8 cups

Special Note
• Pâté will keep 1 week in the refrigerator and frozen for 2 to 3 months.

Pâté Maison

Ingredients

small

8	Tbs (1 stick) butter
1	small onion, chopped
½	lb chicken livers
1	small tart apple, unpeeled, cored and sliced
2	Tbs dry sherry
2	Tbs Madeira
¼	tsp salt
⅛	tsp freshly ground black pepper
2	hard-boiled eggs, coarsely chopped

1	cup (2 sticks) butter
1	medium onion, chopped
1	lb chicken livers
1½	medium tart apples, unpeeled, cored and sliced
¼	cup dry sherry
¼	cup Madeira
½	tsp salt
¼	tsp freshly ground black pepper
4	hard-boiled eggs, coarsely chopped

medium

✽ THE COMPOUND, 653 Canyon Road, Sante Fe, New Mexico

Instructions

1) Melt half the butter over low heat in a ● *10-inch skillet,* ▲ *12-inch skillet.*
2) Add onion and chicken livers; cook until onions are tender.
3) Add apple slices, sherry and Madeira.
4) Cook over moderate heat, stirring occasionally, until chicken livers are brown on the outside and slightly pink within, and liquid is reduced by half.
5) Season to taste with salt and pepper.
6) Add chopped eggs.
7) Put mixture through the finest blade of a meat grinder twice.
8) Pack mixture into a ● *2-cup crock,* ▲ *1-quart crock.*
9) Melt the remaining butter and pour over the crock.
10) Chill 2 to 3 hours before serving.
11) Serve pâté with rye toast, lemon wedges and finely chopped onion.

preparation time: ● 1 hour; ▲ 1½ hours
yield: ● 2 cups; ▲ 4 cups

Special Notes
● Pâté will keep in refrigerator 4 to 5 days.
● As this pâté freezes beautifully, and takes no more than 2 hours to defrost, it's good insurance against unexpected guests. If you intend to freeze it, pack pâté into individual ½-cup crocks.

Beef with Sesame Seeds

Ingredients

2-3

¼	cup chopped scallions
2	Tbs chopped onions
2	Tbs soy sauce
1	Tb sesame oil
1	Tb toasted sesame seeds
2	tsps sugar
⅛	tsp minced garlic
⅛	tsp MSG (optional)
½	lb boneless lean beef cut into strips 1 inch long and ¼ inch thick
2	Tbs vegetable oil

6

½	cup chopped scallions
¼	cup chopped onions
¼	cup soy sauce
2	Tbs sesame oil
2	Tbs toasted sesame seeds
4	tsps sugar
1	large garlic clove, minced
¼	tsp MSG (optional)
1	lb boneless lean beef cut into strips 1 inch long and ¼ inch thick
¼	cup vegetable oil

24

2	cups chopped scallions
1	cup chopped onions
1	cup soy sauce
½	cup sesame oil
½	cup toasted sesame seeds
5	Tbs sugar
4	large garlic cloves, minced
½	tsp MSG (optional)
4	lbs boneless lean beef cut into strips 1 inch long and ¼ inch thick
½	cup vegetable oil

※ HALEKULANI HOTEL, Coral Lanai, 2199 Kalia Road, Honolulu, Hawaii

Instructions

1) Combine scallions, onions, soy sauce, sesame oil, sesame seeds, sugar, garlic and optional MSG in a ● *small bowl,* ▲ *medium bowl,* ■ *large bowl or pot.*
2) Add beef strips and coat them well.
3) Let stand at room temperature, stirring occasionally, for 20 minutes.
4) In ● *an 8-inch skillet,* ▲ *a 10-inch skillet,* ■ *a 12-inch skillet* heat ● ▲ *half,* ■ *¼* the oil.
5) Add enough beef strips to make a single layer in the pan.
6) Cook until lightly browned on one side, turn and cook to desired doneness. Remove to a platter.
7) Repeat with remaining oil and meat.
8) Add sauce and vegetables in bowl to skillet and cook until heated through. Pour sauce over beef strips.

preparation time: ● 45 minutes; ▲ 1 hour; ■ 2 hours
yield: ● 2 to 3 portions as hors d'oeuvre; ▲ 6 portions as hors d'oeuvre or 2 to 3 as entrée, with rice; ■ 24 portions as hors d'oeuvre or 12 as entrée, with rice

Special Notes
● Meat is much easier to slice if it is cut when partially frozen.
● Sesame seeds are toasted according to directions for toasting almonds in Venetian Creme Torte (page 312).
● The beef can be reheated in the top of a double boiler over simmering water or in a preheated 300-degree oven, covered, for 10 to 15 minutes.
● This dish will keep 1 week in the refrigerator; or frozen for 2 to 3 months.

Sauerkraut Balls

Ingredients

1	cup sauerkraut, drained
3	Tbs butter
1	small onion, chopped
½	cup finely chopped ham
½	cup finely chopped lean corned beef
1	small garlic clove, minced
3	Tbs flour
2	Tbs chopped parsley
¼	cup beef broth
1	egg
½	cup flour
¾	cup milk
¾	cup dry bread crumbs
	vegetable oil for deep frying

M

2½	cups sauerkraut, drained
8	Tbs (1 stick) butter
2	medium onions, chopped
1½	cups finely chopped ham
1½	cups finely chopped lean corned beef
2	garlic cloves, minced
9	Tbs flour
6	Tbs chopped parsley
¾	cup beef broth
2	eggs
1	cup flour
1½	cups milk
2	cups dry bread crumbs
	vegetable oil for deep frying

6	cups sauerkraut, drained
1	cup (2 sticks) butter
6	medium onions, chopped
3	cups finely chopped ham
3	cups finely chopped lean corned beef
4	large garlic cloves, minced
1	cup flour
¾	cup chopped parsley
1½	cups beef broth
4	eggs
2	cups flour
3	cups milk
4	cups dry bread crumbs
	vegetable oil for deep frying

❈ The former TOM BROWN'S COACHLIGHT RESTAURANT AND LOUNGE, Chicago, Illinois

Instructions

1) Grind sauerkraut in a meat grinder using the finest blade and reserve.
2) Melt butter over moderate heat in a ● *10-inch skillet,* ▲ *4-quart Dutch oven;* ■ *8-quart Dutch oven.*
3) Add onions and cook until tender.
4) Add ham, corned beef and garlic; cook 5 minutes, stirring occasionally.
5) Sprinkle ● *3 tablespoons flour,* ▲ *9 tablespoons flour,* ■ *1 cup flour,* over meat mixture. Stir well and cook 1 minute.
6) Add sauerkraut, parsley and beef broth; cook until thickened, stirring constantly—mixture will be very thick.
7) Spread the mixture into ● *2-quart shallow baking dish,* ▲ *jelly-roll pan, 15 by 11 inches,* ■ *2 jelly-roll pans,* 15 by 11 inches each.
8) Refrigerate 1 hour, or until cool.
9) Shape the mixture into 1-inch balls.
10) Beat eggs until blended in a ● ▲ *medium bowl,* ■ *large bowl.*
11) Gradually blend in remaining flour. Add milk gradually, beating with a wire whisk until mixture is smooth.
12) Dip balls in batter, coat evenly, and roll in bread crumbs.
13) Heat 2 inches of oil in a heavy saucepan or deep fryer to 375 degrees.
14) Fry 5 to 6 balls at a time about 2 to 3 minutes or until golden brown.
15) Drain on paper towels. Serve immediately.

preparation time (including 1-hour chilling period): ● 2 hours; ▲ 2½ hours; ■ 3½ hours

yield: ● 18 Sauerkraut Balls; ▲ 48 Sauerkraut Balls; ■ 110 Sauerkraut Balls

Special Notes
- To test for frying, let one ball brown. If it has not cooked through; reduce temperature 25 degrees and test again.
- Uncooked, the sauerkraut balls can be frozen after step 9.
- Cooked sauerkraut balls can be frozen after they are completely cooled. Separate layers of balls with wax paper. To reheat, thaw and warm uncovered in a preheated 400-degree oven 5 minutes or until crisp.

Frittura Delizie Romano

Ingredients

1	10-oz package frozen chopped spinach
6	Tbs ricotta cheese
¼	cup freshly grated romano or Parmesan cheese
¼	cup dry bread crumbs
	pinch of MSG (optional)
⅛	tsp salt
	pinch of freshly ground white pepper
1	egg, beaten
2	Tbs flour
	vegetable oil for deep frying
1	cup tomato sauce

2	10-oz packages frozen chopped spinach
¾	cup ricotta cheese
½	cup freshly grated romano or Parmesan cheese
½	cup dry bread crumbs
⅛	tsp MSG (optional)
¼	tsp salt
⅛	tsp freshly ground white pepper
2	eggs, beaten
¼	cup flour
	vegetable oil for deep frying
3	cups tomato sauce

6

8	10-oz packages frozen chopped spinach
3	cups (22 ozs) ricotta cheese
1½	cups freshly grated romano or Parmesan cheese
1½	cups dry bread crumbs
½	tsp MSG (optional)
1	tsp salt
¼–½	tsp freshly ground white pepper
8	eggs, beaten
1	cup flour
	vegetable oil for deep frying
10–12	cups tomato sauce

❄ MARIO'S, 135 Turtle Creek Village, Dallas, Texas

Instructions

1) Cook spinach according to package directions. Drain well in a strainer, squeezing out all liquid with the back of a spoon.
2) Combine spinach, ricotta, romano or Parmesan cheese, bread crumbs, optional MSG, salt, pepper and eggs in a ● ▲ *medium bowl,* ■ *large bowl or pot.*
3) Lightly flour your hands and shape mixture into 1½-inch ovals.
4) Roll ovals lightly in flour.
5) Heat 2 inches of oil in a heavy saucepan or deep fryer to 350 degrees.
6) Fry 5 or 6 balls at a time for 3 to 4 minutes or until lightly brown.
7) Drain on paper towels.
8) Serve with tomato sauce, using ⅓ to ½ cup per serving.

preparation time: ● 30 minutes; ▲ 1 hour; ■ 2 hours
yield: ● 15 balls; ▲ 30 balls; ■ 120 balls

Special Notes
- Although the spinach balls will keep for a week in the refrigerator, their texture will be less crisp than the freshly fried. Preferably freeze them, for as long as 2 or 3 months. Thaw and reheat uncovered in a preheated 350-degree oven for 5 to 10 minutes, until heated through and crisp once again. If you have had them in the refrigerator, reheat as above, or fry in a lightly buttered skillet.
- The spinach balls are also good served as a side dish with poultry or roasts.

Spinach and Cheese Pie

Ingredients

6

1½	Tbs snipped fresh dill
2	Tbs chopped Italian parsley
3	Tbs chopped scallions
½	10-oz package frozen leaf spinach, cooked and squeezed dry
¼	cup olive oil
1½	eggs, beaten
¼	lb feta cheese, crumbled
4	Tbs butter, melted
¼	lb phyllo pastry sheets

24

9	Tbs snipped fresh dill
¾	cup chopped Italian parsley
1	cup + 2 Tbs chopped scallions
3	10-oz packages frozen leaf spinach, cooked and squeezed dry
1½	cups olive oil
9	eggs, beaten
1½	lbs feta cheese, crumbled
1½	cups (3 sticks) butter, melted
1½	lbs phyllo pastry sheets

PARADISE RESTAURANT, 347 West 41 Street, New York City, New York

Instructions

1) Preheat oven to 350 degrees.
2) Combine dill, parsley, scallions and spinach in a ▲ *small bowl*, ■ *large bowl;* blend well.
3) Add oil and blend.
4) Stir in beaten eggs and feta cheese.
5) With a little of the melted butter, brush the bottom of an ▲ *8-by-8-inch square cake pan,* ■ *3 2-quart shallow baking dishes, dividing ingredients evenly between them.*
6) Place 1 sheet of the phyllo on the bottom of the pan, folding the edges to fit against the insides of the pan—no pastry should be above the dish.
7) Brush the pastry sheet thoroughly with butter.
8) Place a second sheet on top of the first, fold edges, brush with butter. Repeat process until half the pastry is in the dish, brushing with butter between each sheet.
9) Pour spinach mixture over pastry.
10) Place 1 sheet of phyllo over spinach mixture fitting it into pan so that it touches the spinach filling and the edges are not sticking out of pan. Fold pastry down against insides of pan, if necessary.
11) Brush with some of the melted butter.
12) Repeat process until all the pastry is used, brushing with butter between each sheet and the top of the final sheet.
13) Bake in the preheated oven 30 minutes or until golden.
14) Cut into pieces approximately 2 by 4 inches and serve immediately.

preparation time: 1½ hours; ■ 2½ hours
yield: ▲ 8 portions ■ 30 portions

Special Notes
- Phyllo pastry sheets can be bought frozen in gourmet and Greek food stores.
- Leftover pie can be frozen for 2 to 3 months. Thaw and place in a preheated 325-degree oven uncovered for 10 to 15 minutes, until thoroughly heated and crisp.

Veal Mousse with Paprika Sauce

SAUCE

4	Tbs butter (½ stick)
2	large shallots, chopped
1	medium carrot, chopped
1	medium onion, chopped
½	celery stalk, chopped
1½	tsps sweet Hungarian paprika
½	tsp salt
1	cup dry white wine
2½	cups chicken broth
½	tsp arrowroot
1	tsp water
1	cup sour cream

MOUSSE

1	lb finely ground lean veal
1	tsp salt
1	tsp freshly ground black pepper
	pinch of ground nutmeg
2	eggs
1½	cups heavy cream

LE MADRIGAL, 216 East 53rd Street, New York, New York

Instructions

1) Melt butter in a 2-quart saucepan.
2) Add shallots, carrot, onion, celery, paprika and salt. Cover pan tightly and cook over low heat for 20 minutes.
3) Add white wine and chicken broth, bring mixture to a boil, and reduce by half (about 1½ cups) over high heat.
4) Strain sauce through a sieve, discard vegetables, and pour liquid into a 1-quart saucepan.
5) Dissolve arrowroot in water.
6) Add to hot liquid, stirring constantly.
7) Boil 1 minute, reduce heat to low, and simmer, partially covered, 45 minutes.
8) Preheat oven to 375 degrees.
9) While sauce is cooking, make veal mousse. Combine ground veal in a medium bowl with salt, pepper and nutmeg; blend well.
10) Beat in 1 egg at a time, very thoroughly.
11) Gradually beat in cream until mixture is smooth.
12) Spoon mixture into a loaf pan, 10 by 3⅜ by 2⅝ inches. Cover with aluminum foil.
13) Place loaf pan in a 2-quart shallow baking dish and fill dish with hot water to come ⅔ up the outside of the loaf pan.
14) Bake in the preheated oven 35 to 45 minutes, or until puffed and set.
15) Drain excess fat from pan. Loosen around edges with a knife and turn out on a warm serving platter. Set aside and complete sauce.
16) Put sour cream in a small bowl. Add a little of the hot sauce and blend well.
17) Off heat, gradually add sour cream to hot sauce, stirring constantly. Sauce must not boil or it will curdle.
18) Slice the mousse and serve with paprika sauce and rice.

preparation time: 2 hours

Special Notes
- If you do not have arrowroot, cornstarch can be substituted.
- Mousse keeps well in refrigerator. It can be reheated by covering with aluminum foil and warming in a preheated 325-degree oven 10 minutes. However, it will not have as light a texture as when freshly made. Sauce, too, should be carefully reheated in a double boiler over simmering water.

SOUPS

Bulgarian Cucumber and Yogurt Soup

Ingredients

1½ cups (about 1 large) peeled, diced cucumber
1 tsp salt
¼ tsp freshly ground black pepper
¼ cup chopped walnuts
2 Tbs olive oil
1 garlic clove, pressed
2 Tbs snipped fresh dill
1 pint plain yogurt

3 cups (about 2 large) peeled, diced cucumber
2 tsps salt
½ tsp freshly ground black pepper
½ cup chopped walnuts
¼ cup olive oil
2 garlic cloves, pressed
¼ cup snipped fresh dill
1 qt plain yogurt

6

24

15 cups (about 10 large) peeled, diced cucumbers
6 tsps salt
2 tsps freshly ground black pepper
2½ cups chopped walnuts
1¼ cups olive oil
10 garlic cloves, pressed
1¼ cups chopped snipped fresh dill
3 qts plain yogurt

❉ LICKETY SPLIT, corner of 4th and South streets, Philadelphia, Pennsylvania

Instructions

1) Combine and blend well the cucumber, salt, pepper, walnuts, olive oil, garlic and dill in a ● *small bowl,* ▲ *medium bowl,* ■ *large bowl.*
2) Cover and refrigerate 12 hours. Do not drain. Add yogurt; mix thoroughly.

preparation time (excluding refrigeration period): ● 15 minutes; ▲ 30 minutes; ■ 1½ hours
yield: ● 3 cups; ▲ 6 cups; ■ 28 cups

Special Note
● Soup will keep in refrigerator 2 to 3 weeks, as long as commercial yogurt.

Iced Lemon Soup

Ingredients

1½	tsps cornstarch
1	cup chicken broth
½	cup light cream
1	egg yolk
½	cup lemon juice
	pinch of cayenne pepper
	lemon slices
	chopped parsley

1	Tb + 1 tsp cornstarch
2⅔	cups chicken broth
1⅓	cups light cream
4	egg yolks
1⅓	cups lemon juice
	pinch of cayenne pepper
	lemon slices
	chopped parsley

24

⅓	cup cornstarch
2½	qts chicken broth
5	cups light cream
16	egg yolks
2¾	cups lemon juice
⅛–¼	tsp cayenne pepper
	lemon slices
	chopped parsley

✳ OLD DROVERS INN, Old Drovers Inn Road, Dover Plains, New York

Instructions

1) Place cornstarch in a ● *1-quart saucepan,* ▲ *2½-quart saucepan,* ■ *8-quart Dutch oven.* Slowly add chicken broth; stir until smooth.
2) Cook over moderate heat, stirring constantly, until mixture thickens and comes to a boil. Remove from heat.
3) Add cream.
4) Beat egg yolks in a small bowl.
5) Pour some of the hot soup into yolks, beating constantly until smooth.
6) Slowly, return mixture to soup, stirring constantly so that the eggs will not curdle.
7) Gradually add lemon juice and cayenne.
8) Cool and chill in refrigerator for at least ● *6 hours,* ▲ *8 hours,* ■ *10 hours.*
9) Serve soup cold, garnished with lemon slices and chopped parsley.

preparation time (excluding chilling period): ● 20 minutes; ▲ 35 minutes; ■ 1 hour

yield: ● 2 cups; ▲ 6 cups; ■ 24 cups

Special Note
● Unfortunately, this soup cannot be frozen, but it will keep in the refrigerator for 3 or 4 days.

Cucumber Soup

Ingredients

1⅓	medium cucumbers
1	Tb butter
1	small bay leaf
½	medium leek, thinly sliced
1	Tb flour
1	tsp salt
1⅓	cups chicken broth
½	cup light cream
¾	tsp lemon juice
1	Tb snipped fresh dill
2	Tbs sour cream

4	medium cucumbers
4	Tbs butter
2	medium bay leaves
1⅓	medium leeks, thinly sliced
2	Tbs + 2 tsps flour
2	tsps salt
4	cups chicken broth
1⅓	cups light cream
2	tsps lemon juice
3	Tbs snipped fresh dill
6	Tbs sour cream

6

15	medium cucumbers
⅔	cup butter
5	large bay leaves
5	medium leeks, thinly sliced
⅓	cup flour
5	tsps salt
15	cups chicken broth
3¾	cups light cream
1	Tb + 1 tsp lemon juice
¾	cup snipped fresh dill
1½	cups sour cream

SCANDIA, 9040 Sunset Boulevard, Los Angeles, California

Instructions

1) Peel and thinly slice ● *1 cucumber,* ▲ *3 cucumbers,* ■ *10 cucumbers.*
2) Melt butter over low heat in a ● *1-quart saucepan,* ▲ *2½ quart saucepan,* ■ *8-quart Dutch oven.*
3) Add cucumber slices, bay leaves and leeks; cook until tender.
4) Add flour and salt; blend with wire whisk.
5) Gradually add chicken broth, stirring constantly, until blended.
6) Cook until soup thickens and comes to a boil, stirring occasionally.
7) Simmer ● ▲ *10 minutes,* ■ *20 minutes.*
8) Pass soup through a food mill, cool and refrigerate for 3 hours. ⑤
9) Peel, seed and coarsely grate the remaining cucumber(s).
10) Dry grated cucumber between paper towels.
11) Stir grated cucumber, cream and lemon juice into chilled soup.
12) Taste for seasoning.
13) Sprinkle chopped dill over each serving and top with 1 tablespoon sour cream.

preparation time (including 3-hour chilling period): ● 3½ hours; ▲ 4 hours; ■ 6 hours
yield: ● 2 cups; ▲ 6 cups; ■ 6 quarts

Special Notes
- Scandia's cucumber soup will keep about 1 week refrigerated.
- Soup may be frozen after step 8. But do not peel the reserved cucumber— maining instructions.
leave that for the day you finish making the soup. Thaw, and follow re-

Iced Avocado Cream

Ingredients

2

1	medium ripe avocado
1	small garlic clove, minced
½	cup light cream
2	Tbs lemon juice
1	cup chicken broth
2	Tbs dry sherry
¼	tsp salt
⅛–¼	tsp freshly ground black pepper
¼	tsp MSG (optional)
2	Tbs chopped scallions

6

2	large ripe avocados
1	large garlic clove, minced
1	cup light cream
4	Tbs lemon juice
2	cups chicken broth
3	Tbs dry sherry
½	tsp salt
¼	tsp freshly ground black pepper
¼	tsp MSG (optional)
4	Tbs chopped scallions

✻ BEN GROSS FAMOUS RESTAURANT, 822 Lincoln Highway West, Irwin, Pennsylvania

✳Ben Gross Famous Restaurant

Instructions

1) Peel avocados and cut in half. Remove stone from center.
2) Put ¾ of the avocado flesh into blender; reserve the rest.
3) Add garlic, half the cream, 1 tablespoon of lemon juice and chicken broth.
4) Blend at medium speed for a few seconds, until mixture is smooth.
5) Pour mixture into a ● *small bowl,* ▲ *medium bowl.*
6) Add remaining cream and lemon juice, and sherry; mix well.
7) Season to taste with salt, pepper and optional MSG.
8) Chill several hours, covered.
9) With a small melon-ball scoop, cut balls out of the reserved avocado flesh.
10) Serve soup garnished with avocado balls and scallions.

preparation time: ● 30 minutes;   ▲ 45 minutes

Special Note
● To keep avocado from turning brown, dip it in a little lemon juice.

Gazpacho

Ingredients

2

1 small garlic clove, halved
1 cup chilled tomato juice
1 medium tomato, peeled, seeded and chopped
⅓ cup peeled, seeded and chopped cucumber
⅓ cup chopped green pepper
1 tsp chopped parsley
1 tsp white vinegar
2 tsps lemon juice
½ tsp Worcestershire sauce
  dash of Tabasco
¼ tsp salt
⅛ tsp freshly ground black pepper
  unflavored croutons for garnish

6

1 garlic clove, halved
3 cups chilled tomato juice
3 medium tomatoes, peeled, seeded and chopped
1 medium cucumber, peeled, seeded and chopped
1 medium green pepper, chopped
1 Tb chopped parsley
1 Tb white vinegar
2 Tbs lemon juice
1 tsp Worcestershire sauce
  dash of Tabasco
½ tsp salt
¼ tsp freshly ground black pepper
  unflavored croutons for garnish

24

2 garlic cloves, halved
3 qts chilled tomato juice
12 medium tomatoes, peeled, seeded and chopped
3 medium cucumbers, peeled, seeded and chopped
3 medium green peppers, chopped
¼ cup chopped parsley
¼ cup white vinegar
½ cup lemon juice
4 tsps Worcestershire sauce
⅛–¼ tsp Tabasco
2 tsps salt
½–1 tsp freshly ground black pepper
  unflavored croutons for garnish

※ THE QUORUM, Grant at Colfax, Denver, Colorado

Instructions

1) With the cut side of garlic, rub the inside of a ● *small bowl,* ▲ *medium bowl,* ■ *large bowl.* Discard garlic.
2) Pour chilled tomato juice into bowl.
3) Add tomatoes, cucumber, green pepper, parsley, vinegar, lemon juice, Worcestershire sauce, Tabasco, salt and pepper.
4) Blend well and chill.
5) Garnish each portion with croutons.

preparation time: ● 30 minutes; ▲ 45 minutes; ■ 1¼ hours
yield: ● 2 cups; ▲ 6 cups; ■ 32 cups

Special Notes
- The soup gets spicier as it stands; therefore, be careful not to overseason at the beginning, and adjust seasoning only after a few hours.
- If soup is too spicy, add a little more tomato juice.
- Soup keeps in refrigerator for 4 to 5 days.

Cold Bisque of Parsley

Ingredients

1	Tb butter
2	large shallots, minced
1	medium potato, peeled and sliced
2	cups chicken broth
½	cup firmly packed chopped parsley
	salt and freshly ground black pepper
¼–½	cup light cream
1	Tb sour cream
⅛	tsp chopped chives

2	Tbs butter
6	large shallots, minced
2	medium potatoes (about ¾ lb), peeled and sliced
4	cups chicken broth
1	cup firmly packed chopped parsley
	salt and freshly ground black pepper
½–1	cup light cream
2	Tbs sour cream
¼	tsp chopped chives

6

8	Tbs (1 stick) butter
1	cup minced shallots (about 20)
8	medium potatoes (about 3 lbs), peeled and sliced
3	qts chicken broth
4	cups firmly packed chopped parsley
	salt and freshly ground black pepper
2–4	cups light cream
½	cup sour cream
1	tsp chopped chives

※ LOVETT'S BY LAFAYETTE BROOK, junction routes 18 and 141, Franconia, New Hampshire

Instructions

1) Melt butter over low heat in a ● *1-quart saucepan,* ▲ *2-quart saucepan,* ■ *8-quart Dutch oven.*
2) Add shallots; cook until tender.
3) Add potatoes and chicken broth; cover and simmer until potatoes are tender, about ● *10 to 15 minutes,* ▲ *25 minutes,* ■ *35 minutes.*
4) Cool slightly.
5) Add parsley and transfer soup to container of blender, filling it only to ⅓ its capacity. Puree until smooth and pour into a ● *small bowl,* ▲ *medium bowl,* ■ *large bowl.*
6) Continue pureeing the remaining soup.
7) Season with salt and pepper to taste. ⬚S
8) Stir in cream.
9) Chill 3 hours or overnight.
10) Serve in chilled cups topped with a teaspoon of sour cream and a sprinkling of chopped chives.

preparation time (excluding chilling period): ● 40 minutes, ▲ 1 hour; ■ 1½ hours

yield: ● 2½ cups, ▲ 6 cups, ■ 24 cups

Special Notes
- This soup is equally good without the cream, hot or cold.
- Soup can be frozen after step 7. To make soup smooth (it's grainy after freezing), thaw and reheat, stirring occasionally. Cool, then add the cream.

Onion Soup

2 Tbs bacon drippings
3 cups (3 large) thinly sliced onions
1½ Tbs flour
⅛–¼ tsp salt
pinch of freshly ground black pepper
⅛ tsp dried thyme
3 cups chicken broth
¾ cup dry white wine
2–3 1-inch slices day-old French bread, toasted
½–¾ cup coarsely grated Gruyère cheese

4 Tbs bacon drippings
6 cups (6 large) thinly sliced onions
3 Tbs flour
¼–½ tsp salt
⅛ tsp freshly ground black pepper
¼ tsp dried thyme
6 cups chicken broth
1½ cups dry white wine
6 1-inch slices day-old French bread, toasted
1½ cups coarsely grated Gruyère cheese

6

¾ cup bacon drippings
24 cups (24 large) thinly sliced onions
¾ cup flour
1–2 tsps salt
¼–½ tsp freshly ground black pepper
1 tsp dried thyme
6 qts chicken broth
6 cups dry white wine
24 1-inch slices day-old French bread, toasted
6 cups coarsely grated Gruyère cheese

❋ LA GRANDE SEINE, at the John F. Kennedy Center for the Performing Arts, Washington, D.C.

Instructions

1) Heat bacon drippings in a ● *1½-quart saucepan,* ▲ *4-quart Dutch oven or heavy saucepan,* ■ *2 7-quart Dutch ovens, dividing ingredients evenly between them.*
2) Add onions; cook, stirring occasionally, until golden brown.
3) Add flour; blend well.
4) Add salt, pepper and thyme; blend well.
5) Add chicken broth and wine.
6 Cover and simmer ● ▲ *30 minutes,* ■ *45 minutes.* Correct seasoning. ⬚S⬚
7) Preheat oven to 400 degrees.
8) Pour soup into individual soup pots or an ovenproof tureen.
9) Top each portion with a slice of toasted French bread.
10) Sprinkle ¼ cup cheese over each slice of bread.
11) Bake in the preheated oven 10 to 15 minutes or until cheese is melted.

preparation time: ● 1¼ hours; ▲ 1¾ hours; ■ 3 hours
yield: ● 4 cups; ▲ 8 cups; ■ 32 cups

Special Notes
- Some people save the fat left from frying bacon in a jar and store in the refrigerator for cooking purposes. If you have not done this, fry some bacon strips and use bacon for something else. Each slice of bacon will yield about 1 tablespoon of drippings.
- Soup will keep in the refrigerator 1 to 2 weeks; and in the freezer for 2 to 3 months.

Armenian Lemon and Meatball Soup

Ingredients

2

1/4	lb ground lean lamb
2	Tbs finely chopped onion
1/4	cup raw, long-grain rice
1/4	cup finely chopped parsley
1/4	tsp salt
	pinch of freshly ground black pepper
1	qt chicken broth
2	Tbs flour
2	egg yolks
2 1/2	Tbs lemon juice

6

1/2	lb ground lean lamb
1/4	cup finely chopped onion
1/2	cup raw, long-grain rice
1/2	cup finely chopped parsley
1/2	tsp salt
1/8	tsp freshly ground black pepper
2	qts chicken broth
1/4	cup flour
4	egg yolks
1/3	cup lemon juice

24

2	lbs ground lean lamb
1	cup finely chopped onion
2	cups raw, long-grain rice
2	cups finely chopped parsley
2	tsps salt
1/4	tsp freshly ground black pepper
8	qts chicken broth
3/4	cup flour
12	egg yolks
1 1/4	cups lemon juice

❄ SAYAT NOVA, 91 Charles Street, New York, New York

Instructions

1) Combine and blend thoroughly the lamb, onion, rice, parsley, salt and pepper in a ● *small bowl,* ▲ *medium bowl,* ■ *large bowl.*
2) Shape the mixture into 1-inch balls.
3) Heat chicken broth over low heat until it comes to a boil in a ● *2-quart saucepan,* ▲ *2½-quart saucepan,* ■ *8-quart Dutch oven.*
4) Roll meat balls in flour to coat lightly on all sides.
5) Drop the meatballs gently, a few at a time, into simmering broth.
6) Simmer, covered, until rice is tender: ● ▲ *20 to 30 minutes,* ■ *40 to 50 minutes.* Stir occasionally to prevent rice from sticking to the bottom of the pan.
7) Remove meatballs and reserve. ⬚S
8) In a ● ▲ *small bowl,* ■ *medium bowl,* combine egg yolks and lemon juice; beat until thick.
9) Gradually add some of the hot broth to egg yolks beating constantly.
10) Gradually return yolks to saucepan to cook over low heat, stirring constantly, until mixture thickens slightly, but do not allow to boil.
11) Return meatballs to soup to warm.

preparation time: ● 35 minutes; ▲ 1 hour; ■ 1½ hours
yield: ● 4 cups; ▲ 8 cups; ■ 32 cups

Special Notes
- The meatballs can be made ahead.
- Completed soup will keep in refrigerator 1 week.
- You can freeze after step 7, before adding egg yolks. Keep soup and meatballs separate.

Zucchini Soup

Ingredients

½ lb zucchini
2 cups chicken broth
1 small onion, sliced
⅛ tsp dried chervil
⅛ tsp dried oregano
⅛ tsp salt
⅛ tsp freshly ground black pepper
¼ cup frozen peas, defrosted

1½ lbs zucchini
6 cups chicken broth
1 medium onion, sliced
¼ tsp dried chervil
¼ tsp dried oregano
¼ tsp salt
¼ tsp freshly ground black pepper
¾ cup frozen peas, defrosted

6

6 lbs zucchini
24 cups chicken broth
3 large onions, sliced
1 tsp dried chervil
1 tsp dried oregano
1 tsp salt
1 tsp freshly ground black pepper
3 cups frozen peas, defrosted

※ CHESTER INN, "On the Green," Chester, Vermont

Instructions

1) Wash zucchini and cut off ends, cut in ¼-inch slices.
2) Combine chicken broth, onion, chervil, oregano, salt and pepper in a
   ● *2-quart saucepan,* ▲ *7-quart Dutch oven,* ■ *2 8-quart Dutch ovens,*
3) Bring mixture to a boil; add zucchini and simmer over low heat for
   ● ▲ *15 minutes,* ■ *20 to 25 minutes.*
4) Add peas; cover and simmer 5 minutes longer or until zucchini is soft.
5) Let soup cool slightly.
6) Pour mixture into blender, filling container only ⅓ full. Cover and puree mixture. Continue with remaining soup.
7) Reheat soup in Dutch oven before serving.

preparation time: ● 45 minutes; ▲ 1 hour; ■ 2 hours
yield: ● 3 cups, ▲ 8 cups, ■ 30 cups

Special Notes
- Do not fill the blender more than ⅓ full with the hot soup. Pressure builds up from the steam and it can explode.
- Soup will keep in refrigerator 1 week. It can be frozen 2 to 3 months.
- Soup can also be served chilled.

Bean Pot Soup

Ingredients

M

¾	lb dried pinto beans, soaked overnight and drained or 2 lbs canned pinto beans, drained	¼	cup dark brown sugar
		1	Tb chili powder
		1	tsp MSG (optional)
		1	tsp salt
		1	tsp crumbled bay leaf
1	lb ham, cut in ½-inch cubes	1	tsp dried oregano
		½	tsp ground cumin
1	qt water	½	tsp dried rosemary
2¾	cups tomato juice	½	tsp celery seeds
1	qt chicken broth	½	tsp dried thyme
3	medium onions, chopped	½	tsp dried marjoram
		½	tsp dried basil
3	garlic cloves, minced	¼	tsp curry powder
3	Tbs chopped parsley	4	whole cloves
¼	cup chopped green pepper	1	cup dry sherry
			chopped scallion

L

2½	lbs dried pinto beans, soaked overnight and drained or 6 lbs canned pinto beans, drained	3	Tbs chili powder
		1	Tb MSG (optional)
		1	Tb salt
		1	Tb crumbled bay leaf
		1	Tb dried oregano
3	lbs ham, cut in ½-inch cubes	1½	tsps ground cumin
		1½	tsps dried rosemary
3	qts water	1½	tsps celery seeds
8½	cups tomato juice	1½	tsps dried thyme
3	qts chicken broth	1	tsp dried marjoram
7	large onions, chopped	1½	tsps dried basil
8	garlic cloves, minced	¾	tsp curry powder
½	cup chopped parsley	12	whole cloves
¾	cup chopped green pepper	3	cups dry sherry
¾	cup dark brown sugar		chopped scallions

✳ TIFFANY'S RESTAURANT-SALOON, Highway 14, Cerrillos, New Mexico

Instructions

1) Combine all ingredients except sherry and scallions in a ▲ *7-quart Dutch oven,* ■ *2 8-quart Dutch ovens, dividing ingredients evenly between them.*
2) Simmer partially covered 3 hours if using dried beans, 1½ hours if using canned; or until beans are tender. Adjust seasoning. Ⓢ
3) Just before serving, add sherry.
4) Sprinkle each serving with chopped scallions.

      preparation time: ▲ dried beans, 4 hours
                                canned beans, 2 hours
                       ■ dried beans, 4½ hours
                                canned beans, 2½ hours
      yield: ▲ 12 cups; ■ 36 cups

Special Notes
- If you use canned beans, cut the amount of salt called for as your brand of beans might be highly seasoned or packed in salted water.
- Soup will keep in refrigerator for 1 week, and freezes perfectly for 2 to 3 months.
- Serve either as a first course or as a main dish—it's quite hearty.

Cream of Peanut Soup

Ingredients

2 Tbs butter
2 Tbs chopped celery
2 Tbs chopped onion
1 Tb flour
1½ cups chicken broth
¾ cup light cream
3 Tbs smooth peanut butter
⅛ tsp salt
  pinch of freshly ground black pepper
⅛ tsp paprika

6 Tbs butter
½ cup chopped celery
½ cup chopped onion
3 Tbs flour
4½ cups chicken broth
2¼ cups light cream
9 Tbs smooth peanut butter
¼ tsp salt
⅛ tsp freshly ground black pepper
¼ tsp paprika

6

1½ cups (3 sticks) butter
2 cups chopped celery
2 cups chopped onion
¾ cup flour
4½ qts chicken broth
5 cups light cream
2½ cups smooth peanut butter
½ tsp salt
⅛–¼ tsp freshly ground black pepper
½ tsp paprika

✳ EVANS FARM INN, 1696 Chain Bridge Road, McLean, Virginia

Instructions

1) Melt butter over low heat in a ● *1-quart saucepan,* ▲ *2-quart sauce-pan;* ■ *8-quart Dutch oven.*
2) Add celery and onion and cook until tender.
3) Stir in flour; blend with a wire whisk until smooth.
4) Gradually add chicken broth; cook until slightly thickened and mixture comes to a boil.
5) Stir in light cream, peanut butter, salt, pepper and paprika and heat thoroughly.

preparation time: ● 30 minutes; ▲ 45 minutes; ■ 1¼ hours
yield: ● 2¼ cups; ▲ 8 cups; ■ 28 cups

Special Notes
● Cream of Peanut Soup will keep 1 week in refrigerator.
● The soup can be frozen 1 to 2 months. Although it can be frozen with the cream, it is better to freeze before the cream is added; thaw, reheat and add cream.

English Cheddar Chowder

Ingredients

2

- 1/8 tsp salt
- 1/2 cup water
- 2 Tbs chopped carrot
- 2 Tbs chopped celery
- 2 Tbs chopped scallions
- 1 cup milk
- 1 cup chicken broth
- 2 Tbs butter
- 1/2 small onion, chopped
- 3 Tbs flour
- 1 cup coarsely grated sharp Cheddar cheese (about 1/4 lb)
- 3/4 tsp prepared brown mustard
- pinch of salt
- pinch of freshly ground white pepper
- pinch of cayenne pepper

6

- 1/4 tsp salt
- 1 cup water
- 3 Tbs chopped carrot
- 3 Tbs chopped celery
- 3 Tbs chopped scallions
- 2 cups milk
- 2 cups chicken broth
- 4 Tbs butter
- 1 small onion, chopped
- 6 Tbs flour
- 1/2 lb coarsely grated sharp Cheddar cheese (about 2 cups)
- 1 1/2 tsps prepared brown mustard
- 1/4–1/2 tsp salt
- up to 1/8 tsp freshly ground white pepper
- up to 1/8 tsp cayenne pepper

24

- 3/4 tsp salt
- 5 cups water
- 1 cup chopped carrot
- 1 cup chopped celery
- 1 cup chopped scallions
- 10 cups milk
- 10 cups chicken broth
- 1 1/4 cups butter
- 2 large onions, chopped
- 1 3/4 cups + 2 Tbs flour
- 2 1/2 lbs (about 10 cups) coarsely grated sharp Cheddar cheese
- 2 Tbs + 2 tsps prepared brown mustard
- 2 tsps salt
- 1/2 tsp freshly ground white pepper
- 1/4 tsp cayenne pepper

❄ BEAUMONT COUNTRY CLUB, Beaumont, Texas

Instructions

1) Bring salt and water to a boil in a ● *small saucepan,* ▲ *1-quart saucepan,* ■ *3-quart saucepan.*
2) Add carrot, celery and scallion; simmer 5 minutes. Reserve vegetables with liquid.
3) Heat milk and chicken broth to the boiling point in a ● *1-quart saucepan,* ▲ *2-quart saucepan,* ■ *8-quart Dutch oven.* Reserve.
4) Melt butter over low heat in ● *1-quart saucepan,* ▲ *2-quart saucepan,* ■ *8-quart saucepan.*
5) Add onion and cook until tender.
6) Stir in flour and blend well with a wire whisk. Cook 1 minute.
7) Gradually add the hot milk and chicken broth, stirring constantly with a wire whisk, until thickened. Bring mixture to a boil. Stir in vegetables with their liquid; blend well.
8) Add cheese and cook until cheese is melted, stirring constantly.
9) Stir in mustard and season to taste with salt, pepper and cayenne.

   preparation time: ● 30 minutes; ▲ 1 hour; ■ 2 hours
   yield: ● 2 cups; ▲ 6 cups; ■ 28 cups

Special Notes
- You can refrigerate for 1 week. If soup becomes too thick, thin with a little milk.
- English Cheddar Chowder freezes perfectly for 2 to 3 months. Simply thaw and reheat over low heat.

Great Bay Clam Chowder

Ingredients

1 pint fresh clams or 2 6½-oz cans of minced clams
4 Tbs finely chopped salt pork or bacon (about 2 ozs)
½ cup chopped onion
6 Tbs chopped green pepper
¾ cup chopped celery
1 cup peeled and diced potatoes (about ½ lb)
¼ tsp dried thyme
pinch of cayenne pepper
2 cups tomato juice

1½ pints fresh clams or 3 6½-oz cans of minced clams
6 Tbs finely chopped salt pork or bacon (about 3 ozs)
¾ cup chopped onion
½ cup chopped green pepper
1¼ cups chopped celery
1½ cups peeled and diced potatoes (about ¾ lb)
½ tsp dried thyme
¼ tsp cayenne pepper
3 cups tomato juice

6

6 pints fresh clams or 9 6½-oz cans of minced clams
1½ cups finely chopped salt pork or bacon (about ¾ lb)
3 cups chopped onion
2¼ cups chopped green pepper
4½ cups chopped celery
6 cups peeled and diced potatoes (about 3 lbs)
1 tsp dried thyme
¼–½ tsp cayenne pepper
12 cups tomato juice

※ HISTORIC SMITHVILLE INN, Town of Smithville, New Jersey

Instructions

1) If using fresh clams, wash well.
2) Cover fresh clams with water in a ● *small saucepan,* ▲ *medium saucepan,* ■ *8-quart Dutch oven.* Bring to a boil over low heat and cook until clams open.
3) Reserve broth; remove clams from shell, discarding any that haven't opened, and chop.
4) If using canned clams, separate clams and liquid and reserve both.
5) Fry salt pork or bacon until crisp and lightly brown in a ● *1-quart saucepan,* ▲ *1½-quart saucepan,* ■ *8-quart Dutch oven.*
6) Add onion, green pepper and celery and cook until tender.
7) If necessary, add enough water to clam broth so liquid measures ● *½ cup,* ▲ *1 cup,* ■ *4 cups.*
8) Add clam broth to vegetables in saucepan.
9) Add potatoes, clams and thyme. Season with salt and cayenne to taste.
10) Cover and simmer until potatoes are tender, about ● ▲ *15 minutes,* ■ *25 to 30 minutes.*
11) Add tomato juice, and heat thoroughly.

preparation time: ● 45 minutes; ▲ 1¼ hours; ■ 1¾ hours
yield: ● 4 cups; ▲ 6 cups; ■ 24 cups

Special Notes
- Flavor of soup improves on standing. Soup can be made 1 or 2 days ahead and refrigerated. Warm thoroughly over low heat.
- Freezes well except that the potatoes will be a little soft from absorbing the liquid. After thawing, if you need more liquid in the soup, add tomato juice.

FISH AND SHELLFISH

Fruits de Mer

Ingredients

⅓	cup olive oil
½	cup chopped onion
3	garlic cloves, pressed
¼	tsp ground fennel seeds
2	sprigs parsley
½	tsp dried thyme
2	bay leaves
¼	tsp dried orange peel
½–1	tsp salt
¼	tsp freshly ground black pepper
½	tsp crushed saffron
6	coriander seeds, crushed
2	large tomatoes, peeled, seeded and chopped
3	lbs sea bass, striped bass or haddock cut into 2-inch pieces, heads and bones included
3	lbs whiting, mackerel or porgy, cut into 2-inch pieces, heads and bones included
	about 8 cups water
1	lb lobster tail, cut in pieces
12	shrimp, cleaned

AÏOLI

½	tsp dry mustard
½	tsp salt
¼	tsp freshly ground black pepper
2	egg yolks
½	cup olive oil
½	tsp lemon juice
2	large garlic cloves, pressed
¼	cup chopped parsley
6	slices day-old French bread

✻ MEDITERRANÉE, Highland Road Exit from Route 6, Pond Road, North Truro, Massachusetts

Instructions

1) Heat oil in a 7-quart Dutch oven over moderate heat.
2) Add onion, garlic, fennel, parsley, thyme, bay leaves, orange peel, salt, pepper, saffron and coriander; cook 2 minutes, stirring occasionally.
3) Add tomatoes; cook until liquid has evaporated.
4) Place firm-fleshed bass or haddock in the pot and add the water.
5) Bring to a boil; simmer 10 minutes; add the whiting, mackerel or porgy. Simmer 5 minutes longer.
6) Add lobster and shrimp; simmer 3 to 4 minutes longer.
7) While fish is simmering, make aïoli: place mustard, salt, pepper, and egg yolks in a small bowl.
8) Beat with a rotary beater or electric mixer until thick.
9) Gradually add olive oil, drop by drop, beating constantly until mixture is thicker than mayonnaise.
10) Add lemon juice and garlic. Taste for seasoning.
11) To serve: remove and discard the fish heads and those bones that you can. Place equal parts of fish in each soup plate. Pour soup into a tureen; sprinkle generously with parsley. Each guest ladles soup over his fish and floats in it a slice of day-old French bread liberally coated with the aïoli.

preparation time: 1 hour

Special Note
• Soup will keep in refrigerator 4 to 5 days; freezes for 2 to 3 months. The aïoli can be stored in the refrigerator for 1 to 2 weeks.

Brook Trout Stuffed with Crabmeat

Ingredients

2

STUFFING

3	Tbs butter
2	large shallots, finely chopped
2	Tbs dry white wine
¼	cup finely chopped mushrooms
½	cup cooked crabmeat, preferably lump
1	Tb flour
2	Tbs clam juice
2	Tbs heavy cream
1	egg yolk
1	tsp finely chopped parsley
⅛	tsp salt
	pinch of freshly ground white pepper

FISH

2	Tbs flour
⅛	tsp salt
	pinch of freshly ground black pepper
2	whole brook trout (about 8 ozs each), cleaned
	olive oil
1	Tb butter, melted
1	tsp lemon juice

STUFFING

8	Tbs (1 stick) butter
¼	cup finely chopped shallots
6	Tbs dry white wine
½	cup finely chopped mushrooms
1½	cups cooked crabmeat, preferably lump
3	Tbs flour
6	Tbs clam juice
6	Tbs heavy cream
3	egg yolks
1	Tb finely chopped parsley
¼	tsp salt
⅛	tsp freshly ground white pepper

6

FISH

4	Tbs flour
½	tsp salt
¼	tsp freshly ground black pepper
6	whole brook trout (about 8 oz each), cleaned
	olive oil
3	Tbs butter, melted
1	Tb lemon juice

※ L'EPUISETTE, 21 West Goethe Street, Chicago, Illinois

Instructions

1) To make stuffing: melt ● *1 tablespoon butter,* ▲ *4 tablespoons butter* in a 10-inch skillet over low heat.
2) Add shallots; cook until tender.
3) Add wine and mushrooms; cook until liquid has evaporated.
4) Stir in crabmeat and set skillet aside.
5) In a 1-quart saucepan, melt remaining butter over low heat.
6) Stir in flour and blend well with a wire whisk. Cook 1 minute.
7) Add clam juice and cream; stirring constantly, cook until mixture thickens and comes to a boil.
8) Beat egg yolks in a small bowl.
9) Beat in a little of the hot clam sauce.
10) Slowly, return yolk mixture to saucepan, beating constantly; cook, stirring constantly, until mixture thickens slightly, but do not allow to boil. Add parsley, salt and pepper.
11) Blend sauce into crabmeat mixture and keep warm in a double-boiler over barely simmering water.
12) Combine flour, salt and pepper on a plate; roll fish in flour mixture to coat well.
13) Heat olive oil ½-inch deep in a heavy 10-inch skillet until a light haze forms.
14) Sauté 2 trout at a time until golden brown on underside, about 3 to 4 minutes.
15) Turn over and brown on other side until fish flakes easily.
16) Remove fish and drain on paper towels. Repeat with remaining fish. (Keep sautéed fish warm in a low oven.)
17) Divide stuffing into equal portions and stuff each fish. S
18) Pour hot melted butter over each fish before serving and sprinkle with a little of the lemon juice.

preparation time: ● 45 minutes; ▲ 1½ hours

Special Note
● Stuffed fish will keep in refrigerator 2 to 3 days; frozen for 2 to 3 months. Reheat in a preheated 350-degree oven for 10 to 15 minutes or until heated through.

Baked Stuffed Red Snapper with Creole Sauce

Ingredients

2-3

STUFFING
- 1 Tb vegetable oil
- 1 small onion, minced
- 1 small celery stalk, chopped
- ½ medium green pepper, chopped
- ½ cup dry French bread crumbs
- ¼ tsp salt
- ⅛ tsp black pepper
- ¼ bay leaf, crumbled
- ⅛ tsp each of dried thyme, marjoram, chervil
- 1 Tb chopped parsley
- ½ cup lump crabmeat
- 1 egg, lightly beaten

SAUCE
- 4 Tbs butter
- 1 medium onion, chopped
- 1 fish head
- 2 cups dry white wine
- 2 cups water
- 1 Tb dry Italian seasoning
- ½ tsp salt
- ⅛ tsp freshly ground black pepper
- ⅛ tsp cayenne pepper
- 1 cup canned tomato puree
- 1½ tsps chicken stock base

FISH
- 1 3-lb red snapper, cleaned
- ¼ tsp salt
- ⅛ tsp freshly ground black pepper
- 1 Tb butter, melted

6-8

STUFFING
- 2 Tbs vegetable oil
- 1 medium onion, minced
- ½ cup chopped celery
- ½ cup chopped green pepper
- 1 cup dry French bread crumbs
- ½ tsp salt
- ¼ tsp freshly ground black pepper
- ½ tsp crumbled bay leaf
- ¼ tsp each of dried thyme, marjoram, chervil
- 2 Tbs chopped parsley
- 1 cup lump crabmeat
- 2 eggs, lightly beaten

SAUCE
- 8 Tbs butter
- 2 large onions, chopped
- 2 fish heads
- 4 cups dry white wine
- 4 cups water
- 2 Tbs dry Italian seasoning
- 1 tsp salt
- ¼ tsp freshly ground black pepper
- ¼ tsp cayenne pepper
- 1½ cups canned tomato puree
- 1 Tb chicken stock base

FISH
- 1 6–7-lb red snapper, cleaned
- ½ tsp salt
- ¼ tsp freshly ground black pepper
- 2 Tbs butter, melted

✲ RESTAURANT NORMANDIE, 1601 Pinhook Road, Lafayette, Louisiana

Instructions

1) Preheat oven to 400 degrees.
2) Heat oil over moderate heat in ● *an 8-inch skillet,* ▲ *a 10-inch skillet.*
3) Add onion, celery and green pepper; cook until tender, stirring occasionally.
4) Add bread crumbs, salt, pepper, bay leaf, thyme, marjoram, chervil, and parsley; blend well. Cook 1 minute. Add crabmeat; blend lightly. Add egg, blend well. Let stuffing cool slightly.
5) Season inside of fish with salt and pepper and place in a well-greased ● *2-quart shallow baking dish;* ▲ *shallow roasting pan or jelly-roll pan, 10¾ by 17 inches.*
6) Stuff cavity of fish and secure opening with skewers.
7) Brush fish with melted butter and set aside.
8) To make creole sauce: over low heat, melt butter in a ● *2-quart saucepan,* ▲ *3-quart saucepan.*
9) Add onions; cook until golden. Add fish heads; cook 1 minute.
10) Add wine, water, Italian seasoning, salt, pepper and cayenne; simmer ½ hour.
11) While sauce is cooking, bake fish in the preheated oven for ● *20 to 25 minutes,* ▲ *30 to 40 minutes,* or until fish flakes easily.
12) Strain stock and discard fish heads.
13) Reduce stock to half over high heat.
14) Add tomato puree and chicken base; simmer until mixture is thickened. Season to taste.
15) If desired, decorate the eyes of the fish with slices of stuffed olive and place parsley sprigs around the fish. Thin lemon slices, cut in half, should be arranged overlapping, down the center of the fish to form a line from head to tail. Carve the fish at the table and serve the sauce on the side. If the fish is not decorated with the parsley and lemon slices, pour the sauce over.

preparation time: ● 1½ hours; ▲ 2½ hours

Special Notes
- If red snapper is not available, a good substitute is sea bass, striped bass or pike. Instead of one large fish use 2 3-pound fish.
- Both prepared fish and sauce freeze very well for 2 to 3 months, but freeze separately.
- If desired, you can make sauce and/or stuff fish and refrigerate before finishing.
- Italian seasoning, which is commercially available, includes oregano, basil, rosemary, garlic and parsley.

Sweet & Sour Fish

Ingredients

FISH

1	2½-lb sea bass or red snapper, cleaned
2	Tbs soy sauce
2	Tbs dry sherry
1	egg, beaten
2	Tbs cornstarch

SAUCE

½	cup sugar
½	cup ketchup
6	Tbs soy sauce
¼	cup wine vinegar
2	cups water
2	Tbs cornstarch
	vegetable oil for deep frying

FISH

2	2½-lb sea bass or red snapper, cleaned
¼	cup soy sauce
¼	cup dry sherry
1	egg, beaten
¼	cup cornstarch

6

SAUCE

1	cup sugar
1	cup ketchup
¾	cup soy sauce
½	cup red wine vinegar
4	cups water
¼	cup cornstarch
	vegetable oil for deep frying

✻ THE MANDARIN, Ghirardelli Square, 900 North Point, San Francisco, California

Instructions

1) Make 3 or 4 parallel deep slashes on both sides of the fish.
2) Successively rub soy sauce, sherry and egg into fish; sprinkle cornstarch over all. Set fish aside.
3) To make sauce: combine sugar, ketchup, soy sauce and vinegar in a ● *2-quart saucepan,* ▲ *4-quart saucepan.*
4) Blend ● *¼ cup water,* ▲ *½ cup water* with the cornstarch in a small bowl until smooth.
5) Stir cornstarch mixture with remaining water into saucepan.
6) Cook over moderate heat, stirring constantly, until mixture thickens and comes to a boil. Keep warm.
7) Heat 2 inches of oil in a large heavy saucepan or deep fryer to 375 degrees.
8) Deep fry fish, one at a time, about 10 to 12 minutes or until golden on both sides and fish flakes easily.
9) Drain on paper towels.
10) Place fish on a serving platter and cover with sauce. If desired, decorate with strips of green pepper and carrots.

preparation time: ● ¾ hour; ▲ 1¼ hours

Special Notes
● To save time and still have a crisp fish, deep fry the fish in advance, keep refrigerated 1 or 2 days and refry for 1 to 2 minutes just before serving.
● Fish should be reheated in the oven, uncovered, at 350 degrees for 10 minutes or until warm. Reheat sauce in a saucepan over low heat.
● To freeze, keep fish and sauce separate. They will keep 2 to 3 months.

Les Merveilles de la Mer en Crêpes

Ingredients

6	Tbs butter
¼	cup chopped scallions or shallots
¼	cup sliced mushrooms
1½	Tbs flour
¼	cup dry white wine
2	cups light cream
2	egg yolks
¼	tsp salt
⅛	tsp freshly ground black pepper
½	cup cooked lobster meat
½	cup cooked crabmeat
½	cup cooked shrimp
2	Tbs Cognac
6	5-inch crêpes (page 252)

12	Tbs (1½ sticks) butter
½	cup chopped scallions or shallots
½	cup sliced mushrooms
3	Tbs flour
½	cup dry white wine
4	cups light cream
4	egg yolks
½	tsp salt
¼	tsp freshly ground black pepper
1	cup cooked lobster meat
1	cup cooked crabmeat
1	cup cooked shrimp
¼	cup Cognac
15	5-inch crêpes (page 252)

6

1½	lbs butter
2	cups chopped scallions or shallots
2	cups sliced mushrooms (about ½ pound)
¾	cup flour
2	cups dry white wine
4	qts light cream
16	egg yolks
1½	tsps salt
¼	tsp freshly ground black pepper
4	cups cooked lobster meat
4	cups cooked crabmeat
4	cups cooked shrimp
1	cup Cognac
60	5-inch crêpes (page 252)

❋ MASSON'S RESTAURANT FRANÇAIS, 7200 Pontchartrain Boulevard, New Orleans, Louisiana

Instructions

1) Melt ● *4 tablespoons butter,* ▲ *8 tablespoons butter,* ■ *1 pound butter* in a ● *10-inch skillet,* ▲ *4-quart Dutch oven,* ■ *2 8-quart Dutch ovens, dividing ingredients evenly between them.*
2) Add scallions and mushrooms and cook until tender.
3) Add flour; blend well with wire whisk. Cook 1 minute.
4) Gradually add wine and cream, blending well with a wire whisk.
5) Cook over moderate heat, stirring constantly, until mixture thickens.
6) Beat egg yolks until thick in a ● ▲ *small bowl,* .. ■ *large bowl.*
7) Pour some of the hot sauce into egg yolks, beating constantly until blended.
8) Gradually return egg yolk mixture to sauce and cook, stirring constantly, until mixture thickens slightly, but do not allow to boil. Remove from heat.
9) Add salt and pepper.
10) Preheat oven to 350 degrees.
11) Over low heat, melt remaining butter in a ● ▲ *10-inch skillet* ■ *4-quart Dutch oven.*
12) Add lobster, crabmeat and shrimp; cook 5 minutes.
13) Add Cognac and warm. Ignite and let flame die.
14) Divide sauce in half. Add seafood to half the sauce.
15) Place ¼ cup of the seafood mixture in each crêpe and roll up.
16) Arrange crêpes in a ● *1½-quart shallow baking dish,* ▲ *2-quart shallow baking dish,* ■ *3 3-quart shallow baking dishes.*
17) Pour remaining sauce over top.
18) Bake in the preheated oven 15 to 20 minutes or until heated through.

preparation time: ● 2 hours (including 30 minutes to prepare crêpes); ▲ 2¾ hours (including 45 minutes to prepare crêpes); ■ 5½ hours (including 2 hours to prepare crêpes)

Special Notes
- This dish can be made ahead—as much as 2 to 3 days—through step 16. When ready to serve, pour sauce over and bake as directed.
- The crêpes can be made 1 to 2 days ahead and kept in the refrigerator.
- The uncooked stuffed crêpes freeze very well for 2 to 3 months. Thaw and continue recipe at step 17. Although it would be best to freeze the sauce separately from the stuffed crêpes, they can be frozen together should you have leftovers.

Shrimp Donatello

Ingredients

2

3	ozs cream cheese, softened
¼	cup commercial blue cheese salad dressing
1	tsp heavy cream
¼	tsp Worcestershire sauce
1	Tb chopped pimiento
1	tsp Madeira
	pinch of salt
	pinch of freshly ground white pepper
1	cup cooked rice
½	lb cooked medium shrimp
2	Tbs canned minced clams, drained
4	Tbs freshly grated romano or Parmesan cheese
2	Tbs dry sherry

6

- 8 ozs cream cheese, softened
- 1 cup commercial blue cheese salad dressing
- 1 Tb heavy cream
- 1 tsp Worcestershire sauce
- 2 Tbs chopped pimiento
- 1 Tb Madeira
- pinch–⅛ tsp freshly ground white pepper
- pinch–⅛ tsp salt
- 3 cups cooked rice
- 2 lbs cooked medium shrimp
- 6 Tbs canned minced clams, drained
- ¾ cup freshly grated romano or Parmesan cheese (about 3 ozs)
- 6 Tbs dry sherry

24

2	lbs cream cheese, softened
32	ozs commercial blue cheese salad dressing
¼	cup heavy cream
4	tsps Worcestershire sauce
¼	cup chopped pimiento
¼	cup Madeira
¼	tsp salt
¼	tsp freshly ground white pepper
12	cups cooked rice
8	lbs cooked medium shrimp
1½	cups canned minced clams, drained
3	cups freshly grated romano or Parmesan cheese (about 12 ozs)
1½	cups dry sherry

✻THE GALLERY, east of Highway 40, Steamboat Springs, Colorado

Instructions

1) Preheat oven to 425 degrees.
2) Beat cream cheese until smooth in a ● *small bowl,* ▲ *medium bowl,* ■ *large bowl or pot.*
3) Add salad dressing, cream, Worcestershire sauce, pimiento, Madeira and salt and pepper to taste.
4) Place ½ cup rice in ● ▲ *individual ovenproof serving dishes,* ■ *3 3-quart baking dishes.*
5) Arrange shrimp on top of rice in each dish.
6) Pour ⅓ cup sauce over each dish.
7) Sprinkle each dish with 1 tablespoon minced clams; then top each with 2 tablespoons grated cheese. ☐S
8) Bake in the preheated oven until sauce is bubbly and cheese is lightly browned, about ● ▲ *10 minutes,* ■ *20 to 30 minutes.*
9) Pour 1 tablespoon sherry over each portion before serving.

preparation time: ● 35 minutes; ▲ 1 hour; ■ 2½ hours

Special Notes
- Sauce can be made in advance and refrigerated for 2 weeks.
- You can also freeze after Step 8.

Shrimp Maisonette

Ingredients

¾ lb cooked shrimp
1 Tb butter
2 large shallots, finely chooped
2 garlic cloves, minced
¼ lb mushrooms, sliced
¼ cup Chablis, or other dry white wine
¼ tsp salt
⅛ tsp freshly ground black pepper
1 Tb chopped parsley
1 tsp lemon juice
2 slices toast, crust removed and cut into triangles

2 lbs cooked shrimp
12 Tbs butter (1½ sticks)
8 large shallots, finely chopped
4 garlic cloves, minced
¾ lb mushrooms, sliced
½ cup Chablis, or other dry white wine
½ tsp salt
¼ tsp freshly ground black pepper
2 Tbs chopped parsley
1 Tb lemon juice
6 slices toast, crust removed and cut into triangles

6

8 lbs cooked shrimp
1¼ lbs butter
1 cup finely chopped shallots
¼ cup minced garlic
3 lbs mushrooms, sliced
1 cup Chablis or other dry white wine
1 tsp salt
½ tsp freshly ground black pepper
½ cup chopped parsley
¼ cup lemon juice
24 slices toast, crust removed and cut into triangles

※ MAISONETTE, 114 East 6th Street, Cincinnati, Ohio

Instructions

1) Split each cooked shrimp down the back and flatten.
2) Melt butter in a ● *10-inch skillet,* ▲ *12-inch skillet,* ■ *8-quart Dutch oven.* Add shallots and garlic; cook until tender.
3) Add mushrooms and cook over moderate heat, stirring occasionally, until they color.
4) Add shrimp and cook 1 to 2 minutes or until heated.
5) Add wine, salt, pepper and parsley and cook until mixture begins to simmer.
6) Add lemon juice and blend well. Serve over toast points.

preparation time: ● 30 minutes;   ▲ 45 minutes;   ■ 3 hours

Special Notes
- This dish will keep in refrigerator 5 to 6 days and should be reheated in a skillet, over low heat. Do not overcook, or shrimp will become tough.
- Mixture freezes well. Will keep 2 to 3 months.

Gallician Scallops

2

4	Tbs olive oil
½	lb bay scallops
¼	cup chopped onion
1	small garlic clove, minced
1	medium tomato, peeled and chopped
⅓	cup cubed ham
½	cup dry white wine
1	Tb beef broth

1	tsp cornstarch
1	tsp water
	pinch of salt
⅛	tsp freshly ground black pepper
¼	cup dry bread crumbs
2	Tbs butter, melted
2	Tbs chopped parsley
2	lemon wedges

6

8	Tbs olive oil
1½	lbs bay scallops
1	cup chopped onion
2	small garlic cloves, minced
3	medium tomatoes, peeled and chopped
1	cup cubed ham
1½	cups dry white wine
3	Tbs beef broth
1	Tb cornstarch
1	Tb water
¼	tsp of salt
¼	tsp freshly ground black pepper
¾	cup dry bread crumbs
6	Tbs butter, melted
¼	cup chopped parsley
6	lemon wedges

24

1	cup olive oil
6	lbs bay scallops
4	cups chopped onion
6	large garlic cloves, minced
12	medium tomatoes, peeled and chopped
4	cups (about 2 lbs) cubed ham
6	cups dry white wine
¾	cup beef broth

4–5	Tbs cornstarch
¼	cup water
¼	tsp salt (optional)
½	tsp freshly ground black pepper
2	cups dry bread crumbs
1	cup (2 sticks) butter, melted
1	cup chopped parsley
24	lemon wedges

✳ SPANISH PAVILION, 475 Park Avenue, New York, New York

Instructions

1) Heat ● *2 tablespoons oil,* ▲ ■ *4 tablespoons oil* over moderate heat in ● *an 8-inch skillet,* ▲ ■ *a 12-inch skillet.*
2) ● ▲ Add scallops and cook, stirring occasionally, 4 to 5 minutes, or until scallops are firm. ■ Add enough scallops to cover bottom of skillet in a single layer and cook until firm. Remove with a slotted spoon. Add oil as needed to cook remaining scallops.
3) Remove scallops and liquid to a bowl and reserve.
4) Add remaining oil to skillet.
5) Add onion and garlic; cook until golden.
6) ● ▲ Add tomatoes and ham. ■ Before adding tomatoes and ham, transfer onion mixture to an 8-quart Dutch oven.
7) Cook until liquid has evaporated.
8) Add the liquid from the scallops, white wine and beef broth.
9) Simmer over low heat for ● *10 minutes,* ▲ *15 minutes,* ■ *20 minutes.*
10) Preheat oven to 400 degrees.
11) In a small dish, mix cornstarch and water until smooth.
12) Stir cornstarch mixture into skillet, stirring constantly, until mixture comes to a boil. Remove from heat.
13) Add scallops, salt and pepper.
14) Spoon mixture into ● *2 individual au gratin dishes,* ▲ *1-quart shallow baking dish,* ■ *3 2-quart soufflé dishes or casseroles.*
15) In a small bowl mix together bread crumbs and melted butter; sprinkle the crumb mixture over top of scallops.
16) Bake in the preheated oven ● ▲ *10 minutes,* ■ *10 to 15 minutes* or until heated through and top is golden.
17) Serve garnished with parsley and lemon wedges.

preparation time: ● 1 hour; ▲ 1¼ hours; ■ 3 hours

Special Note
● Gallician scallops will keep in refrigerator for 2 to 3 days and can be reheated in a preheated 300-degree oven for 10 to 15 minutes, or until heated through. This dish cannot be frozen because of the cornstarch.

Moules à la Marinière

Ingredients

2

1	qt (2 lbs) mussels, scrubbed and debearded
1	small onion, chopped
2	shallots, chopped
2	Tbs chopped parsley
¼	tsp dried thyme
½	bay leaf
⅛	tsp freshly ground black pepper
½	cup dry white wine
3	Tbs butter
1½	Tbs lemon juice
	chopped parsley

3	qts (6 lbs) mussels, scrubbed and debearded
2	medium onions, chopped
8	shallots, chopped
¼	cup chopped parsley
¾	tsp dried thyme
1	large bay leaf
¼	tsp freshly ground black pepper
1½	cups dry white wine
8	Tbs butter
4½	Tbs lemon juice
	chopped parsley

6-8

❋ LE CORDON BLEU, 1201 North Federal Highway, Dania, Florida

Instructions

1) Place mussels in a ● *3-quart Dutch oven,* ▲ *8-quart Dutch oven.*
2) Add remaining ingredients, except chopped parsley for garnish.
3) Cover and cook over moderately high heat 3 minutes.
4) Stir well to bring mussels from top to bottom.
5) Cover and cook 5 minutes longer, or until all the mussels are open.
6) Serve mussels in individual soup dishes with broth. Garnish with chopped parsley.

   preparation time: ● 20 minutes; ▲ 30 minutes

Special Notes
- To clean mussels wash under cold running water, scrub with a stiff brush, and cut beards off with a scissors.
- Mussels can be reheated over low heat.

Crab Cakes

Ingredients

½	lb cooked lump crabmeat
1½	Tbs egg, beaten
¼	tsp salt
¼	tsp freshly ground black pepper
2	Tbs chopped parsley
¼	tsp dry mustard
¼	cup mayonnaise
⅛	tsp Worcestershire sauce
½	cup dry bread crumbs
2–4	Tbs butter

1	lb cooked lump crabmeat
1	egg, beaten
1	tsp salt
½	tsp freshly ground black pepper
¼	cup chopped parsley
¼	tsp dry mustard
½	cup mayonnaise
¼	tsp Worcestershire sauce
1	cup dry bread crumbs
6–8	Tbs butter

6

4	lbs cooked lump crabmeat
4	eggs, beaten
4	tsps salt
1½	tsps freshly ground black pepper
1	cup chopped parsley
2	tsps dry mustard
2	cups mayonnaise
1	tsp Worcestershire sauce
4	cups dry bread crumbs
1½–2	cups (3–4 sticks) butter

❄ CHESAPEAKE RESTAURANT, 1701 North Charles Street, Baltimore, Maryland

Instructions

1) Trying to preserve whole pieces of crabmeat, combine crabmeat, egg, salt, pepper, parsley, mustard, mayonnaise and Worcestershire sauce in a ● *small bowl,* ▲ *medium bowl,* ■ *large bowl or pot.*

2) Using ⅓ to ½ cup for each cake, shape mixture into ● *2 to 3 cakes,* ▲ *6 cakes,* ■ *24 cakes,* each ¾ inch high.

3) Pour ● ▲ *all the bread crumbs,* ■ *¼ of the bread crumbs* on a plate and gently roll crab cakes in crumbs to coat evenly on all sides. ■ As you shape the crab cakes, discard crumbs that become gummy and add fresh crumbs as needed.

4) Place crab cakes on a plate and refrigerate 2 hours.

5) Over moderate heat, melt ● *2 tablespoons butter,* ▲ *3 tablespoons butter,* ■ *¼ cup (½ stick) butter* in ● *an 8-inch skillet,* ▲ *a 10-inch skillet,* ■ *a 12-inch skillet.*

6) Cook ● *2 to 3 crab cakes,* ▲ *half the crab cakes,* ■ *¼ of the crab cakes,* until the underside is golden.

7) Turn cakes over and cook until other side is golden and cakes are heated through.

8) Add remaining butter as needed to sauté remaining cakes.

preparation time (including 2-hour refrigeration): ● 2½ hours; ▲ 3 hours; ■ 4½ hours

Special Notes
- To get 1½ tablespoons egg, beat 1 egg in a small bowl and measure out the amount needed.
- Cakes will keep in refrigerator 3 to 4 days or in freezer 2 months.
- To reheat, wrap in foil and warm in a preheated 325-degree oven for 10 minutes or refry in a skillet with a little butter.

Su Su Lobster Curry

Ingredients

2

- 4 Tbs butter
- ½ cup finely chopped celery
- ½ cup finely chopped onion
- 2 Tbs chopped mushrooms
- 2 Tbs canned bamboo shoots, chopped and drained
- ¾ cup peeled and diced apple
- 1½ Tbs curry powder
- 1 cup heavy cream
- 1 tsp cornstarch
- 2 tsps water
- 1 tsp salt
- 1 cup cooked lobster meat

6

- 8 Tbs (1 stick) butter
- 1 cup finely chopped celery
- 1 cup finely chopped onion
- ¼ cup chopped mushrooms
- ¼ cup canned bamboo shoots, chopped and drained
- 2 cups peeled and diced apple
- 4 Tbs curry powder
- 2 cups heavy cream
- 1 Tb cornstarch
- 2 Tbs water
- 1 Tb salt
- 3 cups cooked lobster meat

24

- 1 lb butter
- 4 cups finely chopped celery
- 4 cups finely chopped onion
- 1 cup chopped mushrooms (about ¼ lb)
- 1 cup canned bamboo shoots, chopped and drained
- 6 cups peeled and diced apple
- ¾–1 cup curry powder
- 6 cups heavy cream
- 4 Tbs cornstarch
- ½ cup water
- 3 Tbs salt
- 12 cups cooked lobster meat

❄ DOBBS HOUSES LUAU, 3135 Poplar Avenue, Memphis, Tennessee

❄ Dobbs Houses Luau

Instructions

1) Melt butter over low heat in a ● *10-inch skillet,* ▲ *12-inch skillet,* ■ *8-quart Dutch oven.*
2) Add celery, onion, mushrooms, bamboo shoots and apple; cook until tender, about 5 minutes.
3) Stir in curry powder and blend well.
4) Gradually add cream and cook until mixture comes to a boil.
5) Blend cornstarch and water until smooth in a ● ▲ *small dish,* ■ *small bowl.*
6) Stir cornstarch mixture into skillet; add salt and cook, stirring constantly, until sauce thickens.
7) Add lobster; cook until heated through.
8) Serve with rice and chutney.

preparation time: ● 30 minutes; ▲ 45 minutes; ■ 1 hour

Special Notes
- This dish is equally delicious with shrimp. Use 1 pound fresh or frozen for 2; 3 pounds for 6; 12 pounds for 24.
- Curry will keep at least 1 week in refrigerator.

POULTRY

Poulet Albert

Ingredients

2   Tbs butter
1   2½-lb chicken, cut into serving pieces
1   cup orange juice
1   3-inch strip of orange peel
½   tsp salt
⅛   tsp freshly ground black pepper
1   tsp peeled, chopped fresh ginger
½   tsp garlic powder
1   tsp onion powder
¼   cup curaçao
    cornstarch
    water
4   peeled orange slices

2   Tbs butter
2   3½-lb chickens, cut into serving pieces
2   cups orange juice
2   3-inch strips of orange peel
¾   tsp salt
¼   tsp freshly ground black pepper
2   tsps peeled, chopped fresh ginger
1   tsp garlic powder
2   tsps onion powder
½   cup curaçao
    cornstarch
    water
12   peeled orange slices

6

8   Tbs (1 stick) butter)
8   3½-lb chickens, cut into serving pieces
8   cups orange juice
8   3-inch strips of orange peel
1   Tb salt
1   tsp freshly ground black pepper
2   Tbs + 2 tsps peeled, chopped fresh ginger
1½   Tbs garlic powder
2   Tbs + 2 tsps onion powder
2   cups curaçao
    cornstarch
    water
48   peeled orange slices

✳   GALLATIN'S, 500 Hartnell, Monterey, California

Instructions

1) Preheat oven to 350 degrees.
2) Over moderate heat, melt butter in a ● *10-inch skillet,* ▲ ■ *12-inch skillet.*
3) Add a few of the chicken pieces and sauté until golden on all sides.
4) Transfer cooked pieces to ● *3-quart saucepan or Dutch oven,* ▲ *a 3-quart shallow baking dish,* ■ *4 3-quart shallow baking dishes, dividing ingredients evenly among them.*
5) Repeat until all pieces are golden.
6) Add orange juice and peel to chicken pieces.
7) Sprinkle chicken with salt, pepper, ginger, garlic powder and onion powder.
8) Pour curaçao over.
9) Cover with aluminum foil and bake in the preheated oven about 40 minutes, or until chicken is tender.
10) Measure liquid. ⬚S
11) Pour into a ● *1-quart saucepan,* ▲ *2-quart saucepan,* ■ *4-quart saucepan.*
12) Combine 2 teaspoons cornstarch with 2 teaspoons water for each cup of liquid. Add to hot liquid; cook over medium heat, stirring constantly, until mixture thickens and comes to a boil.
13) Pour sauce over chicken pieces. Decorate with orange slices. Serve with rice.

preparation time: ●1½ hours; ▲ 1¾ hours; ■ 2 hours

Special Notes
● Chicken and liquid can be frozen at step 9. After thawing, heat sauce with chicken and thicken with cornstarch as directed.
● Chicken keeps in refrigerator 1 week; reheat slowly over low heat, covered.

Chicken and Yellow Rice, Valencia Style

Ingredients

2-3

2	Tbs olive oil
1	2½-lb chicken; cut into serving pieces
1	medium onion, chopped
2	garlic cloves, minced
1	small green pepper, diced
1	small tomato, peeled and chopped
1	cup long-grain rice
2	cups chicken broth
¼	tsp crushed saffron
1	bay leaf
1	tsp salt
½	10-oz package frozen peas, defrosted
1	pimiento, cut into strips
2	hard-boiled eggs, halved
8	cooked asparagus spears
2	Tbs chopped parsley

6

4	Tbs olive oil
4	chicken breasts, halved
3	medium onions, chopped
4	large garlic cloves, minced
2	large green peppers, diced
2	large tomatoes, peeled and chopped
2¼	cups long-grain rice
4½	cups chicken broth
½–¾	tsp crushed saffron
2	bay leaves
1–2	tsps salt
½	10-oz package frozen peas, defrosted
1	pimiento, cut into strips
8	hard-boiled eggs, halved
12	cooked asparagus spears
3	Tbs chopped parsley

12

9	Tbs olive oil
9	chicken breasts, halved
6	medium onions, chopped
10	large garlic cloves, minced
5	medium green peppers, diced
5	medium tomatoes, peeled and diced
4½	cups long-grain rice
9	cups chicken broth
¾–1½	tsps crushed saffron
6	bay leaves
1½	Tbs salt
2	10-oz packages frozen peas, defrosted
3	pimientos, cut in strips
18	hard-boiled eggs, halved
36	cooked asparagus spears
6	Tbs chopped parsley

❊ COLUMBIA RESTAURANT, Seventh Avenue from 21st to 22nd streets, Tampa, Florida

Instructions

1) Preheat oven to 350 degrees.
2) Heat olive oil in a ● *3-quart Dutch oven,* ▲ *4-quart Dutch oven,* ■ *7-quart Dutch oven.*
3) Add chicken pieces; cook until golden on all sides. Remove chicken.
4) Add onions and garlic; cook until onions are soft.
5) Add green pepper and tomato; cook, stirring occasionally until all the liquid evaporates.
6) Add rice and coat well with vegetables.
7) Add chicken broth, saffron, bay leaf and salt; bring to a boil. Pour mixture into ●,▲ *1 3-quart shallow baking dish,* ■ *3 3-quart shallow baking dishes, dividing ingredients evenly among them.*
8) Arrange chicken pieces on top; cover with aluminum foil and bake in the preheated oven 50 minutes.
9) Sprinkle peas around edge of dish, cover and bake 10 minutes longer.
10) Decorate as desired with remaining ingredients

preparation time: ● 1½ hours; ▲ 2½ hours; ■ 3½ hours

Special Notes
- The dish can be decorated by arranging pimiento strips in pie fashion with egg halves in between. Place asparagus spears in center. Sprinkle parsley over top.
- For 2 to 3, if less rice is desired, use half cup rice and 1 cup chicken broth. The larger amount of rice is given as it is basically a 1-dish entrée.
- Valencian chicken and rice will keep refrigerated 1 week; frozen 2 to 3 months, but the rice will be soft. After thawing, heat, covered, in a pre-heated 300-degree oven, for about 20 minutes.

Polynesian Chicken

Ingredients

1	chicken breast, halved
2	chicken legs
2	Tbs vegetable oil
1	Tb soy sauce
1	Tb Worcestershire sauce
1	tsp MSG, optional
1½	tsps garlic powder
½	tsp salt
¼	tsp freshly ground black pepper
¼	tsp dried rosemary
1	ripe pineapple
1	1-lb-14-oz can fruit for salads
1	Tb cornstarch
¼	cup dry white wine
2	Tbs shredded coconut

3	chicken breasts, halved
6	chicken legs
¼	cup vegetable oil
2	Tbs soy sauce
2	Tbs Worcestershire sauce
1	Tb MSG, optional
1	Tb garlic powder
1	tsp salt
1	tsp freshly ground black pepper
1	tsp dried rosemary
3	ripe pineapples
1	1-lb-14-oz can fruit for salads
2	Tbs cornstarch
½	cup dry white wine
⅓	cup shredded coconut

6

❄ The former CURT YOCOM'S RESTAURANT, Iowa City, Iowa

Instructions

1) Preheat oven to 350 degrees.
2) Cut chicken breasts into 2-inch pieces with poultry shears. Place breast pieces and legs in a ● *9-by-9-inch pan,* ▲ *shallow 2-quart baking dish.*
3) Combine oil, soy sauce, Worcestershire sauce, optional MSG, garlic powder, salt, pepper and rosemary in a ● *small bowl,* ▲ *medium bowl.*
4) Brush chicken pieces generously with sauce.
5) Bake in the preheated oven for 20 minutes.
6) Turn pieces over and brush with remaining sauce.
7) Basting occasionally with sauce, bake until chicken is tender and golden brown, an additional ● *20 to 30 minutes,* ▲ *30 minutes.*
8) While chicken is baking, halve pineapples lengthwise, cutting through the leafy crown carefully so it remains intact.
9) Carefully cut around fruit in shells and lift out.
10) Remove core and cut pineapple flesh into 1½-inch cubes. Reserve half the pineapple for this dish—use remaining pineapple as desired.
11) Set fruit and shells aside.
12) Drain liquid from canned fruits and reserve both.
13) Place cornstarch in a ● *1-quart saucepan,* ▲ *1½ quart saucepan.*
14) Gradually add liquid from fruit to cornstarch, stirring until mixture is smooth.
15) Add wine and cook, stirring constantly, until thickened and mixture comes to a boil. Remove from heat.
16) When chicken is done, arrange pieces in pineapple shells.
17) Take chicken basting liquid with drippings and add to fruit sauce.
18) Pour half the sauce into a sauceboat. To the other half of the sauce add drained fruit and pineapple.
19) Spoon the hot sauce with fruits over chicken, arranging fruits in spaces between chicken pieces.
20) Sprinkle coconut over top and serve immediately with extra sauce on side.

preparation time: ● 1 hour; ▲ 1½ hours

Special Note
● Chicken and fruits can be reheated in a saucepan over low heat and arranged in pineapple shells. Do not arrange dish before you are ready to serve because shells will become soggy.

Chicken Jerusalem

Ingredients

2

2	Tbs butter
1	large chicken breast, halved
6	medium mushrooms
½	10-oz package frozen artichoke hearts, partially defrosted
2	Tbs dry sherry
¾	cup light cream
2	egg yolks
1½	tsps lemon juice
¼	tsp salt
⅛	tsp freshly ground black pepper
½	tsp chopped chives

6

3	Tbs butter
3	large chicken breasts, halved
18	medium mushrooms
1½	10-oz packages frozen artichoke hearts, partially defrosted
6	Tbs dry sherry
2	cups light cream
4	egg yolks
1½	Tbs lemon juice
½	tsp salt
¼	tsp freshly ground black pepper
1	tsp chopped chives

❄ JACK'S, 615 Sacramento Street, San Francisco, California

Instructions

1) Over moderate heat, melt butter in a ● *10-inch skillet that has a cover,*
   ▲ *4-quart Dutch oven.*
2) Add chicken and brown evenly on all sides. ▲ Remove pieces as they brown. Return all chicken pieces to the Dutch oven.
3) Reduce heat to low, cover and cook 20 minutes or until chicken is tender. Remove chicken.
4) Add mushrooms and artichoke hearts; cook over moderate heat, stirring occasionally, until vegetables are brown and tender.
5) Add sherry and cook until liquid has almost evaporated.
6) Stir in cream, scraping bottom of pan to loosen brown particles.
7) Simmer until mixture is thickened. Remove from heat.
8) Beat egg yolks in a small bowl with lemon juice.
9) Slowly stir some of the hot sauce into egg yolks, stirring constantly until smooth.
10) Gradually return mixture to pan, stirring constantly; add salt and pepper. Cook over low heat until sauce is hot, but do not let mixture boil.
11) Return chicken to pan and heat through.
12) Sprinkle chives over top and serve immediately.

preparation time: ▲ 40 minutes; ● 1 hour

Special Note
● If you refrigerate the completed dish, the sauce will thicken. On reheating, add a little milk or light cream to correct consistency.

Supremes de Volaille, Elisabeth

Ingredients

2	whole chicken breasts, skinned and boned
1	oz sliced boiled ham
1½	ozs sliced Swiss cheese
2½	Tbs flour
2½	Tbs butter
1	Tb vegetable oil
¼	lb mushrooms, sliced (about 1 cup)
1	Tb chopped shallots
2	small tomatoes, peeled and chopped
¼	cup dry white wine
⅓	cup heavy cream
½	cup light cream
¼	tsp salt
⅛	tsp freshly ground black pepper
1	Tb chopped parsley

6

6	whole chicken breasts, skinned and boned
4	ozs sliced boiled ham
4	ozs sliced Swiss cheese
7	Tbs flour
5	Tbs butter
1	Tb vegetable oil
½	lb mushrooms, sliced (about 2½ cups)
2	Tbs chopped shallots
4	medium tomatoes, peeled and chopped
½	cup dry white wine
1	cup heavy cream
1	cup light cream
½	tsp salt
¼	tsp freshly ground black pepper
2	Tbs chopped parsley

❋ EDITH PALMER'S COUNTRY INN, Virigina City, Nevada

Instructions

1) Open each whole breast so it lies flat. Pound breasts between sheets of wax paper with a mallet until thin, leaving each whole breast intact.
2) Arrange opened breasts on a tray, smoothside down. Cut a piece of ham and a piece of cheese the same size as half the breast and arrange on top of it.
3) Fold breast in half to cover ham and cheese. Seal edges by pounding with mallet. Repeat with remaining breasts.
4) Roll breasts in ● 2 *tablespoons flour,* ▲ 6 *tablespoons flour* to coat; shake off excess.
5) Heat ● 2 *tablespoons butter,* ▲ 4 *tablespoons butter* and the oil in a ● 10-*inch skillet,* ▲ 12-*inch skillet.*
6) Add chicken breasts; cook until underside is golden brown.
7) Turn and cook other side 6 to 8 minutes or until golden brown.
8) Place breasts on a platter and keep warm in a low oven.
9) Add mushrooms and shallots to skillet in which chicken cooked; cook until tender and lightly browned.
10) Add tomatoes and wine; simmer until most of the liquid has evaporated.
11) Stir in heavy cream; cook until reduced by half. Remove from heat.
12) In a 1-quart saucepan melt the remaining butter over low heat.
13) Stir in the remaining flour with a wire wisk; blend well.
14) Add light cream; cook, stirring constantly, until thickened and smooth.
15) Add salt and pepper.
16) Gradually add sauce to tomato mixture in the skillet and cook over low heat until heated through.
17) Pour sauce over chicken and sprinkle with chopped parsley.

preparation time: ● 50 to 60 minutes; ▲ 1½ hours

Special Note
● Dish will keep in the refrigerator up to 1 week. To reheat, arrange chicken breasts in a baking dish with the sauce and bake, covered, in a preheated 325-degree oven 15 to 20 minutes or until heated through. You can freeze this dish for 2 to 3 months.

Baked Chicken with Sour Cream Sauce

Ingredients

CHICKEN

2	Tbs flour
1	tsp freshly grated lemon peel
¼	tsp paprika
¼	tsp dried rosemary
½	tsp salt
¼	tsp freshly ground black pepper
1	large chicken breast, halved
1	Tb butter
1	Tb vegetable oil
¼	cup water
¼	cup dry white wine

SAUCE

1	Tb butter
1	Tb flour
½	tsp salt
½	cup sour cream

CHICKEN

½	cup flour
1	Tb freshly grated lemon peel
1	tsp paprika
1	tsp dried rosemary
1	tsp salt
½	tsp freshly ground black pepper
3	large chicken breasts, halved
2	Tbs butter
1	Tb vegetable oil
½	cup water
½	cup dry white wine

SAUCE

2	Tbs butter
2	Tbs flour
1	tsp salt
1	cup sour cream

✳ FARAWAY HILLS COUNTRY INN, Beverly, West Virginia

Instructions

1) Preheat oven to 350 degrees.
2) In a paper bag combine flour, lemon peel, paprika, rosemary, salt and pepper.
3) Add chicken breasts, 2 halves at a time, and shake bag to coat chicken well. Remove and repeat with remaining breast halves.
4) Place butter and oil in a 10-inch skillet over moderate heat and brown chicken on all sides.
5) Place chicken in a ● *2-quart casserole,* ▲ *4-quart casserole.*
6) Pour in water and wine. Cover.
7) Bake in the preheated oven 30 minutes. Uncover and bake 15 minutes longer.
8) Remove chicken from liquid to a heated serving platter and keep warm.
9) To make sauce: pour cooking liquid into an 8-ounce measuring cup, add water, if necessary, to make ● *½ cup,* ▲ *1 cup.*
10) Melt butter in a ● *1-quart saucepan,* ▲ *2-quart saucepan,* stir in flour and salt.
11) Cook, stirring constantly, 1 minute.
12) Pour in cooking liquid and, stirring constantly, cook until mixture thickens and comes to a boil. ⬚S
13) Put sour cream into a small bowl, stir in some of the hot sauce; slowly return sour cream to saucepan and blend well.
14) Do not allow sauce to boil after adding the sour cream, or mixture will curdle. Pour sauce over chicken and serve immediately.

preparation time: ● 1½ hours; ▲ 2 hours

Special Note
● If you are not serving the dish immediately, or if you are freezing, follow directions through step 12. When ready to serve, warm sauce and chicken, covered, over low heat. When chicken is heated through, remove to a serving dish and keep warm. Complete the sauce.

Coq au Vin

Ingredients

1 Tb olive oil
1 large chicken breast, halved
1 small garlic clove, minced
1 small onion, sliced
2 Tbs chopped shallots
1 small bay leaf
1 small tomato, peeled, seeded and chopped
½ cup sliced mushrooms
¾ tsp salt
¼ tsp freshly ground black pepper
½ cup red Burgundy wine
6 pitted black olives
1 Tb chopped parsley

¼ cup olive oil
3 large chicken breasts, halved
2 garlic cloves, minced
1 medium onion, sliced
4 Tbs chopped shallots
1 bay leaf
2 medium tomatoes, peeled, seeded and chopped
1½ cups sliced mushrooms (about ⅓ lb)
1½ tsps salt
½ tsp freshly ground black pepper
1½ cups red Burgundy wine
½ cup pitted black olives
¼ cup chopped parsley

6

½ cup olive oil
12 large chicken breasts, halved
8 large garlic cloves, minced
3 large onions, sliced
1 cup chopped shallots
4 small bay leaves
2½ lbs tomatoes, peeled, seeded and chopped
6 cups sliced mushrooms (about 1½ lbs)
2 Tbs salt
1 tsp freshly ground black pepper
6 cups red Burgundy wine
2 cups pitted black olives
1 cup chopped parsley

※ CHATEAU LOUISE INN, West Dundee, Illinois

Instructions

1) Heat oil in ● *a 2-quart Dutch oven,* ▲ *a 4-quart Dutch oven,* ■ *2 8-quart Dutch ovens, dividing ingredients evenly between them.*
2) Sauté chicken pieces until golden on both sides, 10 to 15 minutes. ▲ ■ Remove pieces as they brown. Return browned chicken to pan.
3) Add garlic and onions and cook until golden.
4) Add shallots, bay leaf, tomatoes, mushrooms, salt and pepper; simmer 10 minutes.
5) Add wine; simmer partially covered 30 minutes or until chicken is tender.
6) Add olives and sprinkle parsley over top, just before serving.

preparation time: ● 1 hour; ▲ 1¼ hours; ■ 1¾ hours

Special Notes
- Sauce is thin; if a thicker sauce is desired, thicken by making a paste of 1 tablespoon of cornstarch and 1 tablespoon water for each cup of liquid. Add paste to liquid, stirring constantly, and bring to a boil.
- Coq au vin freezes very well and will keep 3 months.

||Sautéed Chicken Livers

Ingredients

1	Tb flour
⅛	tsp salt
⅛	tsp freshly ground black pepper
½	lb chicken livers
1	Tb vegetable oil
3	Tbs butter
1	medium onion, chopped
½	cup sliced mushrooms (about ⅛ lb)
2	Tbs dry sherry
2	Tbs chopped parsley

		6
3	Tbs flour	
½	tsp salt	
¼	tsp freshly ground black pepper	
2	lbs chicken livers	
2	Tbs vegetable oil	
8	Tbs butter	
3	medium onions, chopped	
½	lb mushrooms, sliced	
6–7	Tbs dry sherry	
¼	cup chopped parsley	

❄ NENDEL'S INN, 9900 Southwest Canyon Road, Portland, Oregon

Instructions

1) In a medium bowl, combine flour, salt and pepper.
2) Add chicken livers and toss to coat lightly.
3) Heat oil and butter over moderate heat in ● *an 8-inch skillet,* ▲ *a 12-inch skillet.*
4) Add livers and sauté, stirring occasionally, until livers are brown on the outside and still pink inside.
5) Add onion, cook until tender.
6) Add mushrooms and cook, stirring constantly, until lightly colored.
7) Return livers to the pan and add sherry. Simmer over moderate heat 4 to 5 minutes or until livers are heated through and sauce is slightly thickened.
8) Sprinkle with chopped parsley.

preparation time: ● 30 minutes; ▲ 45 minutes

Special Note
● The livers will keep refrigerated 2 to 3 days and will keep frozen 2 to 3 months.

Roast Duck Normandy

DUCK

8	Tbs (1 stick) butter
¾	cup chopped celery
¾	cup chopped onion
6	Tbs chopped parsley
¾	cup slivered almonds
¾	cup seedless raisins
1½	cups peeled, sliced apples
12	ozs dry stuffing mix
½	cup water
2	4½-lb ready-to-cook ducks
2	carrots, scraped and sliced
2	onions, sliced
4	celery stalks with leaves, sliced

6-8

SAUCE

2	cups sugar
2	Tbs butter
2	cups orange juice
2	Tbs lemon juice
2	Tbs freshly grated orange peel
¼	cup Marsala
½	cup Madeira
¼	tsp vanilla extract
1	tsp salt
4	tsps cornstarch
2	Tbs water
2	oranges, sliced

 FRENCHY'S RESTAURANT, 1901 East North Avenue, Milwaukee, Wisconsin

Instructions

1) Preheat oven to 350 degrees.
2) Melt butter in a 3-quart Dutch oven over low heat.
3) Add celery and onion; cook until soft.
4) Add parsley, almonds, raisins and apples.
5) Add stuffing mix; toss thoroughly.
6) Add water and blend well.
7) Divide stuffing between the ducks. Stuff duck cavities and necks and secure with skewers.
8) Spread sliced carrots, onions and celery on bottom of roaster and place ducks on top. Bake in the preheated oven 1½ hours.
9) Meanwhile, make the sauce: in a heavy 12-inch skillet heat sugar and butter over low heat, stirring constantly, until sugar melts and turns a golden brown.
10) Add orange and lemon juices slowly and carefully; don't worry if sugar hardens, continue cooking until it melts again in the juices.
11) Add orange rind, Marsala, Madeira, vanilla and salt.
12) In a small dish mix cornstarch with water until smooth.
13) Add to sauce, stirring constantly, until mixture thickens and comes to a boil. Reserve.
14) After ducks have cooked 1½ hours, remove and discard vegetables and accumulated fat.
15) Baste with sauce every 10 minutes and continue to cook 30 minutes longer or until ducks are done and golden brown.
16) Decorate ducks with orange slices and serve remaining sauce on the side.

preparation time: 2½ to 3 hours

Special Notes
• Duck will keep in refrigerator 1 week. Warm uncovered in a preheated 350-degree oven until heated through, 20 to 30 minutes.
• Duck with sauce can be frozen for 2 to 3 months.

MEAT

Braised Lamb Shanks Gemüse

Ingredients

4

2	Tbs olive oil
4	¾-lb lamb shanks
½	cup chopped onion
½	cup chopped carrots
½	cup chopped celery
2	bay leaves
2	garlic cloves, crushed
12	black peppercorns
¼	tsp dried summer savory
¼	tsp dried thyme
¼	tsp dried marjoram
3	cups beef broth
3	cups red Burgundy wine
½	cup string beans, cut in ½-inch pieces
½	cup peas
	flour
	water
	Kitchen Bouquet
	salt and black pepper

12

6	Tbs olive oil
12	¾-lb lamb shanks
1½	cups chopped onions
1½	cups chopped carrots
1½	cups chopped celery
6	bay leaves
6	garlic cloves, crushed
2	tsps black peppercorns
1	tsp dried summer savory
1	tsp dried thyme
1	tsp dried marjoram
9	cups beef broth
9	cups red Burgundy wine
1½	cups sring beans, cut in ½-inch pieces
1½	cups peas
	flour
	water
	Kitchen Bouquet
	salt and black pepper

❄ KARL RATZSCH'S, 320 East Mason, Milwaukee, Wisconsin

Instructions

1) Heat ● *2 tablespoons oil,* ▲ *3 tablespoons oil* in ● *a 4-quart Dutch oven,* ▲ *each of 2 8-quart Dutch ovens, dividing all ingredients evenly between them.*
2) Add shanks and brown evenly on all sides. Remove.
3) Cook onions, carrots and celery in the same Dutch oven until golden.
4) Preheat oven to 375 degrees.
5) With bay leaves, garlic, peppercorns, savory, thyme and marjoram make ● *1 herb bouquet,* ▲ *2 herb bouquets.*
6) Place herb bouquet in Dutch oven.
7) Return shanks to pot and add broth and wine. Cover pot.
8) Bake in the preheated oven 2 to 2½ hours, or until tender. Add string beans and peas for the last 30 minutes of cooking.
9) Place Dutch oven on top of range and discard the herb bouquet.
10) Remove shanks and measure liquid.
11) For every 1 cup of liquid blend 1 tablespoon flour into 1 tablespoon water and add ½ teaspoon Kitchen Bouquet.
12) Return liquid to pan. Stir in flour mixture and cook, stirring constantly, until thickened and mixture comes to a boil. Lower heat.
13) Return shanks to pot and reheat gently.
14) Season to taste with salt and pepper.

preparation time: ● 3 hours; ▲ 3½ hours

Special Note
● As the flavor of the braised lamb shanks improves after a day or 2 in the refrigerator, and even freezes well, it seems impractical to make only two shanks, the quantity for two. But it can easily be done by halving the recipe for 4.

Beef Tenderloin in Claret

Ingredients

2-3

1	lb trimmed beef tenderloin
⅛ – ¼	tsp salt
⅛	tsp freshly ground black pepper
4	Tbs butter
4	large shallots, sliced
½	cup Claret wine or any dry red wine
1	tsp cornstarch
½	cup beef broth
½	tsp lemon juice
1	Tb brandy

6

3	lbs trimmed beef tenderloin
½	tsp salt
¼	tsp freshly ground black pepper
8	Tbs (1 stick) butter
8	large shallots, sliced
1	cup Claret wine or any dry red wine
2	tsps cornstarch
1	cup beef broth
1	tsp lemon juice
2	Tbs brandy

24

2	6-lb trimmed beef tenderloins
1	tsp salt
½	tsp freshly ground black pepper
1	lb butter
1½	cups sliced shallots
4	cups Claret wine or any dry red wine
2	Tbs + 2 tsps cornstarch
4	cups beef broth
4	tsps lemon juice
½	cup brandy

※ ZODIAC ROOM RESTAURANT at NEIMAN-MARCUS, Dallas, Texas

Instructions

1) Preheat oven to 325 degrees.
2) Rub the tenderloin with salt and pepper
3) Roast in the preheated oven until meat reaches an internal temperature of 160 degrees (for medium), about ● *35 minutes,* ▲ *1¾ hours,* ■ *3 hours.*
4) While meat is roasting, melt butter over moderate heat in a ● ▲ *small skillet,* ■ *3-quart saucepan.*
5) Add shallots and cook until tender.
6) Add wine and boil until liquid is reduced by half.
7) In a small dish blend cornstarch and ¼ cup beef broth until smooth.
8) Gradually stir into wine mixture with remaining beef broth, stirring constantly until mixture thickens and comes to a boil.
9) Stir in lemon juice and pour over cooked roast.
10) Run meat under broiler until sauce is bubbly.
11) Heat brandy in a small saucepan until warm. Ignite and pour flaming over meat. Serve immediately.

preparation time: ● 45 minutes; ▲ 2¼ hours; ■ 3½ hours

Sliced Peppered Tenderloin Casserole

Ingredients

2

4	Tbs butter
1	Tb olive oil
½	tsp freshly ground black pepper
	pinch of dried sage
	pinch of ground cumin
½	lb beef tenderloin, cut into ½-inch strips
½	lb mushrooms, quartered
1	garlic clove, minced
1	small onion, cut into 8 wedges
1	medium green pepper, seeded and cut into 1-inch pieces
1	medium tomato, peeled and cut into 8 wedges
1	Tb tomato paste
¼	cup soy sauce
1	Tb white vinegar
¼–½	tsp salt

6-8

8	Tbs (1 stick) butter
2	Tbs olive oil
1	tsp freshly ground black pepper
¼	tsp dried sage
¼	tsp ground cumin
2	lbs beef tenderloin, cut into ½-inch strips
1	lb mushrooms, quartered
2	garlic cloves, minced
1	medium onion, cut into 8 wedges
2	medium green peppers, seeded and cut into 1-inch pieces
2	medium tomatoes, peeled and cut into 8 wedges
2	Tbs tomato paste
½	cup soy sauce
2	Tbs white vinegar
½–1	tsp salt

24

1	cup (2 sticks) butter
4	Tbs olive oil
2	tsps freshly ground black pepper
1	tsp dried sage
1	tsp ground cumin
8	lbs beef tenderloin, cut into ½-inch strips
4	lbs mushrooms, quartered
8	garlic cloves, minced
4	medium onions, cut into 8 wedges
8	medium green peppers, seeded and cut into 1-inch pieces
8	medium tomatoes, peeled and cut into 8 wedges
½	cup tomato paste
2	cups soy sauce
½	cup white vinegar
1–2	tsps salt

❄ CHARLIE'S CAFE EXCEPTIONALE, 701 Fourth Avenue South, Minneapolis, Minnesota

Instructions

1) Heat half the butter and the oil in ● *an 8-inch skillet,* ▲ *a 12-inch skillet,* ■ *a 7-quart casserole.*
2) Stir in pepper, sage and cumin.
3) Add some beef slices to skillet and sauté over moderately high heat until meat is medium rare, about 1 minute. Remove from skillet and set aside. Sauté rest of meat.
4) Add remaining butter and oil to skillet.
5) Add mushrooms and sauté until golden.
6) Add garlic, onion wedges and green pepper; cook, stirring occasionally, 4 to 5 minutes or until barely tender.
7) Add remaining ingredients and simmer 2 minutes.
8) Return meat to skillet, mix ingredients and cook till heated through
9) Do not overcook; vegetables should retain their texture.
10) Carefully taste for salt. Serve with rice.

preparation time: ● 30 to 40 minutes; ▲ 1 hour; ■ 1¼ hours

Special Notes
- This dish is tangy and quite salty due to the soy sauce. Add salt gradually, if at all.
- Peppered tenderloin freezes well; will keep 2 to 3 months.

Beef Tenderloin Tips au Vin

Ingredients

2

- 2 Tbs vegetable oil
- ½ lb beef tenderloin, cut diagonally into ¼-inch strips
- 1½ cups red Burgundy wine
- ¼ tsp coarsely ground black peppercorns
- 2 Tbs finely minced shallots
- ¼ cup finely chopped mushrooms
- 2 Tbs butter, melted
- 2 Tbs Madeira
- 2 slices white toast, crusts removed and cut into triangles
- 1 Tb chopped parsley
- ⅛ tsp salt

6

- 4 Tbs vegetable oil
- 2 lbs beef tenderloin, cut diagonally into ¼-inch strips
- 6 cups red Burgundy wine
- 1 tsp coarsely ground black peppercorns
- 6 Tbs finely minced shallots
- ¾ cup finely chopped mushrooms
- 4 Tbs butter, melted
- ½ cup Madeira
- 6 slices white toast, crusts removed and cut into triangles
- ¼ cup chopped parsley
- ¼ tsp salt

24

- ¾ cup vegetable oil
- 8 lbs beef tenderloin, cut diagonally into ¼-inch strips
- 6 qts red Burgundy wine
- 4 tsps crushed black peppercorns
- 1½ cups finely minced shallots
- 3 cups fine chopped mushrooms (about ¾ lb)
- 1 cup (2 sticks) butter, melted
- 2 cups Madeira
- 24 slices white toast, crusts removed and cut into triangles
- 1 cup chopped parsley
- ½ tsp salt

❊ CAFÉ DE PARIS at the PARK DEARBORN HOTEL, 1260 North Dearborn Parkway, Chicago, Illinois

Instructions

1) Heat ● *2 tablespoons oil,* ▲ *4 tablespoons oil,* ■ *½ cup oil* in a ● *10-inch skillet,* ▲ ■ *12-inch skillet.* ● ▲ Add beef tips and brown quickly over moderately high heat. Meat should be rare ■ Add some of the beef slices, brown quickly and remove to a platter. Repeat with remaining beef slices adding oil as needed.

2) Remove skillet from heat.

3) In ● *a 1-quart saucepan,* ▲ *a 2-quart saucepan,* ■ *2 8-quart Dutch ovens* combine Burgundy and peppercorns and bring to a boil. Boil rapidly until liquid is reduced to ● *½ cup,* ▲ *2 cups,* ■ *4 cups in each pot.*

4) Strain and discard pepper.

5) Return wine to saucepan; add mushrooms and shallots; simmer 3 to 4 minutes.

6) Stir in ● *1½ tablespoons melted butter,* ▲ *3 tablespoons melted butter,* ■ *¾ cup melted butter* and the Madeira.

7) Add meat and bring to a boil; remove from heat. Season to taste.

8) To serve: dip toast points in remaining melted butter and then in parsley. Insert 2 toast points in each portion with parsley ends sticking out.

preparation time: ● 30 minutes; ▲ 45 minutes; ■ 3 hours

Special Note
● This wine sauce can be stored in refrigerator for 2 weeks, or frozen for 2 to 3 months.

Boeuf Braisé

Ingredients

2-3

1½	lbs lean short ribs, well trimmed	1	small garlic clove, minced
¼	tsp salt	1	Tb brandy
⅛	tsp freshly ground black pepper	¾	cup red Burgundy wine
1	Tb flour	1	cup beef broth
1	oz salt pork, diced	1	sprig parsley
¼	cup diced celery	⅛	tsp dried thyme
1	medium onion, chopped	1	small bay leaf
1	small carrot, chopped	1	Tb butter
2	Tbs chopped green pepper	¼	cup sliced mushrooms
1	shallot, minced	½	tsp Worcestershire sauce
		3	cooked small onions

6

3	lbs lean short ribs, well trimmed	2	shallots, minced
½	tsp salt	1	large garlic clove, minced
¼	tsp freshly ground black pepper	1	Tb brandy
2	Tbs flour	1½	cups red Burgundy wine
2	ozs salt pork, diced	2	cups beef broth
½	cup diced celery	2	sprigs parsley
2	medium onions, chopped	¼	tsp dried thyme
1	medium carrot, chopped	1	small bay leaf
4	Tbs chopped green pepper	2	Tbs butter
		½	cup sliced mushrooms
		1	tsp Worcestershire sauce
		6	cooked small onions

24

16	lbs lean short ribs, well trimmed	3	large garlic cloves, minced
2½	tsps salt	5	Tbs brandy
1¼	tsps freshly ground black pepper	7½	cups red Burgundy wine
10	Tbs flour	10	cups beef broth
10	ozs salt pork, diced	8	sprigs parsley
5	cups diced celery	1	tsp dried thyme
5	cups chopped onions (7 large onions)	4	bay leaves
5	large carrots, chopped	4	Tbs butter
1¼	cups chopped green pepper	2	cups sliced mushrooms
½	cup minced shallots	5	tsps Worcestershire sauce
		2	lbs cooked small onions

❄ LE CHAMBERTIN, 348 West 46th Street, New York, New York

Instructions

1) Preheat oven to 500 degrees.
2) Sprinkle short ribs with salt and pepper, and coat well with flour.
3) Arrange ribs in ● ▲ *a jelly-roll pan,* ■ *2 jelly-roll pans.*
4) Bake ribs in the preheated oven until well browned, about 8 to 10 minutes. Turn and brown other side, another 8 to 10 minutes. Reduce oven heat to 350 degrees.
5) In ● *a 2-quart Dutch oven,* ▲ *a 4-quart Dutch oven,* ■ *2 8-quart Dutch ovens, dividing ingredients evenly between them,* brown diced salt pork over moderate heat; remove with slotted spoon and reserve.
6) In remaining pork fat, sauté celery, onions, carrots, green pepper, shallots and garlic until onions begin to brown .
7) Add the browned short ribs.
8) Pour brandy over meat, heat slightly and ignite.
9) In a ● *1-quart saucepan,* ▲ *2-quart saucepan,* ■ *4-quart sauce-pan* bring the Burgundy to a boil and ignite it. When the flame dies pour the wine over the meat.
10) Pour in beef broth.
11) With parsley, thyme and bay leaf, make ● ▲ *1 herb bouquet,* ■ *2 herb bouquets* and add to Dutch oven.
12) Cover and bake in the preheated oven for 1½ to 2 hours, or until tender.
13) While ribs are baking, melt butter over moderate heat in a ● ▲ *small skillet,* ■ *10-inch skillet.* Add mushrooms and sauté until they color.
14) When ribs are done, remove from oven, skim fat, remove ribs and reserve.
15) Discard herb bouquet.
16) Remove sauce from Dutch oven and put through a food mill; return to pot. Add Worcestershire sauce, onions and mushrooms. Add ribs and reheat.
17) Sprinkle top with reserved salt pork and serve.

preparation time: ● 3 hours; ▲ 3½ hours; ■ 5 hours

Special Notes
- Flavor improves as dish stands. It will keep refrigerated up to a week and frozen for 2 to 3 months.
- An herb bouquet or a bouquet garni is made by cutting a 6-inch square of cheesecloth. Put herbs in center and bring corners together. Tie with long piece of string.

Ragout of Beef Huntsman

Ingredients

1	lb dried kidney beans
	cold water
	salted water
4	lbs boneless beef chuck, cut into 1½-inch cubes
1	tsp salt
¼	tsp freshly ground black pepper
3	Tbs vegetable oil
4	medium onions, sliced
1¾	tsps paprika
3	cups dry red wine
¼	cup peeled and cubed turnip
3	medium potatoes, peeled and cubed
3	medium carrots, scraped and cut into strips
3	cups water
1	tsp chili powder
1	1-lb-10-ozs can tomatoes
1	10-oz package frozen French-style green beans, partially defrosted
3	Tbs flour
3	Tbs water
1	Tb salt
½	tsp freshly ground black pepper
1	pint sour cream, chilled

12

HO-HO-KUS INN, Franklin Turnpike and Sheridan Avenue, Ho-Ho-Kus, New Jersey

Instructions

1) Wash kidney beans; put into a large bowl and cover with cold water. Let stand overnight.
2) Drain beans, put into a 4-quart casserole, cover with salted water.
3) Bring to a boil, reduce heat, cover and simmer 1½ hours or until tender. Drain and reserve beans.
4) Sprinkle salt and pepper over beef.
5) Heat oil in an 8-quart casserole. Add some beef cubes and brown over moderate heat on all sides. Remove and brown more meat. Return browned meat to pot.
6) Add onions and ½ teaspoon paprika; cook until onions are golden.
7) Add wine and blend well. Simmer, covered, 2 hours.
8) Stir in turnips, potatoes and carrots, water, chili powder, and 1 teaspoon paprika.
9) Simmer, covered, 45 minutes, or until vegetables are tender.
10) Add tomatoes with their liquid, kidney beans and green beans. Heat through.
11) In a small dish, blend flour and water.
12) Stir into stew and bring to a boil. Reduce heat and simmer 10 minutes, until thickened.
13) Season with salt and pepper.
14) Cool and refrigerate overnight to develop flavors. $\boxed{S}$
15) Heat slowly. Sprinkle the remaining ¼ teaspoon paprika over sour cream and serve in a separate bowl, with the stew.

preparation time: 4 hours (without soaking beans)

Special Notes
- Make the stew 1 or 2 days before you plan to serve. Kidney beans must be soaked overnight before cooking, or if you are in a hurry, beans can be covered with water, brought to a boil, covered and left to stand 1 hour. Drain and continue with instructions from step 3.
- Stew will keep in refrigerator for 1 week, and each day the flavor improves.
- Stew can be frozen for 2 to 3 months after step 14.

Anticuchos (Marinated Beef)

Ingredients

2-3

1	small dried hot, red chili pepper, crushed
1	small bay leaf
½	garlic clove, chopped
2	Tbs lemon juice
1	Tb lime juice
1	Tb vegetable oil
1	Tb water
¼	tsp salt
10	ozs boneless sirloin, cut into 1½-inch cubes
6	ozs chicken livers

SAUCE

1½	Tbs vegetable oil
1½	tsps chopped onion
½	garlic clove, chopped
1	Tb flour
1½	tsps chili powder
1	cup chicken broth
1½	Tbs canned tomato puree

6

2	small dried hot, red chili peppers, crushed
1	bay leaf
1	small garlic clove, chopped
¼	cup lemon juice
2	Tbs lime juice
2	Tbs vegetable oil
2	Tbs water
½	tsp salt
1¼	lbs boneless sirloin, cut into 1½-inch cubes
¾	lb chicken livers

SAUCE

3	Tbs vegetable oil
1	Tb chopped onion
1	small clove garlic, chopped
2	Tbs flour
1	Tb chili powder
2	cups chicken broth
3	Tbs canned tomato puree

24

6–8	small dried hot, red chili peppers, crushed
2	large bay leaves
4	garlic cloves, chopped
1	cup lemon juice
½	cup lime juice
½	cup vegetable oil
½	cup water
2	tsps salt
5	lbs boneless sirloin, cut into 1½-inch cubes
3	lbs chicken liver

SAUCE

¾	cup vegetable oil
¼	cup chopped onions
4	cloves garlic, chopped
½	cup flour
¼	cup chili powder
8	cups chicken broth
¾	cup canned tomato puree

❄ THE DELEGATES' DINING ROOM of the UNITED NATIONS, New York, New York

❄ The Delegates' Dining Room of the UN

Instructions

1) Combine chili peppers, bay leaf, garlic, lemon juice, lime juice, vegetable oil, water and salt in a ● *small bowl,* ▲ *medium bowl,* ■ *large bowl.*
2) Add beef and marinate in refrigerator 2½ hours.
3) Add chicken livers; marinate in refrigerator 30 minutes longer.
4) While meat is marinating, prepare the sauce: heat the oil in a ● *small saucepan,* ▲ *1-quart saucepan,* ■ *3-quart saucepan or Dutch oven.*
5) Add onions and garlic; cook until tender.
6) Stir in flour and chili powder; cook, stirring, 1 minute.
7) Add chicken broth and tomato puree; bring to a boil.
8) Reduce heat and simmer ● *10 minutes;* ▲ *15 to 20 minutes,* ■ *20 to 25 minutes.* Keep warm.
9) Alternating them, thread marinated beef and livers on skewers.
10) Broil over hot coals of a barbeque grill, 4 to 5 inches from the source of heat.
11) Broil 4 to 5 minutes on each side or until cooked to desired degree of doneness.
12) Serve with hot sauce on the side.

preparation time (including 3-hour marination): ● 3½ hours; ▲ 4 hours; ■ 4½ hours

Special Notes
- Instead of a barbeque you can use a preheated broiler, keeping meat 4 inches from the heat, turning once.
- Do not marinate meat more than 4 or 5 hours as it will become too tart. If you cannot cook it right away, remove from marinade, thread on skewers and refrigerate.
- Meat and sauce, packed separately, will freeze for 2 to 3 months.

Moussaka

Ingredients

<table>
<tr><td colspan="2">

MEAT SAUCE
4	Tbs butter
2	Tbs olive oil
2	medium onions, chopped
2	lbs lean ground beef
1	1-lb-12-oz can tomatoes
3	Tbs tomato paste
¼	cup chopped parsley
1½	tsps salt
½	tsp ground cinnamon
1	large garlic clove, minced
½	tsp dried oregano
¼	tsp ground allspice
⅛	tsp ground cloves
½	cup freshly grated Parmesan cheese (about 2 oz)
1	egg

</td><td>

CHEESE SAUCE
4	Tbs butter
3	Tbs flour
1½	cups milk
6	Tbs light cream or half-and-half
6	Tbs freshly grated Parmesan cheese
2	egg yolks
½	tsp salt
⅛–¼	tsp freshly ground black pepper

TO ASSEMBLE
2	medium eggplants
4	Tbs olive oil
4	Tbs vegetable oil
¾	tsp salt
2	Tbs butter
⅓	cup dry bread crumbs
¼	tsp ground nutmeg

</td></tr>
</table>

6

24

MEAT SAUCE

8	Tbs (1 stick) butter
¼	cup olive oil
8	medium onions, chopped
8	lbs ground lean beef
4	1-lb 12-oz cans tomatoes
1	cup tomato paste
1	cup chopped parsley
4	tsps salt
2	tsps ground cinnamon
4	large garlic cloves, minced
2	tsps dried oregano
1	tsp ground allspice
½	tsp ground cloves
2	cups freshly grated Parmesan cheese (about 8 ozs)
4	eggs

CHEESE SAUCE

1	cup (2 sticks) butter
¾	cup flour
6	cups milk
1½	cups light cream or half-and-half
1½	cups freshly grated Parmesan cheese
8	egg yolks
2	tsps salt
1	tsp freshly ground black pepper

TO ASSEMBLE

8	medium eggplants
1	cup olive oil
1	cup vegetable oil
3½	tsps salt
8	Tbs (1 stick) butter
1⅓	cups dry bread crumbs
1	tsp ground nutmeg

✷EDITH PALMER'S COUNTRY INN, Virginia City, Nevada

136

Instructions

1) To make meat sauce: combine butter and oil over moderate heat in a ▲ *4-quart Dutch oven,* ■ *2 8-quart Dutch ovens, dividing all ingredients evenly between them.*

2) Add onions and cook until golden. Add beef, breaking up pieces with a fork; cook until brown. Drain off fat.

3) Add tomatoes with their liquid, tomato paste, parsley, salt, cinnamon, garlic, oregano, allspice, cloves and half the cheese. Cover; simmer over low heat 1 hour. Remove from heat and add remaining cheese.

4) Beat eggs in a ▲ *small bowl,* ■ *medium bowl.* Stir a little of the hot sauce into eggs, stirring constantly. Slowly return egg mixture to pot and blend well. Reserve meat sauce. Preheat oven to 400 degrees.

5) To make cheese sauce: melt butter over low heat in a ▲ *1-quart saucepan,* ■ *3-quart saucepan.*

6) Blend flour into butter with a wire whisk until smooth. Slowly add milk and cream, stirring constantly, until mixture thickens and comes to a boil. Stir in cheese and cook 1 minute.

7) Beat egg yolks in a small bowl. Stir a little of the hot white sauce into yolks and blend well. Slowly return egg mixture to saucepan, stirring constantly, until blended.

8) Peel eggplants and cut lengthwise into ¼-inch slices.

9) Mix together olive oil and vegetable oil and brush eggplant slices well with oil. Arrange slices on cookie sheets and bake in the preheated oven until golden, about 4 minutes.

10) Turn over and brown slices on other side, brushing slices with more oil as needed. Do not overcook, or eggplant will fall apart. Remove from oven, lower temperature to 350 degrees, season with salt.

11) To assemble dish: butter a ▲ *3-quart shallow baking dish,* ■ *4 3-quart shallow baking dishes.*

12) Place half the eggplant slices on bottom of dish(es). Sprinkle half the bread crumbs over eggplant. Spoon meat sauce over and spread evenly. Sprinkle remaining crumbs over meat sauce. Cover with remaining eggplant slices. Spread cheese sauce over eggplant to cover completely. Sprinkle nutmeg over top.

13) Bake in the oven for 30 minutes. Let cool 5 minutes before cutting.

preparation time: ▲ 2½ to 3 hours; ■ 4 hours

Special Notes
- Moussaka can be made and refrigerated for 3 or 4 days before baking.
- Completed dish freezes well for 3 months. Defrost, cover and warm in a preheated 325-degree oven for 20 minutes.
- As this dish is a lot of work for 2, it would be best to make the 6-portion quantity and freeze in small containers, perhaps freezer-to-oven dishes.

Stuffed Cabbage

Ingredients

6-8

1 large head green cabbage
2 lbs ground lean beef
1 cup cooked rice
½ cup chopped onions
2 Tbs sugar
2 eggs
¼ tsp garlic powder
1 tsp salt
¼ tsp freshly ground black pepper
4 cups canned tomatoes, drained
2 cups brown gravy
1 cup raisins
½ cup crushed ginger snaps
⅓ cup lemon juice
4 Tbs dark brown sugar
½ tsp salt

24

3 large heads green cabbage
6 lbs ground lean beef
3 cups cooked rice
1½ cups chopped onions
6 Tbs sugar
6 eggs
1 tsp garlic powder
1 Tb salt
1 tsp freshly ground black pepper
12 cups canned tomatoes, drained
6 cups brown gravy
3 cups raisins
1½ cups crushed ginger snaps
1 cup lemon juice
¾ cup dark brown sugar
1½ tsps salt

❄ PUMPERNIK's, 6700 Collins Avenue, Miami Beach, Florida

Instructions

1) Fill an 8-quart Dutch oven ¾ full with water, bring to a boil and add cabbage. (■ Blanch each cabbage separately.)
2) Remove outer leaves as they become pliable and continue until you have ▲ *16 leaves,* ■ *48 leaves.*
3) Shred remaining cabbage and reserve.
4) In a medium bowl combine ground beef, rice, onions, sugar, eggs, garlic powder, salt and pepper; blend well.
5) Place about ¼ cup of the meat mixture in the center of each cabbage leaf
6) Bring stem end of leaf over meat. Bring the two outer corners to the center. Roll into a package. Secure with a tooth pick.
7) With half the shredded cabbage, line ▲ *an 8-quart Dutch oven,* ■ *2 8-quart Dutch ovens, dividing ingredients evenly between them.*
8) Arrange stuffed cabbage leaves on top.
9) Cover with remaining shredded cabbage.
10) Combine tomatoes, brown gravy, raisins, ginger snaps, lemon juice, brown sugar and salt; pour over cabbage.
11) Cover and simmer 2½ hours.

preparation time: ▲3½ hours; ■ 4½ hours

Special Notes
- Stuffed cabbage freezes perfectly for 2 to 3 months.
- There is much too much work to make only 2 portions. Strongly recommend making in larger quantity and freezing leftovers.

Kofta (Meatball) Curry

Ingredients

2-3

1	lb ground lean beef
½	tsp ground coriander
½	tsp ground ginger
	pinch of ground cloves
	pinch of ground cinnamon
¼	tsp salt
	pinch of freshly ground black pepper

1½	Tbs curry powder
1	Tb butter
1	Tb vegetable oil
1	medium onion, chopped
1	large garlic clove, minced
1	Tb canned tomato puree
2	cups beef broth

2 lbs ground lean beef
1 tsp ground coriander
1 tsp ground ginger
¼ tsp ground cloves
¼ tsp ground cinnamon
1 tsp salt
¼ tsp freshly ground black pepper
3 Tbs curry powder
1 Tb butter
2 Tbs vegetable oil
2 medium onions, chopped
3 garlic cloves, minced
2 Tbs canned tomato puree
4 cups beef broth

6

24

8	lbs ground lean beef
4	tsps ground coriander
4	tsps ground ginger
1	tsp ground cloves
1	tsp ground cinnamon
4	tsps salt
1	tsp freshly ground black pepper

¾	cup curry powder
4	Tbs butter
¼	cup vegetable oil
5	large onions, chopped
10	garlic cloves, minced
½	cup canned tomato puree
4	qts beef broth

Instructions

1) In a ● ▲ *medium bowl,* ■ *large bowl or pot,* combine beef, coriander, ginger, cloves, cinnamon, salt, pepper and ● *1½ teaspoons curry powder,* ▲ *1 tablespoon curry powder,* ■ *4 tablespoons curry powder.*
2) Mix together until well blended; shape into 1-inch balls.
3) Heat butter and oil in a ● *10-inch skillet,* ▲ *3-quart Dutch oven,* ■ *8-quart Dutch oven.*
4) Add half the meatballs and brown on all sides. Remove meatballs with a slotted spoon and reserve. Brown remaining meatballs; remove and reserve.
5) Add onions and garlic to pan and cook until tender. Drain off fat.
6) Stir in tomato puree and remaining curry powder; cook, stirring constantly, 1 minute.
7) Add beef broth and meatballs; blend well.
8) Cover and simmer 10 minutes. Remove meatballs and keep warm.
9) Reduce sauce to half, or until thickened.
10) Return meatballs to sauce and reheat.
11) Serve curried meatballs with rice and side dishes of chutney, chopped hard-boiled egg whites and yolks and shredded coconut.

preparation time: ● 45 minutes; ▲ 1¼ hours; ■ 2½ hours

Special Notes
- Curry can be refrigerated 5 to 6 days; frozen for 2 to 3 months.
- On cooling or freezing, skim and discard fat which comes to the surface.
- Curry usually gets stronger on standing. If it is too hot for your taste, add more beef broth.

Beef Tacos with Green Chili Salsa

Ingredients

2-3

SALSA
- 1 medium tomato, chopped
- 1 small onion, chopped
- 1 jalapeño or green chili pepper, chopped
- 1 small garlic clove, minced
- ¼ ·tsp salt
- ¼ tsp MSG (optional)

TACOS
- 1 Tb butter
- ½ lb ground lean beef
- 1 small onion, chopped
- ½ cup tomato sauce
- 1½ tsps soy sauce
- 1½ tsps Worcestershire sauce
- 1 small garlic clove, minced
- vegetable oil for deep frying
- 9 tortillas
- 1 medium tomato, chopped
- 1 cup shredded romaine
- ½ cup grated Cheddar cheese

6

SALSA
- 2 medium tomatoes, chopped
- 1 medium onion, chopped
- 2 jalapeños or green chili peppers, chopped
- 1 garlic clove, minced
- ½ tsp salt
- ¼ tsp MSG (optional)

TACOS
- 2 Tbs butter
- 1 lb ground lean beef
- 1 medium onion, chopped
- 1 cup canned tomato sauce
- 1 Tb soy sauce
- 1 Tb Worcestershire sauce
- 1 garlic clove, minced
- vegetable oil for deep frying
- 18 tortillas
- 2 large tomatoes, chopped
- 2 cups shredded romaine
- 1 cup grated Cheddar cheese

24

SALSA
- 8 large tomatoes, chopped
- 3 large onions, chopped
- 8 jalapeños or green chili peppers, chopped
- 4 garlic cloves, minced
- 1–2 tsps salt
- ½ tsp MSG (optional)

TACOS
- 8 Tbs (1 stick) butter
- 4 lbs ground lean beef
- 3 large onions, chopped
- 4 cups tomato sauce
- ¼ cup soy sauce
- ¼ cup Worcestershire sauce
- 4 garlic cloves, minced
- vegetable oil for deep frying
- 72 tortillas
- 8 large tomatoes, chopped
- 8 cups shredded romaine
- 4 cups grated Cheddar cheese

✳ TIFFANY'S RESTAURANT-SALOON, Highway 14, Cerrillos, New Mexico

Instructions

1) To make green chili salsa: combine tomato, onion, jalapeños, garlic, salt and optional MSG in a ● *small bowl,* ▲ *medium bowl,* ■ *large bowl.*
2) Let salsa stand at least 15 minutes.
3) Heat butter over moderate heat in a ● ▲ *10-inch skillet,* ■ *8-quart Dutch oven.*
4) Add beef and onion; cook, stirring occasionally, until meat crumbs are no longer pink.
5) Drain off excess fat.
6) Add tomato sauce, soy sauce, Worcestershire sauce and garlic; simmer over low heat 10 minutes.
7) Heat 2 inches of oil to 375 degrees in a heavy 2-quart saucepan or deep fryer.
8) Fold tortillas in half to form a U and fry 2 or 3 at a time in oil for 2 minutes, or until golden; use tongs to turn.
9) Drain on paper towels.
10) Preheat oven to 425 degrees.
11) Spoon 2 tablespoons of the meat filling into each tortilla.
12) Sprinkle chopped tomato over top, then a layer of romaine, and finally cheese.
13) Arrange tacos (fried filled tortillas) in ● *a 2-quart shallow baking dish,* ▲ *a 3-quart shallow baking dish,* ■ *4 3-quart shallow baking dishes.*
14) Bake in the preheated oven for 5 minutes, or until cheese melts. Serve with green chili salsa.

preparation time: ● 1½ hours; ▲ 2¼ hours; ■ 5 hours

Special Notes
- Meat filling and tacos can be made in advance, but assemble only before baking as filled tacos become soggy.
- Leftover tacos can be reheated, uncovered, in a preheated 350-degree oven for 10 to 15 minutes.

143

Blanquette de Veau

Ingredients

2-3

2	Tbs butter	¼	lb ground lean veal
¾	lb boneless veal, cut into 1½-inch cubes	2	ozs ground pork
		¼	cup fresh bread crumbs
3	Tbs chopped scallions	1	egg
⅓	cup beef broth	2	Tbs butter
	pinch of ground nutmeg	6	small mushrooms
	pinch of dried thyme	1	Tb butter
½	bay leaf	1½	tsps flour
¼	tsp salt	½	cup beef broth
⅛	tsp freshly ground black pepper	1	egg yolk
		1½	tsps lemon juice
¼	cup water		

6

3	Tbs butter	½	lb ground lean veal
2	lbs boneless veal, cut into 1½-inch cubes	¼	lb ground pork
		½	cup fresh bread crumbs
½	cup chopped scallions	2	Tbs milk
1	cup beef broth	1	egg
⅛	tsp ground nutmeg	4	Tbs butter
⅛	tsp dried thyme	12	small mushrooms
1	small bay leaf	2	Tbs butter
½	tsp salt	1	Tb flour
¼	tsp freshly ground black pepper	1	cup beef broth
		2	egg yolks
½	cup water	1	Tb lemon juice

24

12	Tbs (1½ sticks) butter	2	lbs ground lean veal
8	lbs boneless veal, cut into 1½-inch cubes	1	lb ground pork
		2	cups fresh bread crumbs
2	cups chopped scallions	½	cup milk
4	cups beef broth	4	eggs
½	tsp ground nutmeg	1	cup (2 sticks) butter
½	tsp dried thyme	1½	lbs small mushrooms
4	bay leaves	8	Tbs (1 stick) butter
2	tsps salt	4	Tbs flour
1	tsp freshly ground black pepper	4	cups beef broth
		16	egg yolks
2	cups water	¼	cup lemon juice

❈ TAVERN ON THE GREEN, 67th Street and Central Park West, New York, New York

Instructions

1) Melt ● *2 tablespoons butter,* ▲ ■ *3 tablespoons butter* in ● *a 1½-quart Dutch oven or heavy saucepan;* ▲ *a 4-quart Dutch oven,* ■ *each of 2 7- or 8-quart Dutch ovens.*

2) ● ▲ Add all the cubed veal, and cook until lightly browned on all sides. ■ Brown some of the veal in each pot, remove with a slotted spoon and continue with remaining butter and veal.

3) Add scallion; cook 1 to 2 minutes.

4) Stir in beef broth, nutmeg, thyme, bay leaf, salt, pepper and water.

5) Cover and simmer over low heat ½ hour.

6) While veal is cooking, make meatballs: in a small bowl combine ground veal and pork, bread crumbs, ▲ ■ *milk* (● *no milk needed*) and egg; blend well.

7) Shape mixture into 1-inch meatballs.

8) Over moderate heat, melt butter in a ● ▲ *10-inch skillet,* ■ *12-Inch skillet;* add meatballs and brown. Turn meatballs carefully as they are quite delicate.

9) Place meatballs in Dutch oven and sauté mushrooms in skillet.

10) Add mushrooms to cubed veal and meatballs and continue cooking, covered, 30 minutes longer or until veal is tender.

11) Meanwhile, prepare sauce: melt butter in a ● ▲ *1-quart saucepan,* ■ *3-quart saucepan.*

12) Stir in flour and blend well.

13) Gradually add beef broth and cook, stirring constantly, until thickened.

14) Add this sauce to veal and simmer 10 minutes longer. Remove from heat.

15) Beat egg yolks and lemon juice until thick in a ● ▲ *small bowl,* ■ *medium bowl.*

16) Pour some of the hot veal sauce into egg yolks, beating constantly.

17) Slowly return egg mixture to Dutch oven; blend well. Be careful not to break up meatballs. Do not boil.

18) Serve over rice or noodles.

preparation time: ● 1½ hours; ▲ 1¾ hours; ■ 6 hours

Special Note
● You can keep this dish in the refrigerator for 1 week and in the freezer for 2 to 3 months. When reheating, warm over low heat in a heavy saucepan, covered, being careful not to let it come to a boil.

Osso Buco

Ingredients

2

1½	lbs veal shank crosscuts
1–2	Tbs flour
3	Tbs olive oil
3	Tbs chopped celery
1	small onion, chopped
1	small carrot, chopped
⅓	cup peeled and chopped fresh tomato
½	tsp salt
⅛	tsp freshly ground black pepper

	pinch of dried rosemary
	pinch of dried sage
⅔	cup dry white wine
½	anchovy fillet, mashed
½	small garlic clove, minced
1	tsp freshly grated lemon peel
2	tsps chopped parsley

6

4½	lbs veal shank crosscuts
2–3	Tbs flour
½	cup olive oil
½	cup chopped celery
1	large onion, chopped
2	medium carrots, chopped
1	cup peeled and chopped fresh tomatoes (about ¾ lb)
1¼	tsps salt
½	tsp freshly ground black pepper
	pinch of dried rosemary
	pinch of dried sage
2	cups dry white wine
1	anchovy fillet, mashed
1	garlic clove, minced
1	Tb freshly grated lemon peel
2	Tbs chopped parsley

24

18	lbs veal shank crosscuts
½	cup flour
¾	cup olive oil
2	cups chopped celery
4	cups chopped onions
2½	cups chopped carrots
4	cups peeled and chopped fresh tomatoes (about 2¼ lbs)

1	Tb salt
2	tsps freshly ground black pepper
½	tsp dried rosemary
½	tsp dried sage
8	cups dry white wine
4	anchovy fillets, mashed
5	garlic cloves, minced
3	Tbs grated lemon peel
½	cup chopped parsley

✳ THE BLUE HORSE, 1355 University Avenue, St. Paul, Minnesota

Instructions

1) Roll veal shanks in flour to coat evenly.
2) Heat ● *3 tablespoons olive oil,* ▲ *½ cup olive oil,* ■ *¼ cup oil,* in ● *a 3-quart Dutch oven,* ▲ *an 8-quart Dutch oven,* ■ *each of 2 8-quart Dutch ovens, adding more oil as needed. Divide all ingredients evenly between the 2 pots.*
3) Brown shanks on all sides. Remove as they brown.
4) Place celery, onion, carrots, tomato, salt, pepper, rosemary and sage in the pot; blend well.
5) Cook over low heat 10 minutes, stirring occasionally. Return meat to pot.
6) Add wine, cover and simmer until tender, ● *1½ hours,* ▲ *2 hours,* ■ *2 to 2½ hours.*
7) After cooking, skim fat from liquid and discard.
8) Just before serving, stir in anchovy and garlic. Sprinkle lemon peel and parsley over top.
9) Serve over rice.

preparation time: ● 2 hours; ▲ 2½ hours; ■ 5 hours

Special Notes
- Osso Buco will keep in refrigerator 4 to 5 days; in freezer for 3 months. Reheat over low heat.
- When buying the shanks choose the least bony cuts sawed into 3-inch pieces.

Piccata Milanese

Ingredients

2-3

5	Tbs butter
2	ozs boiled ham, diced
6	canned tomatoes, drained
	pinch of salt, black pepper, ground nutmeg
1½	ozs bacon, diced
½	small onion, chopped
1	tsp tomato paste
½	cup dry white wine
1	small garlic clove
	pinch of dried marjoram
	pinch of sugar
⅛	tsp black pepper
½	lb veal scallops, seasoned with salt and pepper
1	tsp olive oil
2	eggs
6	Tbs freshly grated Parmesan cheese
¼	cup flour
4	Tbs butter
4	ozs spaghetti, cooked and drained

6

10	Tbs butter
6	ozs boiled ham, diced
1	35-oz can tomatoes, drained
⅛	tsp each of salt, black pepper, nutmeg
6	slices bacon, diced
1	medium onion, chopped
1	Tb tomato paste
1½	cups dry white wine
1	large garlic clove
⅛	tsp dried marjoram
⅛	tsp sugar
¼	tsp black pepper
1½	lbs veal scallops, seasoned with salt and pepper
1	Tb olive oil
3	eggs
¾	cup freshly grated Parmesan cheese
½	cup flour
⅓	cup butter
10	ozs spaghetti, cooked and drained

24

1	lb butter
1½	lbs boiled ham, diced
4	35-oz cans tomatoes, drained
½	tsp salt
¼	tsp black pepper
½	tsp ground nutmeg
1½	lbs bacon, diced
3	large onions, chopped
¼	cup tomato paste
4	cups dry white wine
3	large garlic cloves
½	tsp dried marjoram
½	tsp sugar
½	tsp black pepper
7	lbs veal scallops, seasoned with salt and pepper
¼	cup olive oil
10	eggs
3	cups freshly grated Parmesan cheese
2	cups flour
1	cup (2 sticks) butter
2½	lbs spaghetti, cooked and drained

❊ BELLEVUE RESTAURANT at the PIONEER INN, 1000 Pioneer Drive, Oshkosh, Wisconsin

148

Instructions

1) Over low heat, melt butter in ● *an 8-inch skillet,* ▲ *a 10-inch skillet,* ■ *a 4-quart Dutch oven.*
2) Add ham and ⅓ of the tomatoes; cook 5 minutes.
3) Add salt, pepper and nutmeg. Reserve.
4) Cook bacon over moderate heat until brown and crisp in ● *an 8-inch skillet,* ▲ *a 10-inch skillet,* ■ *a 4-quart Dutch oven.*
5) Remove bacon pieces with a slotted spoon and reserve.
6) Add onion to the bacon fat; cook until soft.
7) Stir in remaining tomatoes, tomato paste, wine, garlic, marjoram, sugar and pepper.
8) Cook over moderate heat until reduced by half, stirring occasionally.
9) Add reserved bacon; set sauce aside.
10) Sprinkle olive oil over the veal.
11) Beat together eggs and ⅔ of the Parmesan cheese in a ● *small bowl,* ▲ *medium bowl,* ■ *large bowl.*
12) Preheat oven to 350 degrees.
13) Dip veal slices in egg mixture and coat well; then dust lightly with flour.
14) Melt 2 tablespoons of butter over low heat in ● *an 8-inch skillet,* ▲ *a 10-inch skillet,* ■ *a 12-inch skillet.*
15) Add the veal slices, a few at a time, and cook over moderate heat until lightly browned on one side.
16) Turn and quickly brown on the other side. Remove from skillet and keep warm in a very low oven.
17) Repeat with remaining butter and veal slices.
18) Mix together the cooked spaghetti and the ham-tomato mixture in a ● *1½-quart shallow baking dish,* ▲ *2-quart shallow baking dish,* ■ *3 3-quart shallow baking dishes, dividing ingredients evenly among them.*
19) Sprinkle remaining Parmesan cheese over mixture.
20) Pour bacon-tomato sauce over top, but do not mix.
21) Arrange veal slices on top of sauce.
22) Bake in the preheated oven until heated through, ● ▲ *15 to 20 minutes,* ■ *20 to 25 minutes.*

preparation time: ● 1½ hours; ▲ 2 hours; ■ 3 to 4 hours

Special Notes
- Any part or all of this dish can be made in advance and refrigerated. Continue the recipe or reheat the dish when ready.
- This dish is equally good made with skinned and boned chicken breasts.
- Piccata Milanese can be frozen 2 to 3 months. Thaw; warm, covered, in a preheated 350-degree oven 10 to 15 minutes.

Veal in Cream with Dill

Ingredients

1 Tb olive oil
1 Tb butter
¾ lb veal scallops, pounded thin
½ cup heavy cream
1 tsp dried dill weed
  dash of Tabasco
⅛ tsp Worcestershire sauce
1 Tb dry sherry
½ Tb Cognac

3 Tbs olive oil
3 Tbs butter
1½ lbs veal scallops, pounded thin
1 cup heavy cream
2 tsps dried dill weed
⅛ tsp Tabasco
¼ tsp Worcestershire sauce
2 Tbs dry sherry
1 Tb Cognac

Instructions

1) Heat oil and butter in ● *an 8-inch skillet,* ▲ *a 12-inch skillet.*
2) Add veal scallops and sauté quickly on each side until they are lightly brown.
3) Remove veal to a pan and keep warm in a very low oven.
4) Add cream and dill to skillet; cook over high heat, scraping bottom of pan to loosen drippings, until cream has reduced to the consistency of thick sauce.
5) Stir in Tabasco, Worcestershire sauce, sherry and Cognac; cook until mixture bubbles.
6) Return veal scallops to sauce and serve immediately with white rice.

preparation time: ● 20 minutes; ▲ 35 minutes

Special Note
● To reheat: place veal with sauce in a casserole, cover and warm in a preheated 300-degree oven for 10 minutes or until heated through.

Petite Veal Cutlet Cordon Bleu

Ingredients

2

8	1-oz veal scallops, pounded thin
¼	tsp salt
⅛	tsp freshly ground black pepper
2	1-oz slices Swiss cheese
2	1-oz slices ham, preferably Virginia
1	Tb flour
1	egg, beaten
½	cup dry bread crumbs
3	Tbs butter
1	tsp lemon juice

6

24	1-oz veal scallops, pounded thin
½	tsp salt
¼	tsp freshly ground black pepper
6	1-oz slices Swiss cheese
6	1-oz slices ham, preferably Virginia
¼	cup flour
2	eggs, beaten
1½	cups dry bread crumbs
8	Tbs (1 stick) butter
1	Tb lemon juice

6	lbs 1-oz veal scallops, pounded thin
1	tsp salt
½	tsp freshly ground black pepper
24	1-oz slices Swiss cheese
24	1-oz slices ham, preferably Virginia
1	cup flour
4	eggs, beaten
5–6	cups dry bread crumbs
1	lb (4 sticks) butter
¼	cup lemon juice

❈ CHEF TÉTART'S Highway 86 East, Branson, Missouri

Instructions

1) Season veal with salt and pepper.
2) Trim Swiss cheese and ham slices to size of veal scallops.
3) Place 1 slice of cheese and 1 slice of ham on 1 slice of veal.
4) Cover with a second slice of veal.
5) Beat the edges of the veal together with a mallet to seal completely.
6) Repeat with remaining veal, ham and cheese.
7) ● ▲ Roll each packet lightly in flour, dip in egg, then cover completely with bread crumbs. ■ Place ¼ cup flour, 1 egg and 1 cup crumbs in separate bowls. Dip veal as directed. If coating ingredients become gummy, discard and start afresh.
8) Melt ● *3 tablespoons butter,* ▲ ■ *4 tablespoons (½ stick) butter* in a ● *10-inch skillet,* ▲ ■ *12-inch skillet.*
9) ● Brown veal scallops quickly on one side. Turn and brown on other side, about 3 to 4 minutes. ▲ ■ Sauté a few veal scallops at a time. Remove from skillet and keep warm. Add more butter as needed and sauté remaining veal.
10) Sprinkle with lemon juice and serve immediately.

preparation time: ● 35 minutes; ▲ 1½ hours; ■ 4 hours

Special Notes
- Veal cutlets can be reheated in a preheated 350-degree oven for 10 minutes.
- Veal can be assembled in advance through step 7; refrigerate and continue just before serving.

Vitello Tonnato

Ingredients

1	3-lb boneless veal roast, tied
1	tsp flour
2	Tbs olive oil
2	small celery stalks
1	medium onion, sliced
1	7-oz can tuna fish, undrained
6	anchovy fillets
½	cup dry white wine
1½	cups chicken broth
⅓	cup mayonnaise
1	Tb lemon juice
	capers

6-8

24

2	4-lb boneless veal roasts, tied
2	tsps flour
6	Tbs olive oil
4	large celery stalks
2	large onions, sliced
2	7-oz cans tuna fish, undrained
16	anchovy fillets
1½	cups dry white wine
4	cups chicken broth
1	cup mayonnaise
2	Tbs lemon juice
	capers

✻ QUO VADIS, 26 East 63rd Street, New York, New York

Instructions

1) Dust veal roast with flour.
2) Heat oil in a ▲ *4-quart Dutch oven,* ■ *a 10-quart Dutch oven or 2 4-quart Dutch ovens, dividing ingredients evenly between them.*
3) Add meat and brown well on all sides. Remove meat.
4) Add celery and onion; cook until golden.
5) Return meat to pan, add tuna fish, anchovies, white wine and chicken broth. Cover and simmer until meat is tender, about 2 hours, ■ *2½ hours if 10-quart Dutch oven is used.*
6) Remove meat. Let cool to room temperature, then chill in refrigerator.
7) Reduce sauce to half.
8) Puree liquid and vegetables in a blender a little at a time. Allow sauce to cool to room temperature. Ⓢ
9) Stir in mayonnaise and lemon juice. Chill.
10) At serving time remove strings from roast. Slice veal very thin and arrange on a serving platter. Pour chilled sauce over veal. Decorate with capers. Serve dish with cold boiled rice.

preparation time: ▲ 2¾ hours; ■ 3 hours

Special Notes
- When pureeing a hot liquid in the blender, do not fill it more than ⅓ full. Pressure develops if the container is too full, and there is the danger that it will explode.
- The sauce for this dish will not keep for more than 4 or 5 days in the refrigerator.
- The sauce can be frozen after step 8, and will keep for 2 to 3 months. To serve, defrost and add mayonnaise and lemon juice. Veal should be frozen separately.

Roast Pork with Sweet and Sour Sauce

Ingredients

2	loin pork chops, 1 inch thick
½	cup sugar
¼	cup white vinegar
¼	cup water
1	Tb chopped green pepper
¼	tsp salt
1	tsp cornstarch
1	tsp water
½	tsp paprika
1	tsp chopped parsley

1	4½-lb rib or loin pork roast	
1½	cups sugar	
1	cup white vinegar	
1	cup water	
¼	cup chopped green pepper	**6**
1	tsp salt	
4	tsps cornstarch	
2	Tbs water	
2	tsps paprika	
2	Tbs chopped parsley	

✹ THE VINEYARDS, 29230 Franklin Road, Southfield, Michigan

Instructions

1) Preheat oven to 450 degrees.
2) Place pork in a ● *1½-quart shallow baking dish,* ▲ *3-quart shallow baking dish.*
3) Bake in the preheated oven until brown, ● *20 to 30 minutes,* ▲ *30 minutes.*
4) Meanwhile, to make sauce: in a 1-quart saucepan, combine sugar, vinegar, the ● *¼ cup water,* ▲ *1 cup water,* green pepper and salt; bring to a boil over high heat.
5) Reduce heat and simmer 5 minutes.
6) In a small dish combine cornstarch and remaining water; blend well.
7) Stir cornstarch mixture into saucepan and cook, stirring constantly, until mixture thickens slightly.
8) Add paprika and parsley and reserve.
9) After pork has browned, reduce oven heat to 325 degrees. Pour sauce over meat and bake an additional ● *40 to 50 minutes,* ▲ *1½ hours,* or until done. Baste pork occasionally with the sauce.
10) Serve roast with sauce over it or separately.

preparation time: ● 1 to 1½ hours; ▲ 2 to 2½ hours

Special Notes
- Sauce gets very thick when it cools; reheating will restore consistency.
- Pork and sauce will keep in the refrigerator 1 week. Reheat pork in a preheated 325-degree oven, wrapped in aluminum foil, until heated through, about ½ hour.

Pork Chops Orientale

Ingredients

2   loin pork chops, 1 inch thick
1   Tb tarragon vinegar
1   Tb vegetable oil
¼   tsp dry mustard
2   Tbs dark brown sugar
⅓   cup orange juice
¼   cup whole pickled onions, drained
¼   cup whole cooked or canned baby carrots, drained
4   thin orange slices

6   loin pork chops, 1 inch thick
3   Tbs tarragon vinegar
3   Tbs vegetable oil
¾   tsp dry mustard
6   Tbs dark brown sugar
1   cup orange juice
¾   cup whole pickled onions, drained
¾   cup whole cooked or canned baby carrots, drained
12 thin orange slices

6

24   loin pork chops, 1 inch thick
¾   cup tarragon vinegar
¾   cup vegetable oil
1   Tb dry mustard
1½   cups dark brown sugar
4   cups orange juice
3   cups whole pickled onions, drained
3   cups whole cooked or canned baby carrots, drained
48   thin orange slices

✳ CHALET SUZANNE, Highway 27A North, Lake Wales, Florida

Instructions

1) Arrange pork chops in ● *a shallow 1½-quart baking dish,* ▲ *a 3-quart shallow baking dish,* ■ *4 3-quart shallow baking dishes.*
2) Combine vinegar, oil, mustard and brown sugar in a ● ▲ *small bowl,* ■ *medium bowl.*
3) Cover all sides of chops with marinade and let stand 2 hours.
4) Preheat oven to 350 degrees.
5) Add orange juice and bake in the preheated oven until tender, ● ▲ *40 to 50 minutes,* ■ *60 to 70 minutes,* basting and turning every 15 minutes.
6) Add vegetables and orange slices; baste; cook 15 minutes longer.

preparation time (including standing time): ● ▲ 3¼ hours; ■ 4 hours.

Special Note
● Pork chops orientale will keep in refrigerator 2 to 3 days, in freezer 2 to 3 months. Reheat, covered, in a preheated 325-degree oven for 15 minutes.

Beef Wellington with Périgourdine Sauce

Ingredients

4

1	2-lb trimmed beef tenderloin
⅛	tsp salt
⅛	tsp freshly ground black pepper
1	Tb olive oil
1	Tb butter
2	Tbs finely chopped onion
¼	lb mushrooms, finely chopped
2	Tbs Cognac
¼	tsp dried rosemary
1	5-oz can pâté de foie gras

1	10-oz package frozen puff-pastry patty shells, defrosted
1	egg
1	Tb milk

SAUCE

2	Tbs butter
⅓	cup chopped shallots
¾	cup Madeira
1¼	cups brown gravy
1	truffle, chopped

8-10

1	4-lb trimmed beef tenderloin
¼	tsp salt
¼	tsp freshly ground black pepper
2	Tbs olive oil
2	Tbs butter
¼	cup finely chopped onion
½	lb mushrooms, finely chopped
¼	cup Cognac
½	tsp dried rosemary
2	5-oz cans pâté de foie gras

2	10-oz packages frozen puff-pastry patty shells, defrosted
1	egg
1	Tb milk

SAUCE

6	Tbs butter
⅔	cup chopped shallots
1¾	cups Madeira
3	cups brown gravy
2	truffles, chopped

24

3	4-lb trimmed beef tenderloins
¾	tsp salt
¾	tsp freshly ground black pepper
¼	cup olive oil
8	Tbs (1 stick) butter
¾	cup finely chopped onion
1½	lbs mushrooms, finely chopped
¾	cup Cognac
1½	tsps dried rosemary
6	5-oz cans pâté de foie gras

6	10-oz packages frozen puff-pastry patty shells, defrosted
2	eggs
2	Tbs milk

SAUCE

1½	cups (3 sticks) butter
2	cups chopped shallots
5	cups Madeira
12	cups brown gravy
6	truffles, chopped

✳ MAISONETTE, 114 East 6th, Cincinnati, Ohio

160

Instructions

1) Preheat oven to 450 degrees.
2) Season beef on all sides with salt and pepper.
3) Heat oil in a roasting pan; place tenderloin in oil and roast in the preheated oven ● *10 minutes,* ▲ *15 minutes,* ■ *25 minutes.* Be sure meat stays very rare.
4) Remove meat and cool.
5) Lower oven to 425 degrees (for step 19).
6) Place butter in a 10-inch skillet and melt over moderate heat.
7) Add onion and mushrooms and cook until tender.
8) Add Cognac and let cool.
9) Stir in rosemary and pâté with a fork to blend well.
10) When beef is cool, spread paste generously over meat. (If mixture seems loose, chill 10 minutes to set while rolling out pastry.)
11) ● ▲ Work the defrosted dough together to form a ball. ■ Work with only 2 packages of dough and 1 piece of meat at a time; continue through step 13. Repeat with remaining dough and meat.
12) Roll out dough on lightly floured board into a rectangle about ● *12 by 13 inches,* ▲ ■ *17 by 16 inches,* or about 4 or 5 inches longer than the roast and ⅛ inch thick.
13) Place meat, rounded side down, in center of dough and wrap the dough completely around the meat. Trim off excess and tuck in ends; reserve excess dough for decoration.
14) Pinch edges to seal.
15) In a small dish beat together egg and milk.
16) With a pastry brush glaze the dough with the egg mixture.
17) Make two slits with a knife in top of dough (to let steam escape).
18) Decorate crust by cutting any desired shapes out of reserved dough. Use the egg wash to apply the decorations and also brush the decorations with glaze. ⬚S
19) Bake in the preheated oven for ● *15 to 20 minutes,* ▲ *30 to 35 minutes,* ■ *45 minutes.*
20) Meanwhile, prepare périgourdine sauce: melt ● *1 tablespoon butter,* ▲ *2 tablespoons butter,* ■ *8 tablespoons butter* in a ● *1-quart saucepan,* ▲ *3-quart saucepan,* ■ *8-quart Dutch oven.*
21) Add shallots and cook until golden.
22) Add ● *½ cup Madeira,* ▲ *1 cup Madeira,* ■ *3½ cups Madeira;* boil until reduced by half.
23) Add brown gravy and simmer 10 minutes.
24) Strain.
25) Add remaining butter and Madeira, and truffles; bring to a boil.
26) Serve périgourdine sauce in a sauceboat with beef Wellington.

preparation time: ● 1½ hours; ▲ 2½ hours ■ 4½ hours
(over)

Special Notes
- You can prepare beef Wellington ahead through step 18 and store in refrigerator. When ready, let stand at room temperature for 1 hour and then proceed to step 19.
- The périgourdine sauce can be made the day before and refrigerated. Reheat over low heat.
- Périgourdine sauce freezes for 2 to 3 months. Use with roasts and steaks.

VEGETABLES, GRAINS AND POTATOES

Carrots Mountainside

Ingredients

1 cup water
¼ tsp salt
8 medium carrots, scraped and sliced
6 Tbs butter, softened
1 Tb sugar
½ tsp ground nutmeg
½ tsp salt
¼ tsp freshly ground white pepper
2 Tbs Grand Marnier

3 cups water
1 tsp salt
2 dozen medium carrots, scraped and sliced
18 Tbs (2¼ sticks) butter, softened
3 Tbs sugar
1½ tsps ground nutmeg
1½ tsps salt
¾ tsp freshly ground white pepper
6 Tbs Grand Marnier

6

3 quarts water
1 Tb + 1 tsp salt
8 dozen medium carrots (about 12 bags), scraped and sliced
4½ cups butter (2¼ lbs), softened
¾ cup sugar
2 Tbs ground nutmeg
2 Tbs salt
1 Tb freshly ground white pepper
1½ cups Grand Marnier

❄ MOUNTAINSIDE INN, River Road, Point Pleasant, Pennsylvania

Instructions

1) Combine water, salt and sliced carrots in a ● *1-quart saucepan,* ▲ *2-quart saucepan,* ■ *8-quart saucepan.*
2) Simmer until carrots are tender, about 20 to 30 minutes.
3) Drain carrots and puree in a food mill or blender, or press through a sieve.
4) Return carrot puree to saucepan and add butter, sugar, nutmeg, salt and pepper.
5) Cook over low heat, stirring constantly, until heated through. ⑤
6) Add Grand Marnier just before serving.

preparation time: ● 50 to 60 minutes; ▲ 1½ hours; ■ 2 hours
yield: ● 1 cup; ▲ 3 cups; ■ 12 cups

Special Note
● Carrots can be made ahead and refrigerated or frozen after step 5. Thaw and reheat in a saucepan over low heat; add Grand Marnier before serving.

Eggplant Provençale

Ingredients

2

1	medium eggplant
1/8–1/4	tsp salt
4	Tbs olive oil
1/2	garlic clove, minced
3	medium tomatoes, peeled, seeded and chopped
1/2	tsp dried oregano
1/8	tsp salt
pinch–1/8	tsp freshly ground black pepper
1	tsp capers, rinsed and drained

6

3	medium eggplants
1/2	tsp salt
3/4	cup olive oil
1	large garlic clove, minced
8	large tomatoes, peeled, seeded and chopped
1 1/2	tsps dried oregano
1/2	tsp salt
1/4	tsp freshly ground black pepper
1	Tb capers, rinsed and drained

24

12	medium eggplants
1 1/2	tsps salt
2 1/2	cups olive oil
4	large garlic cloves, minced
2	dozen large tomatoes, peeled, seeded and chopped
4 1/2	tsps dried oregano
1 1/2	tsps salt
1/2	tsp freshly ground black pepper
1/4	cup capers, rinsed and drained

❄ PETITE MARMITE RESTAURANT, Worth Avenue, Palm Beach, Florida

Instructions

1) Trim eggplants and cut them in half lengthwise.
2) Cut several gashes in eggplant pulp, being careful not to pierce the skin. Sprinkle with salt; place eggplant, cutside down, on paper towels and let stand 30 minutes.
3) Wipe dry.
4) Preheat oven to 450 degrees.
5) Dip eggplant halves in ● *1 tablespoon olive oil,* ▲ *½ cup olive oil,* ■ *2 cups olive oil,* to coat all sides well.
6) Place halves, cutside up, on a baking sheet and bake in the preheated oven 20 to 30 minutes or until tender.
7) Meanwhile, prepare tomato mixture: heat the remaining oil in ● *an 8-inch skillet,* ▲ *a 10-inch skillet,* ■ *a 6-quart Dutch oven.*
8) Add garlic and cook for a moment.
9) Add tomatoes, oregano, salt and pepper; cook, stirring occasionally, until all the liquid has evaporated and mixture is thick, about ● *5 to 10 minutes,* ▲ *10 minutes,* ■ *15 to 20 minutes.*
10) Spread mixture evenly over hot eggplant halves.
11) Sprinkle with capers and serve immediately.

preparation time: ● 1 hour; ▲ 1¼ hours; ■ 2 hours

Special Note
● Prepared eggplant will keep in the refrigerator 1 week: warm, covered, in a preheated 325-degree oven for 10 minutes.

Eggplant à la Russe

Ingredients

EGGPLANT

1   small eggplant
2   Tbs flour
6   Tbs olive oil
¼   tsp salt

SAUCE

2   Tbs butter
1   Tb flour
1   cup sour cream
¼   cup heavy cream
4   Tbs freshly grated Parmesan cheese

EGGPLANT

2   medium eggplants
¼   cup flour
¾   cup olive oil
1   tsp salt

SAUCE

4   Tbs butter
2   Tbs flour
2   cups sour cream
½   cup heavy cream
¾   cup freshly grated Parmesan cheese

6

✳ RUSSIAN BEAR, 139 East 56 Street, New York, New York

Instructions

1) Peel eggplant and cut lengthwise into slices ½ inch thick.
2) Coat slices slightly with flour.
3) Heat 2 tablespoons of the oil in a 10-inch skillet.
4) Sauté 2 to 3 eggplant slices until tender and golden. Drain on paper towels.
5) Season slices with salt.
6) Repeat with remaining slices, adding oil as needed.
7) To make sauce: melt butter in a ● *1-quart saucepan,* ▲ *1½-quart saucepan.* Remove from heat.
8) Add flour and blend well.
9) Add sour cream and heavy cream gradually; blend well.
10) Heat sauce over low heat until heated through and slightly thickened.
11) Preheat broiler.
12) Arrange eggplant on a ● *9-inch pie plate,* ▲ *15-by-13-inch jelly-roll pan or other shallow ovenproof dish.*
13) Pour sauce over eggplant, covering well.
14) Sprinkle Parmesan cheese over top.
15) Broil under preheated broiler until cheese is browned, about 2 to 3 minutes. Serve immediately.

preparation time: ● 30 minutes; ▲ 45 minutes to 1 hour

Special Note
● This dish is best served immediately from the broiler. If you wish to reheat it, cover with aluminum foil and warm in a preheated 350-degree oven 10 minutes, or until heated through.

Onion Pie

Ingredients

¼	cup unsalted saltine cracker crumbs
2	Tbs butter, melted
1	cup thinly sliced onions
1	egg
⅓	cup prepared instant nonfat dry milk
¼	tsp salt
⅛	tsp freshly ground black pepper
2	Tbs coarsely grated sharp Cheddar cheese

1	cup unsalted saltine cracker crumbs
8	Tbs (1 stick) butter, melted
4	cups thinly sliced onions
4	eggs
1½	cups prepared instant nonfat dry milk
½	tsp salt
⅛	tsp freshly ground black pepper
½	cup coarsely grated sharp Cheddar cheese (about 2 ozs)

6

4½	cups unsalted saltine cracker crumbs
2¼	cups (4½ sticks) butter, melted
18	cups thinly sliced onions
24	eggs
9	cups prepared instant nonfat dry milk
2	Tbs salt
1½	tsps freshly ground black pepper
4½	cups coarsely grated sharp Cheddar cheese (about 18 ozs)

❄ WIN SCHULER'S, 115 South Eagle Street, Marshall, Michigan

Instructions

1) Preheat oven to 350 degrees.
2) In a small bowl, combine crumbs with half the melted butter.
3) Press mixture into the bottom and sides of ● *a 5-inch au gratin dish,* ▲ *a 10-inch pie plate,* ■ *3 3-quart shallow baking dishes, dividing ingredients evenly among them.*
4) Melt remaining butter in ● *an 8-inch skillet,* ▲ *a 12-inch skillet,* ■ *a 7-inch Dutch oven.*
5) Add onions; sauté until soft but not brown.
6) Spread onions over crumbs in pie plate.
7) Lightly beat the eggs in a ● *small bowl,* ▲ *medium bowl,* ■ *large bowl.*
8) Add salt, pepper and prepared milk gradually and beat with a wire whisk to blend.
9) Pour liquid over onions.
10) Sprinkle cheese over top and bake in the preheated oven ● *10 to 15 minutes,* ▲ *25 to 30 minutes,* ■ *20 to 25 minutes.*

preparation time: ● 30 minutes; ▲ 1 hour; ■ 1½ hours

Special Note
● Onion pie can be reheated. Cover dish with aluminum foil; place in a pre-heated 325-degree oven for 10 to 15 minutes, or until heated through.

Baked Pumpkin

Ingredients

1 cup canned pumpkin
3 Tbs butter, melted
5 Tbs sugar
3 Tbs milk
1 egg, beaten
  pinch of ground nutmeg
  pinch of ground allspice
  pinch of salt

1 1-lb-13-oz can pumpkin
8 Tbs (1 stick) butter, melted
1 cup sugar
¾ cup milk
2 eggs, beaten
¼ tsp ground nutmeg
¼ tsp ground allspice
⅛ tsp salt

2 1-lb-13-oz cans pumpkin
1 lb butter, melted
4 cups sugar
3 cups milk
8 eggs, beaten
1 tsp ground nutmeg
1 tsp ground allspice
½ tsp salt

✳ CORINNE DUNBAR'S 1617 St. Charles Avenue, New Orleans, Louisiana

Instructions

1) Preheat oven to 350 degrees.
2) Pour pumpkin into a ● *small bowl,* ▲ *medium bowl,* ■ *large bowl or pot.*
3) Add remaining ingredients and blend well.
4) Pour mixture into ● *a 20-ounce casserole;* ▲ *a 2-quart shallow baking dish,* ■ *2 3-quart shallow baking dishes.*
5) Bake in the preheated oven until lightly brown on top and almost set, ● *30 to 35 minutes,* ▲ *50 to 60 minutes;* ■ *60 to 70 minutes.*

preparation time: ● 50 minutes; ▲ 1½ hours; ■ 2 hours

Special Notes
- Pumpkin will keep in refrigerator 1 to 2 weeks. Reheat in a preheated 325-degree oven 15 to 20 minutes or in a saucepan on top of the stove, stirring occasionally, until warm.
- You can freeze prepared pumpkin; it will keep 2 to 3 months.
- On standing some of the butter may settle to bottom of dish; stir to blend.

Spinach Rockefeller

Ingredients

1 10-oz package frozen chopped spinach
2 Tbs dry bread crumbs
2 Tbs minced scallions
1 egg
2 Tbs butter, melted
2 Tbs freshly grated Parmesan cheese
⅛ tsp MSG (optional)

¼ tsp minced garlic
¼ tsp dried thyme
pinch of freshly ground black pepper
pinch of cayenne pepper
¼ tsp salt
4 ¼-inch-thick tomato slices
⅛ tsp garlic salt

2 10-oz packages frozen chopped spinach
¼ cup dry bread crumbs
¼ cup minced scallions
2 eggs
4 Tbs butter, melted
¼ cup freshly grated Parmesan cheese
¼ tsp MSG (optional)
½ tsp minced garlic
½ tsp dried thyme
⅛–¼ tsp freshly ground black pepper
⅛ tsp cayenne pepper
¼ tsp salt
6–8 ¼-inch-thick tomato slices
½ tsp garlic salt

6-8

6 10-oz packages frozen chopped spinach
¾ cup dry bread crumbs
¾ cup minced scallions
4 eggs
12 Tbs (1½ sticks) butter, melted
1 cup freshly grated Parmesan cheese

½ tsp MSG (optional)
1 tsp minced garlic
1½ tsps dried thyme
½ tsp freshly ground black pepper
⅛–¼ tsp cayenne pepper
2 tsps salt
24 ¼-inch-thick tomato slices
1½ tsps garlic salt

❋ BAKERS DOZEN at the BAKER HOTEL, 1400 Commerce Street, Dallas, Texas

174

Instructions

1) Preheat oven to 350 degrees.
2) Cook spinach according to package directions; drain well.
3) Place spinach, bread crumbs, scallions, eggs, melted butter, Parmesan cheese, optional MSG, garlic, thyme, black pepper, cayenne and salt in a ● ▲ *medium bowl;* ■ *large bowl or pot.* Blend well.
4) Arrange tomato slices in ● *a 9-inch pie plate,* ▲ *a 2-quart shallow baking dish,* ■ *3 3-quart shallow baking dishes.*
5) Sprinkle slices with garlic salt.
6) Spoon about ¼ cup of the spinach mixture onto each of the tomato slices. Shape into a dome.
7) Bake in the preheated oven 15 minutes, or until set and heated through.

preparation time: ● 45 minutes; ▲ 1 hour; ■ 1½ hours

Special Note
● Spinach mixture can be made ahead; it will keep refrigerated for 1 week. Just before serving, stir spinach, arrange on top of tomato slices and bake.

Sour Creamed Spinach

Ingredients

2-3

1	10-oz package frozen chopped spinach
½	cup sour cream
2	tsps prepared horseradish
¼	tsp dried fines herbes
½	tsp seasoned salt
3	tomato slices, ¼ inch thick

6

2	10-oz packages frozen chopped spinach
1	cup sour cream
4	tsps prepared horseradish
½	tsp dried fines herbes
1	tsp seasoned salt
6	tomato slices, ¼ inch thick

24

8	10-oz packages frozen chopped spinach
4	cups sour cream
4½–5	Tbs prepared horseradish
2	tsps dried fines herbes
3–4	tsps seasoned salt
24	tomato slices, ¼ inch thick

✳ TIFFANY'S RESTAURANT-SALOON, Highway 14, Cerrillos, New Mexico

Instructions

1) Cook spinach according to package directions; drain well, squeezing out as much liquid as possible.
2) Place in a ● *1-quart saucepan,* ▲ *2-quart saucepan,* ■ *8-quart Dutch oven;* add sour cream, horseradish, fines herbes and seasoned salt.
3) Cook over low heat, stirring constantly, until heated through, but do not boil.
4) Spoon mixture on top of tomato slices and serve immediately.

   preparation time: ● 25 minutes; ▲ 30 minutes; ■ 1 hour

Special Note
● Spinach keeps in the refrigerator 1 to 2 weeks. It can be reheated in the top of a double-boiler over simmering water.

Spanish Baked Squash

Ingredients

1	¾-lb acorn squash
1	medium-thick slice bacon
¼	cup chopped onion
¼	cup chopped celery
¼	cup chopped green pepper
2	Tbs tomato sauce
⅛	tsp salt
2	tsps butter, softened
1	Tb dry bread crumbs
2	Tbs butter, melted

3	¾-lb acorn squashes
3	medium-thick slices bacon
1	cup chopped onion
1	cup chopped celery
1	cup chopped green pepper
6	Tbs tomato sauce
½	tsp salt
2	Tbs butter, softened
3	Tbs dry bread crumbs
6	Tbs butter, melted

6

12	¾-lb acorn squashes
12	medium-thick slices bacon
4	cups chopped onion
4	cups chopped celery
4	cups chopped green pepper
1½	cups tomato sauce
1½	tsps salt
½	cup butter, softened
¾	cup dry bread crumbs
1½	cups (3 sticks) butter, melted

❋ McKAY'S WINGS, Municipal Airport, Marshall, Missouri

Instructions

1) Preheat oven to 350 degrees.
2) Cut squash in half and remove seeds and membranes.
3) Arrange halves in a buttered ● *9-inch pie plate,* ▲ *3-quart shallow baking dish,* ■ *4 3-quart shallow baking dishes.*
4) In ● *an 8-inch skillet,* ▲ *a 10-inch skillet,* ■ *a 4-quart Dutch oven,* fry bacon slices until brown. Remove bacon and drain on paper towels; crumble bacon and reserve.
5) In the bacon fat sauté onion, celery and green pepper until tender.
6) Stir in tomato sauce.
7) Sprinkle inside of each squash with salt and dot with softened butter.
8) Put about ¼ cup of the vegetable mixture into each squash half.
9) Sprinkle bread crumbs over top.
10) Pour 1 tablespoon melted butter over each half.
11) Bake in the preheated oven for 35 to 45 minutes or until tender.
12) Sprinkle crumbled bacon over top before serving.

preparation time: ● 1¼ hours; ▲ 1½ hours; ■ 2 hours

Special Notes
- Squash can be reheated. Cover dish with aluminum foil and warm in a preheated 325-degree oven 15 to 20 minutes or until heated through.
- Stuffed squash can be frozen for 2 to 3 months.

Tomato Timbale

Ingredients

1	Tb butter
1	Tb minced onion
1	Tb flour
¼	tsp dried basil
⅛	tsp ground nutmeg
2	Tbs dry sherry
2	Tbs chicken broth
½	cup chopped cooked broccoli
⅛	tsp freshly ground black pepper
⅛–¼	tsp salt
2	tomatoes
	salt and freshly ground black pepper

3	Tbs butter
¼	cup minced onion
3	Tbs flour
¾	tsp dried basil
¼	tsp ground nutmeg
6	Tbs dry sherry
6	Tbs chicken broth
1½	cups chopped cooked broccoli
¼	tsp freshly ground black pepper
¼–½	tsp salt
6	tomatoes
	salt and freshly ground black pepper

6

12	Tbs (1½ sticks) butter
1	cup minced onion
¾	cup flour
4	tsps dried basil
1	tsp ground nutmeg
1½	cups dry sherry
1½	cups chicken broth
6	cups chopped cooked broccoli
1	tsp freshly ground black pepper
1–2	tsps salt
24	tomatoes
	salt and freshly ground black pepper

❄ BLUE FOX, 659 Merchant Street, San Francisco, California

Instructions

1) Melt butter in ● *an 8-inch skillet,* ▲ *a 10-inch skillet,* ■ *a 12-inch skillet;* cook onion until tender.
2) Add flour, basil and nutmeg; blend with a wire whisk.
3) Gradually add sherry and chicken broth, stirring constantly with whisk. Bring mixture to a boil. It will be thick.
4) Add broccoli and blend. Remove from heat.
5) Add pepper and season to taste with salt. Reserve mixture.
6) Fill a small saucepan ¾ full with water and bring to a boil.
7) Add tomatoes 2 at a time and simmer 10 to 20 seconds. Remove with slotted spoon and peel.
8) Slice off ¼ inch from stem end of tomato and scoop out center, leaving a firm empty tomato shell.
9) Turn tomatoes upside down and drain well.
10) Preheat oven to 350 degrees.
11) Put each tomato shell, openside up, into a 5-ounce custard cup.
12) Season inside of shells with salt and pepper.
13) Stuff with broccoli mixture.
14) Place cups in ● *a 1-quart shallow baking dish,* ▲ *a 2-quart shallow baking dish,* ■ *4 3-quart shallow baking dishes.* Fill baking dish with boiling water to reach ⅔ up the outside of the custard cups.
15) Bake in the preheated oven 20 to 25 minutes, or until heated through.
16) Invert on serving plate and serve tomatoside up.

preparation time: ● 1 hour; ▲ 1½ hours; ■ 2 hours

Special Notes
- Broccoli mixture can be stored in refrigerator 1 week, or frozen 2 months.
- If you are not serving dish immediately, do not fill tomatoes. Leave tomatoes draining on paper towels and fill when ready to bake. (Tomatoes water on standing and will make the filling runny.)

Turnips au Gratin

Ingredients

½	pound turnips, pared and diced
1½	tsps butter
1½	tsps flour
½	cup milk
6	Tbs coarsely grated sharp Cheddar cheese
⅛	tsp salt
	pinch of freshly ground black pepper
3	Tbs dry bread crumbs
1	Tb butter, melted
¼	tsp paprika

1½	lbs turnips, pared and diced
1½	Tbs butter
1½	Tbs flour
1½	cups milk
1¼	cups shredded sharp Cheddar cheese (about ⅓ lb)
½	tsp salt
¼	tsp freshly ground black pepper
½	cup dry bread crumbs
3	Tbs butter, melted
1	tsp paprika

6

24

6	lbs turnips, pared and diced
6	Tbs butter
6	Tbs flour
6	cups milk
5	cups coarsely grated sharp Cheddar cheese (about 1¼ lbs)
2	tsps salt
1	tsp freshly ground black pepper
2	cups dry bread crumbs
¾	cup butter, melted
2	Tbs paprika

※ FERNALD-HACKETT RESTAURANT, 1 South Main Street, Rochester, New Hampshire

Instructions

1) Preheat oven to 350 degrees.
2) Place turnips in a ● *1-quart saucepan,* ▲ *3-quart saucepan,* ■ *8-quart Dutch oven.* Cover with lightly salted boiling water (¼ teaspoon salt to 1 cup water); cook until fork-tender, 15 to 20 minutes.
3) Drain well; place turnips in ● *a 1½-cup casserole,* ▲ *a 1½-quart casserole,* ■ *2 3-quart shallow baking dishes, dividing all ingredients evenly between them.*
4) Melt butter over low heat in a ● ▲ *1-quart saucepan,* ■ *3-quart saucepan.*
5) Stir in flour with a wire whisk; cook 1 minute, stirring constantly.
6) Add milk and blend well.
7) Cook over moderate heat, stirring occasionally, until mixture thickens and comes to a boil.
8) Stir in cheese, salt and pepper; stir until cheese is melted.
9) Pour sauce over turnips and toss to coat well.
10) Combine bread crumbs and butter in a ● ▲ *small bowl,* ■ *medium bowl.*
11) Sprinkle bread-crumb mixture over turnips.
12) Sprinkle paprika over top. Bake in the preheated oven until bubbly and lightly browned, ● ▲ *15 to 20 minutes,* ■ *20 to 25 minutes.*

preparation time: ● 50 minutes; ▲ 1 hour; ■ 1½ hours

Special Notes
- Cooked turnips will keep in refrigerator 1 week; warm, covered, in a pre-heated 300-degree oven 10 to 15 minutes.
- Freeze for 2 to 3 months; thaw and reheat as above.

Zucchini Soufflé

Ingredients

2

1	small zucchini (about ¼ lb)
2	Tbs butter
½	garlic clove, minced
1	scallion, chopped
2	Tbs Sauterne
½	tsp lemon juice
	pinch of ground nutmeg
1	tsp chopped parsley
¼	tsp salt
⅛	tsp freshly ground black pepper
½	pimiento, chopped
1	egg yolk
2	Tbs freshly grated Parmesan cheese
1	egg white, at room temperature

2 to 3	small zucchini (about 1 lb)
4	Tbs butter
1	garlic clove, minced
3	large scallions, chopped
⅔	cup Sauterne
1	Tb lemon juice
⅛	tsp ground nutmeg
1	Tb chopped parsley
1	tsp salt
¼	tsp freshly ground black pepper
2	pimientos, chopped
6	egg yolks
4	Tbs freshly grated Parmesan cheese
6	egg whites, at room temperature

6-8

✴ BLUE FOX, 659 Merchant Street, San Francisco, California

Instructions

1) Wash zucchini. Cut off tops and bottoms and cut into strips ¼ inch wide and 1 inch long.
2) In a ● *10-inch skillet* ▲ *12-inch skillet,* melt butter and add garlic and scallions. Cook until tender.
3) Add zucchini; cook over moderate heat 2 to 3 minutes, stirring occasionally, until zucchini is lightly browned.
4) Add wine, lemon juice, nutmeg, parsley, salt and pepper; blend well.
5) Cook over moderate heat, stirring occasionally, until liquid has almost evaporated and zucchini is fork-tender.
6) Add pimientos and blend.
7) Remove from heat and let cool.
8) Preheat oven to 400 degrees.
9) Beat egg yolks and Parmesan cheese until fluffy in a ● *medium bowl,* ▲ *large bowl.*
10) Stir in zucchini mixture.
11) In another ● *medium bowl,* ▲ *large bowl,* beat egg whites until stiff peaks form.
12) Fold egg whites gently into zucchini mixture.
13) Pour mixture into ● *2 well-greased 6-inch au gratin dishes,* ▲ *a well-greased 2-quart shallow baking dish.*
14) Place dish in a larger deep-sided pan; pour in enough cold water to reach ⅔ up the outside of the baking dish.
15) Bake in the preheated oven until mixture is set and lightly browned, ● *10 to 15 minutes,* ▲ *20 to 25 minutes.* Remove pan from water bath. Serve immediately.

preparation time: ● 1 hour; ▲ 1¼ hours

Special Notes
- Mixture can be made in advance through step 10. When ready to bake, beat egg whites and continue with remaining instructions.
- Dish does not reheat well. It should be served immediately, although it is not as precarious as most soufflés.

Barley Mère Jacques

Ingredients

2	Tbs butter
3	Tbs chopped onion
⅓	cup sliced mushrooms (less than ⅛ lb)
⅓	cup pearl barley
1	cup chicken broth

6	Tbs butter
½	cup chopped onion
1	cup sliced mushrooms (about ¼ lb)
½	lb pearl barley
3	cups chicken broth

6

1¼	cups (2½ sticks) butter
2	cups chopped onion
4	cups sliced mushrooms (about 1 lb)
2	lbs pearl barley
12	cups chicken broth

✳ AU PÈRE JACQUES, 34105 Chagrin Boulevard, Chagrin Falls, Ohio

Instructions

1) Preheat oven to 350 degrees.
2) Melt butter over low heat in ● *a 1½-quart ovenproof casserole,* ▲ *a 4-quart Dutch oven,* ■ *2 6-quart Dutch ovens, dividing ingredients evenly between them.*
3) Add onions and mushrooms; cook until tender.
4) Add barley and mix well.
5) Cook over moderate heat, stirring occasionally, until barley is lightly browned.
6) Add ⅓ of the chicken broth.
7) Cover and bake in the preheated oven 20 minutes.
8) Add another ⅓ of the chicken broth; bake 30 minutes longer.
9) Add remaining chicken broth; cook 30 minutes longer or until barley is tender. If necessary, add more chicken broth while cooking.

preparation time: ● 1½ hours; ▲ 1¾ hours; ■ 2 hours
yield: ●1½ cups; ▲ 4 cups; ■ 18 cups

Special Notes
- Do not cook barley for 24 in one large pot because it will not cook properly. If you do not have 2 6-quart Dutch ovens use any two pots and adjust measurements proportionally.
- Barley keeps in refrigerator 1 to 2 weeks. Reheat in a covered casserole in a preheated 325-degree oven 10 to 15 minutes or until heated through.

Green Rice

Ingredients

2

¾ cup cooked rice
¼ cup chopped parsley
2 Tbs coarsely grated Cheddar cheese
2 Tbs chopped onion
1 Tb chopped green pepper
1 small garlic clove, minced
6 Tbs evaporated milk
1 egg

2 Tbs vegetable oil
¼ tsp salt
⅛ tsp seasoned salt
⅛ tsp freshly ground black pepper
pinch of MSG (optional)
1 tsp lemon juice
½ tsp freshly grated lemon peel
⅛ tsp paprika

6

2½ cups cooked rice
¾ cup chopped parsley
⅓ cup coarsely grated Cheddar cheese
⅓ cup chopped onion
3 Tbs chopped green pepper
1 garlic clove, minced
1 13-oz can evaporated milk
2 eggs
¼ cup vegetable oil
¾ tsp salt
½ tsp seasoned salt
¼ tsp freshly ground black pepper
⅛ tsp MSG (optional)
1 Tb lemon juice
1 tsp freshly grated lemon peel
¼ tsp paprika

24

10½ cups cooked rice
3 cups chopped parsley
2 cups coarsely grated Cheddar cheese (about ½ lb)
1½ cups chopped onion
¾ cup chopped green pepper
3 large garlic cloves, minced
7½ cups evaporated milk

9 eggs
¾ cup vegetable oil
1 Tb salt
1½ tsps seasoned salt
¾ tsp freshly ground black pepper
¼ tsp MSG (optional)
6 Tbs lemon juice
2 Tbs freshly grated lemon peel
1½ tsps paprika

✳ STEPHENSON'S APPLE FARM RESTAURANT, Lees Summit Road, Kansas City, Missouri

✳Stephenson's Apple Farm Restaurant

Instructions

1) Preheat the oven to 350 degrees.
2) Mix together rice, parsley, cheese, onion, green pepper and garlic in a ● *small bowl,* ▲ *medium bowl,* ■ *large bowl or pot.*
3) Pour mixture into ● *a 3-cup casserole,* ▲ *a 2-quart casserole,* ■ *3 3-quart shallow baking dishes, dividing ingredients evenly among them.*
4) In the same bowl combine milk, eggs, vegetable oil, salt, seasoned salt, pepper, optional MSG, lemon juice and lemon peel; blend well.
5) Pour over rice mixture; blend well.
6) Sprinkle with paprika.
7) Bake in the preheated oven until set and golden brown, ● *20 to 25 minutes,* ▲ *35 to 40 minutes,* ■ *30 to 35 minutes.*

preparation time: ● 45 minutes; ▲ 1 hour; ■ 1½ hours
yield: ● 2½ cups; ▲ 7 cups; ■ 28 cups

Special Notes
- Reheat by placing dish covered with aluminum foil in a preheated 300-degree oven for 10 to 15 minutes.
- You can prepare ahead by arranging rice mixture in dish (steps 2 and 3). Put liquids together in bowl (step 4) and reserve. When ready to bake, beat liquid to blend, pour over rice and bake as directed.

Escalloped Sweet Potatoes

Ingredients

1	medium sweet potato (about ¾ lb) cooked, peeled and halved
2	thin slices of peeled orange
2	thin slices of cored, unpeeled apple
2	thin slices of peeled peach
¼	cup water
1	Tb honey
2	Tbs orange or pineapple juice
2	Tbs dark brown sugar
1	Tb butter
1	Tb dry bread crumbs
2	marshmallows

3	medium sweet potatoes (about 2½ lbs), cooked, peeled and halved
1	orange, peeled and cut into 6 thin slices
1	apple, unpeeled, cored, and cut into 6 thin slices
1	peach, peeled and cut into 6 thin slices
½	cup water
2	Tbs honey
4	Tbs orange or pineapple juice
4	Tbs dark brown sugar
2	Tbs butter
3	Tbs dry bread crumbs
6	marshmallows

6

12	medium sweet potatoes (about 10 lbs), cooked, peeled and halved
4	oranges, peeled and cut into 24 thin slices
4	apples, unpeeled, cored, and cut into 24 thin slices
4	peaches, peeled and cut into 24 thin slices
2	cups water
½	cup honey
1	cup orange or pineapple juice
1	cup dark brown sugar
8	Tbs (1 stick) butter
¾	cup dry bread crumbs
24	marshmallows

※ STEPHENSON'S APPLE FARM RESTAURANT, Lees Summit Road, Kansas City, Missouri

✳ **Stephenson's Apple Farm Restaurant**

Instructions

1) Preheat oven to 350 degrees.
2) Arrange potato halves in ● *an 8-inch square pan,* ▲ *a 2-quart shallow baking dish,* ■ *3 3-quart shallow baking dishes.*
3) Arrange 1 slice of each fruit on top of each potato half.
4) Combine water, honey, orange or pineapple juice, half the brown sugar and half the butter in a ● ▲ *1-quart saucepan,* ■ *2-quart saucepan.* Bring mixture to a boil.
5) Pour over potatoes and fruit.
6) In a small bowl combine remaining brown sugar and crumbs; work in remaining butter until mixture is crumbly.
7) Sprinkle over top of potatoes.
8) Bake in the preheated oven for 20 minutes.
9) Put a marshmallow on top of each potato and bake 10 minutes longer or until marshmallows are brown.

preparation time: ● 1 hour; ▲ 80 minutes; ■ 1½ hours

Special Notes
- Escalloped sweet potatoes can be assembled ahead of time, but bring the sauce to a boil and continue the recipe just before baking.
- The completed dish can be frozen for 2 months.

191

SALADS AND RELISHES

Aquacote Rejeños (Stuffed Avocado)

Ingredients

1 medium tomato	¼ green pepper, chopped
1 small green pepper	1 Tb chopped onion
1 small onion	½ cup flaked crabmeat
½ hot chili pepper or	¼ cup mayonnaise
⅛ tsp chili powder	½ tsp prepared mustard
¼ tsp salt	1 Tb lemon juice
pinch of cayenne pepper	lettuce leaves
1 ripe avocado	tomato wedges
1½ hard-boiled eggs, chopped	hard-boiled egg wedges
1 small celery stalk, chopped	black olives
	pearl onions

3 medium tomatoes	1 small green pepper, chopped
2 medium green peppers	¼ cup chopped onion
2 medium onions	1½ cups flaked crabmeat
1 hot chili pepper or	¾ cup mayonnaise
¼ tsp chili powder	1½ tsps prepared mustard
½ tsp salt	3 Tbs lemon juice
⅛ tsp cayenne pepper	lettuce leaves
3 ripe avocados	tomato wedges
4½ hard-boiled eggs, chopped	hard-boiled egg wedges
3 medium celery stalks, chopped	black olives
	pearl onions

6

24

12 medium tomatoes	4 medium green peppers, chopped
8 medium green peppers	1 cup chopped onion
8 medium onions	6 cups flaked crabmeat
4 hot chili peppers or	3 cups mayonnaise
½ tsp chili powder	2 Tbs prepared mustard
1–2 tsps salt	12 Tbs lemon juice
¼ tsp cayenne pepper	lettuce leaves
12 ripe avocados	tomato wedges
18 hard-boiled eggs, chopped	hard-boiled egg wedges
12 medium celery stalks, chopped	black olives
	pearl onions

❄ CAFÉ JOHNELL, 2529 South Calhoun, Fort Wayne, Indiana

Instructions

1) Put tomatoes, green peppers, onion and chili pepper through the fine blade of a meat grinder.
2) Drain liquid and discard; add salt and cayenne to vegetables and chili.
3) Cut avocados in half lengthwise. Remove pit and carefully scoop out pulp. Reserve skins.
4) Mash pulp in a ● ▲ *medium bowl,* ■ *large bowl,* until smooth.
5) Stir in eggs, celery, green pepper, onion and crabmeat; blend.
6) Add mayonnaise, mustard and lemon juice.
7) Fill avocado skins with crabmeat mixture.
8) Spoon 2 tablespoons of the vegetable sauce over each filled half.
9) Serve remaining vegetable sauce separately in a sauceboat.
10) Decorate the platter with lettuce leaves, tomato wedges, egg wedges, black olives and pearl onions.

preparation time: ● 45 minutes; ▲ 1 hour; ■ 1½ hours

Special Notes
- Filled avocados should be covered; they can be kept in refrigerator for 1 or 2 days.
- If you have any leftover sauce and avocado mixture, combine them and make a cracker dip.

Bean Sprout Salad

Ingredients

2

½	cup red wine vinegar
3	Tbs sugar
3	Tbs Japanese soy sauce
1½	tsps salt
1½	tsps brown mustard
3	Tbs sesame oil
1	lb fresh bean sprouts

1½	cups red wine vinegar
9	Tbs sugar
9	Tbs Japanese soy sauce
4½	tsps salt
4½	tsps brown mustard
9	Tbs sesame oil
3	lbs fresh bean sprouts

6

✳ THE COPPER KETTLE, 535 East Dean, Aspen, Colorado

Instructions

1) In a ● *medium bowl,* ▲ *large bowl,* combine vinegar, sugar, soy sauce, salt and mustard; beat with a wire whisk until thick.
2) Gradually beat in sesame oil, beating until thick.
3) Add washed and dried bean sprouts; toss with dressing to coat well.
4) Chill, covered, 24 hours.

preparation time: ● 15 minutes; ▲ 25 minutes

Special Notes
- The volume of the bean sprouts will reduce by half as they absorb the marinade. Transfer bean sprouts to a smaller container after marination.
- Salad keeps 1 to 2 weeks in refrigerator.
- This recipe really must be made with fresh bean sprouts. They can be found in oriental food or gourmet shops.

Cucumbers in Cream-Dill Sauce

Ingredients

2-3

- 1 large cucumber
- ¼ tsp salt
- ½ cup white vinegar
- ½ cup sugar
- ⅛ tsp freshly ground white pepper
- ½ cup mayonnaise
- ¼ cup whipped cream
- ¼ cup sour cream
- 1 Tb snipped fresh dill
- ⅛ tsp salt
- pinch of white pepper

6-8

- 3 medium cucumbers
- 1 tsp salt
- 1½ cups white vinegar
- 1½ cups sugar
- ¼ tsp freshly ground white pepper
- 1 cup mayonnaise
- ¼ cup heavy cream, whipped
- ½ cup sour cream
- 2 Tbs snipped fresh dill
- ¼ tsp salt
- ⅛ teaspoon white pepper

24

- 8 large cucumbers
- 1 Tb salt
- 6 cups white vinegar
- 6 cups sugar
- ½ tsp freshly ground white pepper
- 4 cups mayonnaise
- 1 cup heavy cream, whipped
- 2 cups sour cream
- ½ cup snipped fresh dill
- 1 tsp salt
- ¼ tsp white pepper

❄ VICTOR HUGO INN, 361 Cliff Road, Laguna Beach, California

Instructions

1) Slice cucumbers very thin; place in a ● *small bowl,* ▲ *medium bowl,* ■ *large bowl.*
2) Sprinkle cucumbers with the ● *¼ teaspoon salt,* ▲ *1 teaspoon salt,* ■ *1 tablespoon salt;* toss well and let stand 20 minutes.
3) Meanwhile, combine vinegar, sugar and ● *⅛ teaspoon white pepper,* ▲ *¼ teaspoon white pepper,* ■ *½ teaspoon white pepper* in a ● ▲ *medium bowl,* ■ *large bowl.*
4) Press as much liquid as possible from the cucumber slices.
5) Add cucumber to vinegar mixture and let marinate 2 hours.
6) Combine mayonnaise, whipped cream, sour cream and dill in a ● ▲ *medium bowl,* ■ *large bowl.*
7) Press all liquid out of cucumbers.
8) Add cucumbers to dressing; blend well to coat slices evenly; taste for seasoning.
9) Chill in refrigerator 3 hours before serving.

preparation time (including 2-hour marination): ● ▲ 2½ hours; ■ 3 hours

Special Note
● You can refrigerate cucumbers for 1 week, but stir well before serving.

German Salad

Ingredients

2-3

½	tsp sugar
⅛	tsp salt
	pinch of freshly ground black pepper
2	small potatoes, boiled and peeled
¼	cup chopped onion
¼	cup hot water
1	small head Bibb or Boston lettuce, torn into small pieces
5	ozs sliced bacon
¼	cup red wine vinegar

6-8

1½	tsps sugar
¼	tsp salt
⅛	tsp freshly ground black pepper
5	medium potatoes, boiled and peeled
¾	cup chopped onion
¾	cup hot water
2	large heads Bibb or Boston lettuce, torn into small pieces
1	lb sliced bacon
¾	cup red wine vinegar

24

2	Tbs sugar
½	tsp salt
¾	tsp freshly ground black pepper
7	lbs potatoes, boiled and peeled
3	cups chopped onion
3	cups hot water
7	medium heads Bibb or Boston lettuce, torn into small pieces
4	lbs sliced bacon
2½	cups red wine vinegar

❄ BELLEVUE RESTAURANT at THE PIONEER INN, 1000 Pioneer Drive, Oshkosh, Wisconsin

Instructions

1) Combine sugar, salt, pepper, potatoes and onion in ● *a small bowl,* ▲ *a medium bowl,* ■ *2 large bowls or pots.* Blend together until smooth.
2) Add hot water; beat until light.
3) Carefully blend in lettuce.
4) ● ▲ Fry bacon until brown and crisp in a ● *10-inch skillet,* ▲ *12-inch skillet.* Remove and drain on paper towels. Crumble bacon and reserve. ■ Fry bacon, 6 to 8 strips at a time, in a 12-inch skillet; drain on paper towels. Pour drippings into a measuring cup as you fry, and reserve. When all the bacon is fried, reheat bacon drippings in a 3-quart sauce-pan and continue with recipe. Crumble bacon and reserve.
5) Add vinegar to hot bacon fat and immediately pour mixture over po-tatoes. Toss and coat well. Stir in crumbled bacon.
6) Serve at room temperature.

preparation time: ● 20 minutes; ▲ 30 minutes; ■ 3 hours
yield: ● 2 cups; ▲ 6½ cups; ■ 28 cups

Special Note
● Salad is at its best served soon after preparation, but it can be refriger-ated for 3 to 4 days. Restore to room temperature before serving.

Langosta à la Mallorquina

Ingredients

2

½	lb frozen lobster tails
	boiling water
1	Tb white vinegar
1	tsp salt
1	bay leaf
1	small banana, sliced
½	medium apple, peeled, cored and cubed
½	medium pear, peeled, cored and cubed
2	Tbs mayonnaise
1	Tb dry sherry
1	Tb whipped cream
1½	tsps ketchup
⅛	tsp Worcestershire sauce
⅛	tsp dried tarragon

1½	lbs frozen lobster tails
	boiling water
2	Tbs white vinegar
2	tsps salt
2	bay leaves
2	medium bananas, sliced
1	large apple, peeled, cored and cubed
1	large pear, peeled, cored and cubed
6	Tbs mayonnaise
3	Tbs dry sherry
3	Tbs whipped cream
1½	Tbs ketchup
½	tsp Worcestershire sauce
½	tsp dried tarragon

SPANISH PAVILION, 475 Park Avenue, New York, New York

Instructions

1) Place lobster tails in a ● *1-quart saucepan,* ▲ *3-quart saucepan.* Add boiling water to cover, vinegar, salt and bay leaves; cook as long as package directs. Drain and cool.
2) Remove meat from shell and cut into bite-size pieces.
3) Combine lobster meat with the banana, apple and pear in a ● *small bowl,* ▲ *medium bowl.*
4) In a small bowl, combine mayonnaise, sherry, cream, ketchup, Worcestershire sauce and tarragon; blend.
5) Pour dressing over lobster mixture; lightly toss to coat all pieces evenly.
6) Chill 1 hour before serving as entrée.

preparation time (excluding final chilling): ● 25 minutes; ▲ 45 minutes

Special Note
● The lobster and dressing may be prepared as far as 2 to 3 days in advance. The fruit, however, should be added no more than 1 hour before serving.

Leek Salad

Ingredients

3	medium, or 2 large, leeks
	boiling water
¼	tsp salt
1	tsp lemon juice
2	tsps beaten egg
1	Tb Dijon mustard
½	tsp red wine vinegar
	pinch of salt
	pinch of freshly ground black pepper
¼	cup peanut oil
1	tomato, wedged
1	hard-boiled egg, wedged

6	large leeks
	boiling water
½	tsp salt
1	Tb lemon juice
1½	Tbs beaten egg
2	Tbs Dijon mustard
1	tsp red wine vinegar
⅛	tsp salt
	pinch of freshly ground black pepper
½	cup peanut oil
2	tomatoes, wedged
2	hard-boiled eggs, wedged

6

24	large leeks
	boiling water
2	tsps salt
¼	cup lemon juice
2	eggs, beaten
½	cup Dijon mustard
4	tsps red wine vinegar
½	tsp salt
¼	tsp freshly ground black pepper
2	cups peanut oil
8	tomatoes, wedged
8	hard-boiled eggs, wedged

※ THE FLYING FRENCHMAN, 844 North Wabash Avenue, Chicago, Illinois

Instructions

1) Cut off root-end of leeks and trim all but 3 inches of green top.
2) Halve the leeks lengthwise to within 1 inch of root-end. Carefully run leeks under cold water to rinse off dirt.
3) With string, securely tie 3 leeks in a bundle.
4) Place leeks in a ● *2-quart saucepan,* ▲ *4-quart saucepan,* ■ *8-quart Dutch oven.* Pour in boiling water to cover, salt and lemon juice.
5) Simmer, partially covered, over low heat until barely fork-tender, but not soft, about ● *5 to 10 minutes,* ▲ *15 to 20 minutes,* ■ *20 to 30 minutes.*
6) Drain on paper towels and cool.
7) Remove string and chill. Meanwhile, prepare dressing: combine egg, mustard, vinegar, salt and pepper in a ● *small bowl,* ▲ *medium bowl,* ■ *large bowl.* Gradually add oil, beating constantly with a wire whisk until thick.
8) Arrange a leek on each salad plate; garnish with tomato and hard-boiled egg wedges. Serve dressing on the side or pour over leeks.

   preparation time: ● 40 minutes; ▲ 1 hour; ■ 2 hours

Special Note
● Cooked leeks and the dressing, kept separately, will keep in refrigerator for 1 to 2 weeks.

Pickled Mostaccioli

Ingredients

2

3 ozs mostaccioli pasta
boiling water
¼ tsp salt
1 tsp vegetable oil
3 Tbs olive oil
2 tsps yellow mustard
1 tsp Worcestershire
sauce
1½ Tbs cider vinegar
¼ tsp coarsely ground
black pepper

½ small garlic clove,
minced
1 tsp sugar
¼ tsp salt
dash of Tabasco
¼ cup chopped scallion
3 Tbs peeled, chopped
cucumber
3 Tbs chopped parsley
2 Tbs chopped pimiento

6

8 ozs mostaccioli pasta
boiling water
1 tsp salt
1 Tb vegetable oil
½ cup olive oil
1½ Tbs yellow mustard
1 Tb Worcestershire sauce
¼ cup cider vinegar
1 tsp coarsely ground black pepper
1 small garlic clove, minced
1 Tb sugar
1 tsp salt
dash of Tabasco
½ cup chopped scallion
½ cup peeled, chopped cucumber
⅓ cup chopped parsley
¼ cup chopped pimiento

24

2 lbs mostaccioli pasta
boiling water
1 Tb salt
2 Tbs vegetable oil
2 cups olive oil
6 Tbs yellow mustard
¼ cup Worcestershire
sauce
1 cup cider vinegar
1 Tb coarsely ground
black pepper

3 large cloves garlic,
minced
¼ cup sugar
1 Tb salt
3–4 dashes of Tabasco
2 cups chopped scallion
2 cups peeled, chopped
cucumber
1½ cups chopped parsley
1 cup chopped pimiento

❄ The former CURT YOCOM'S RESTAURANT, Iowa City, Iowa

206

Instructions

1) Cook pasta in plenty of boiling water to which salt and vegetable oil have been added until pasta is al dente.
2) Drain and rinse in cold water.
3) Put pasta in a ● ▲ *medium bowl,* ■ *large bowl or pot.*
4) Add olive oil and toss well.
5) Add mustard, Worcestershire sauce, vinegar, pepper, garlic, sugar, salt and Tabasco; blend well.
6) Add scallion, cucumber, parsley and pimiento.
7) Marinate, covered, 8 to 12 hours in the refrigerator. Serve cold or at room temperature as a salad or as a first course.

preparation time (excluding marination time): ● 45 minutes; ▲ 1¼ hours; ■ 2 hours

Special Notes
- Pasta will keep in refrigerator at least 1 week.
- You can substitute other macaroni about 2 inches long for the mostaccioli.

Mushroom Salad

Ingredients

½   lb mushrooms, sliced (about 2 cups)
2   Tbs + ¾ tsp Dijon mustard
2   Tbs + ¾ tsp wine vinegar
¼   tsp salt
¼   tsp dried oregano
¼   tsp dried tarragon
⅛   tsp freshly ground black pepper
6   Tbs olive oil
2   Tbs chopped parsley

1   lb mushrooms, sliced (about 4 cups)
4½   Tbs Dijon mustard
4½   Tbs wine vinegar
½   tsp salt
½   tsp dried oregano
½   tsp dried tarragon
¼   tsp freshly ground black pepper
¾   cup olive oil
¼   cup chopped parsley

6

4   lbs mushrooms, sliced (about 16 cups)
¾   cup Dijon mustard
¾   cup wine vinegar
1½   tsps salt
1½   tsps dried oregano
1½   tsps dried tarragon
¾   tsp freshly ground black pepper
2¼   cups olive oil
½   cup chopped parsley

❊ CHANTAL RESTAURANT, 11712 San Vicente Boulevard, Los Angeles, California

Instructions

1) Place sliced mushrooms in a ● *small bowl,* ▲ *medium bowl,* ■ *large bowl.*
2) Combine mustard, vinegar, salt, oregano, tarragon and pepper in a ● ▲ *small bowl,* ■ *medium bowl.* Blend well.
3) Add olive oil, very gradually, by beating with an electric mixer until mixture is thick and smooth.
4) Pour dressing over mushrooms; toss gently but coat well.
5) Sprinkle with parsley and serve.

   preparation time: ● 20 minutes; ▲ 45 minutes; ■ 1¼ hours

Special Notes

● Mushroom salad will stay exactly as made for 3 or 4 hours. After that, the mushrooms will water a little into the dressing. It is as delicious— only you may want to drain off a little dressing.
● You can make the dressing 1 day in advance, refrigerate and toss with mushrooms when ready to serve. The oil will congeal when refrigerated so let dressing come to room temperature before using.

Rice Salad, Bit-O-Sweden

Ingredients

1¼ cups cooked rice
¼ cup chopped celery
½ cup finely chopped
 bread and butter
 pickles, drained
½ small onion, chopped
1 small green pepper,
 chopped
¼ cup chopped stuffed
 green olives
2 Tbs sliced ripe olives

2 small radishes, thinly
 sliced
½ 0.6-oz package Italian
 salad-dressing mix
¼ tsp salt
 pinch of freshly ground
 black pepper
1½ Tbs white vinegar
2 Tbs olive oil
3 cherry tomatoes, halved

2½ cups cooked rice
½ cup chopped celery
1 cup finely chopped bread and butter pickles, drained
1 small onion, chopped
1 medium green pepper, chopped
½ cup chopped stuffed green olives
¼ cup sliced ripe olives
3 large radishes, thinly sliced
1 0.6-oz package Italian salad-dressing mix
¾ tsp salt
⅛ tsp freshly ground black pepper
3 Tbs white vinegar
4 Tbs olive oil
5 cherry tomatoes, halved

6

---

10 cups cooked rice
2 cups chopped celery
4 cups finely chopped
 bread and butter
 pickles, drained
3 medium onions, chopped
4 medium green peppers,
 chopped
2 cups chopped stuffed
 green olives
1 cup sliced ripe olives

12 large radishes, thinly
 sliced
4 0.6-oz packages Italian
 salad-dressing mix
2 tsps salt
¼ tsp freshly ground black
 pepper
¾ cup white vinegar
1 cup olive oil
20 cherry tomatoes, halved

BIT-O-SWEDEN, Route 2, Eureka Springs, Arkansas

Instructions

1) Place rice in a ● *small bowl,* ▲ *medium bowl,* ■ *large bowl or pot.*
2) Add celery, pickles, onion, green pepper, stuffed and ripe olives and radishes; toss lightly but blend well.
3) Combine dressing mix, salt and pepper in a ● ▲ *small bowl,* ■ *medium bowl.*
4) Add vinegar.
5) Gradually add olive oil, beating with a wire whisk until thick.
6) Pour dressing over rice mixture and toss lightly and coat evenly.
7) Add cherry tomatoes.
8) Let stand in refrigerator, covered, for at least 5 hours to blend flavors before serving.

preparation time (excluding refrigeration time): ● 30 minutes; ▲ 1 hour; ■ 1½ hours

yield: ● 3 cups; ▲ 6 cups; ■ 25 cups

Special Note
● Rice salad will keep in refrigerator about 2 weeks.

Rice Salad, Zodiac Room

Ingredients

1	cup cooked, cooled rice
¼	cup cooked flaked or lump crabmeat or cubed lobster
¼	cup slivered ham
¼	cup finely chopped celery
1	hard-boiled egg, finely chopped
2	tsps chopped chives
2	Tbs chopped parsley
2	tsps olive oil
2	tsps wine vinegar
¼	cup mayonnaise
⅛	tsp salt
⅛	tsp freshly ground black pepper

3	cups cooked, cooled rice
¾	cup cooked flaked or lump crabmeat or cubed lobster
¾	cup slivered ham
¾	cup finely chopped celery
3	hard-boiled eggs, finely chopped
2	Tbs chopped chives
⅓	cup chopped parsley
2	Tbs olive oil
2	Tbs wine vinegar
¾	cup mayonnaise
¼	tsp salt
¼	tsp freshly ground black pepper

6

12	cups cooked, cooled rice
3	cups cooked flaked or lump crabmeat or cubed lobster
3	cups slivered ham
3	cups finely chopped celery
9	hard-boiled eggs, finely chopped
½	cup chopped chives
1¼	cups chopped parsley
½	cup olive oil
½	cup + 2 Tbs wine vinegar
3	cups mayonnaise
½	tsp salt
½	tsp freshly ground black pepper

❄ ZODIAC ROOM RESTAURANT at NEIMAN-MARCUS, Dallas, Texas

Instructions

1) Combine rice, crabmeat, ham, celery, eggs, chives and parsley in ● *a small bowl,* ▲ *a medium bowl,* ■ *2 large bowls or pots, dividing ingredients evenly between them.*
2) Sprinkle oil and vinegar over rice mixture.
3) Add mayonnaise; blend well.
4) Season to taste with salt and pepper.
5) Chill 3 hours before serving as entrée.

preparation time (excluding final chilling): ● 20 minutes; ▲ 40 minutes; ■ 1 hour

yield: ● 1½ cups; ▲ 5 cups; ■ 20 cups

Special Notes
● Cook rice for large quantity in small separate batches, no more than 3 cups raw rice at a time.
● Salad will keep 2 or 3 days in the refrigerator.

Special Salad

Ingredients

2-3

3	Tbs olive oil
⅛	tsp salt
1	small garlic clove, minced
1	tomato, peeled and wedged
1	head romaine lettuce, torn into pieces
2	Tbs chopped scallion
¼	cup freshly grated romano cheese
½	lb bacon, fried and crumbled
½	cup unseasoned croutons
2	Tbs lemon juice
¼	tsp freshly ground black pepper
⅛	tsp chopped fresh mint
⅛	tsp dried oregano
1	coddled egg

6

6	Tbs olive oil
¼	tsp salt
1	large garlic clove, minced
2	tomatoes, peeled and wedged
2	heads romaine lettuce, torn into pieces
¼	cup chopped scallion
½	cup freshly grated romano cheese
1	lb bacon, fried and crumbled
1	cup unseasoned croutons
¼	cup lemon juice
½	tsp freshly ground black pepper
¼	tsp chopped fresh mint
¼	tsp dried oregano
1	coddled egg

24

¾	cup olive oil
½	tsp salt
2	large garlic cloves, minced
4	tomatoes, peeled and wedged
4	heads romaine lettuce, torn into pieces
½	cup chopped scallion
1	cup freshly grated romano cheese
2	lbs bacon, fried and crumbled
2	cups unseasoned croutons
½	cup lemon juice
¾	tsp freshly ground black pepper
½	tsp chopped fresh mint
½	tsp oregano
2	coddled eggs

❄CANLIS' RESTAURANT, 2100 Kalakaua Avenue, Honolulu, Hawaii

Instructions

1) Pour ● *1 tablespoon oil,* ▲ ■ *2 tablespoons oil* into ● *a medium salad bowl,* ▲ *a large salad or punch bowl,* ■ *each of 2 large salad bowls.*

2) Add salt, garlic, tomatoes, lettuce, scallion, cheese, bacon and croutons; toss lightly.

3) Combine remaining oil, lemon juice, pepper, mint, oregano and coddled egg in a ● ▲ *small bowl,* ■ *medium bowl.* Beat vigorously with a wire whisk until thick.

4) Pour dressing over salad. Toss well and let stand 10 minutes before serving.

preparation time: ● 25 minutes; ▲ 45 minutes; ■ 1¼ hours
yield: ● 2 to 3 servings as entree; 6 as salad
    ▲ 6 servings as entree; 12 as salad
    ■ 24 salads

Tabuli

Ingredients

½ cup bulgur (cracked wheat)
  ice water
1 medium tomato, peeled and chopped
¼ cup chopped parsley
¼ cup chopped fresh mint
1 small onion, chopped
¼ cup olive oil
2 Tbs lemon juice
¾ tsp salt
⅛ tsp freshly ground black pepper
  romaine lettuce leaves

---

1 cup bulgur (cracked wheat)
  ice water
1 large tomato, peeled and chopped
½ cup chopped parsley
½ cup chopped fresh mint
1 medium onion, chopped
½ cup olive oil
¼ cup lemon juice
1¼ tsps salt
¼ tsp freshly ground black pepper
  romaine lettuce leaves

6

4 cups bulgur (cracked wheat)
  ice water
4 large tomatoes, peeled and chopped
2 cups chopped parsley
2 cups chopped fresh mint
4 large onions, chopped
2 cups olive oil
1 cup lemon juice
4 tsps salt
½ tsp freshly ground black pepper
  romaine lettuce leaves

❄ CANLIS' RESTAURANT, 2576 Aurora Avenue, Seattle, Washington

Instructions

1) Soak bulgur in ice water to cover for 2 hours in a ● *small bowl,* ▲ *medium bowl,* ■ *large bowl or pot.* Drain well.
2) Replace bulgur in the same bowl. Add tomato, parsley, mint and onion; blend well.
3) Combine olive oil, lemon juice, salt and pepper in a jar with a tight-fitting lid and shake well to blend.
4) Pour over bulgur and toss lightly but thoroughly.
5) Chill, covered, 2 hours or overnight.
   Serve over romaine lettuce leaves as a side salad or appetizer.

   preparation time (including 2-hour soaking): ● 2½ hours, ▲ 2½ hours, ■ 3 hours

Special Notes
- Tabuli will keep in refrigerator for 1 week. If it begins to water, just drain it.
- Bulgur can be found in health food shops and Middle Eastern grocery stores.

Beet and Apple Relish

½	cup peeled and chopped apples
½	cup canned or cooked julienne beets, drained
¼	cup sour cream
¼	cup mayonnaise
1	Tb honey
⅛	tsp salt

2	cups peeled and chopped apples
2	cups canned or cooked julienne beets, drained
¾	cup sour cream
¾	cup mayonnaise
3	Tbs honey
¼	tsp salt

6

8	cups peeled and chopped apples
8	cups canned or cooked julienne beets, drained
3	cups sour cream
3	cups mayonnaise
¾	cup honey
1	tsp salt

❄ COPENHAGEN RESTAURANT, 68 West 58 Street, New York, New York

Instructions

1) Combine apples and beets in a ● *small bowl,* ▲ *medium bowl,* ■ *large bowl or pot.*
2) Blend sour cream, mayonnaise, salt and honey in a ● ▲ *small bowl,* ■ *medium bowl.*
3) Pour over beets and apples; blend well.
4) Chill 3 hours before serving.

preparation time (excluding chilling period): ● 30 minutes; ▲ 45 minutes; ■ 1¼ hours

yield: ● 1¼ cups; ▲ 4 cups; ■ 16 cups

Special Note
● Relish refrigerates perfectly for about 2 weeks.

Cold Relish

½ cup vegetable oil
⅓ cup white vinegar
¼ tsp celery seed
¼ tsp dried basil
¼ tsp MSG (optional)
¼ tsp chopped chives
¼ – ½ tsp salt
⅛ tsp freshly ground black pepper
1 medium cauliflower, broken into flowerets
  boiling water
1 Tb lemon juice
1 medium onion, thinly sliced

medium

3 cups vegetable oil
2 cups white vinegar
1½ tsps celery seed
1½ tsps dried basil
1½ tsps MSG (optional)
1½ tsps chopped chives
1 tsp salt
¼ tsp freshly ground black pepper
3 medium cauliflowers, broken into flowerets
  boiling water
3 Tbs lemon juice
3 large onions, thinly sliced

❈BROWN PALACE HOTEL, Tremont and 17th streets, Denver, Colorado

Instructions

1) Combine oil, vinegar, celery seed, basil, optional MSG, chives, salt and pepper in a ▲ *1-quart saucepan,* ■ *2-quart saucepan.* Bring to a boil over moderate heat. Cover and simmer 5 minutes.
2) Add lemon juice and cauliflower to a ▲ *3-quart saucepan,* ■ *8-quart Dutch oven,* ⅔ full of boiling water. Boil 8 minutes.
3) Add onions and cook 2 minutes longer or until cauliflower is almost tender, but not soft. Drain and place in a ▲ *medium bowl,* ■ *large bowl or pot.*
4) Pour hot pickling mixture over hot cauliflower.
5) Cool to room temperature. Chill, covered, for at least 12 hours before serving.

preparation time: ▲ 30 minutes; ■ 1 hour
yield: ▲ 1 quart; ■ 3 quarts

Special Notes
• Relish will keep in refrigerator for several weeks.
• If desired, relish can be preserved. Pour hot relish into hot sterilized jars and seal.

Corn Relish

Ingredients

1	10-oz package frozen corn kernels
1	cup finely shredded cabbage
½	cup thinly sliced celery
½	medium sweet red pepper, finely chopped
1	cup water
¼	cup sugar
1	Tb salt
1	Tb dry mustard
½	cup white vinegar

2	10-oz packages frozen corn kernels
2	cups finely shredded cabbage
1	cup thinly sliced celery
1	medium sweet red pepper, finely chopped
2	cups water
½	cup sugar
2	Tbs salt
2	Tbs dry mustard
1	cup white vinegar

medium

4	10-oz packages frozen corn kernels
4	cups finely shredded cabbage
2	cups thinly sliced celery
2	medium sweet red peppers, finely chopped
4½	cups water
¾	cup sugar
2½	Tbs salt
3	Tbs dry mustard
1½	cups white vinegar

❄ LEVAS, 119 South Limestone Street, Lexington, Kentucky

Instructions

1) Cook corn according to package directions. Drain and reserve kernels.
2) Combine cabbage, celery, red pepper and half the water into a ● *1-quart saucepan,* ▲ *2-quart saucepan,* ■ *7-quart saucepan.*
3) Cover; cook over low heat 5 minutes or until barely tender.
4) Drain. Combine corn and vegetables in the same pot.
5) Combine sugar, salt, mustard, vinegar and remaining water in a ● *small bowl,* ▲ *medium bowl,* ■ *large bowl.*
6) Pour over vegetables and simmer, stirring occasionally, 5 minutes.
7) Pour into a ● *small bowl,* ▲ *medium bowl,* ■ *large bowl;* let cool to room temperature.
8) Cover and store in refrigerator.

preparation time: ● 30 minutes; ▲ 40 minutes; ■ 1 hour
yield: ● 2½ cups; ▲ 5 cups; ■ 10 cups

Special Notes
- Relish will keep 2 weeks in refrigerator.
- Corn Relish can be preserved after Step 6; pour hot relish into hot sterilized jars and seal.

Health Relish

Ingredients

1	large carrot
2	medium onions
1	medium red pepper
1	medium green pepper
1½	lbs green cabbage
2	Tbs salt
¾	tsp celery seed
¾	tsp mustard seed
	dash of Tabasco
½	cup white vinegar
¾	cup sugar

3	large carrots
5	large onions
3	medium red peppers
3	medium green peppers
4½	lbs green cabbage
4	Tbs salt
2	tsps celery seed
2	tsps mustard seed
⅛	tsp Tabasco
1½	cups white vinegar
2¼	cups sugar

WOODBINE COTTAGE, River Road at the Harbor, Sunapee, New Hampshire

Instructions

1) Chop the carrots, onions, peppers and cabbage very finely and put in a ▲ *medium bowl,* ■ *large bowl or pot.*
2) Add salt and toss well. Let stand 2 to 3 hours.
3) Drain liquid from vegetables, squeezing out excess with your hands.
4) Add celery seed, mustard seed, Tabasco, vinegar and sugar; blend well.
5) Chill in refrigerator at least 3 hours before serving.

preparation time (excluding chilling period): ▲ 45 minutes; ■ 1½ hours

yield: ▲ 6 cups; ■ 18 cups

Special Note
• Relish keeps in refrigerator 2 to 3 weeks.

BREADS AND MUFFINS

Apricot Bread

Ingredients

8 muffins

⅔ cup dried apricots
⅓ cup boiling water
2 Tbs butter, softened
½ cup sugar
3 Tbs beaten egg
1 cup sifted flour
¾ tsp baking soda
⅛ tsp salt
⅓ cup chopped walnuts

8-by-4½-by-2¼-inch loaf

1 cup dried apricots
½ cup boiling water
3 Tbs butter, softened
¾ cup sugar
1 egg
1½ cups sifted flour
1 tsp baking soda
¼ tsp salt
½ cup chopped walnuts

❊ The former HARBOURSIDE INN, Northeast Harbor, Maine

Instructions

1) Use scissors to cut apricots into small pieces; place in a small bowl, cover with boiling water, and let stand 15 minutes.
2) Preheat oven to 350 degrees.
3) Cream butter and sugar until smooth in the ● *small bowl,* ▲ *medium bowl* of an electric mixer.
4) Add egg; beat until well blended.
5) Sift together flour, baking soda and salt. Reserve 1 tablespoon of flour mixture in a small dish.
6) Add flour mixture and apricots with its soaking liquid alternately to batter, and stir until well blended.
7) Toss walnuts with the reserved tablespoon flour and fold into batter.
8) Pour batter into ● *8 greased and floured 2½-inch muffin tins; fill to ⅔ capacity,* ▲ *a greased and floured 8-by-4½-by-2¼-inch loaf pan.*
9) Bake in the preheated oven until tester inserted in center comes out clean, about ● *15 to 20 minutes,* ▲ *1 hour.*
10) Remove to wire rack and cool.

preparation time: ● 1 hour; ▲ 1½ hours
yield: ● 8 muffins; ▲ 8 to 10 portions.

Special Notes
- For a better flavor, let bread or muffins stand at room temperature wrapped in foil, for 1 or 2 days.
- Bread and muffins freeze well. Thaw and serve at room temperature, or reheat wrapped in aluminum foil in a preheated 300-degree oven, about 15 minutes.

Hot Banana Bread

Ingredients

8 muffins

1	cup sifted flour
¾	tsp baking powder
¼	tsp baking soda
⅛	tsp salt
¼	cup seedless raisins
¼	cup dried apricots
½	cup mashed banana (about 1 large)
1	egg
½	cup sugar
4	Tbs butter, melted
1	Tb buttermilk
½	tsp lemon juice
¼	cup chopped walnuts

1 round loaf

2	cups sifted flour
1½	tsps baking powder
½	tsp baking soda
¼	tsp salt
½	cup seedless raisins
½	cup dried apricots
1	cup mashed banana (about 2 large)
2	eggs
1	cup sugar
8	Tbs (1 stick) butter, melted
1½	Tbs buttermilk
1	tsp lemon juice
½	cup chopped walnuts

❋ THE HARBOR, Route 46, Parsippany, New Jersey

Instructions

1) Preheat oven to 350 degrees.
2) Sift together sifted flour, baking powder, baking soda and salt into a ● *small bowl,* ▲ *medium bowl.*
3) Rinse raisins and dried apricots under cold water and dry well with paper towels. Put fruits through the coarse blade of a food grinder. Reserve.
4) In a large mixing bowl, combine bananas, eggs, sugar, melted butter, buttermilk and lemon juice; beat until mixture is smooth.
5) Combine ground raisins and apricots with chopped nuts in a small bowl; blend well.
6) Sprinkle ● *1 tablespoon flour mixture,* ▲ *2 tablespoons flour mixture* over fruit and nuts and toss to coat all pieces. Reserve.
7) Gradually add remaining flour to banana mixture; stir until well blended.
8) Stir in fruit and nut mixture.
9) Pour batter into ● *8 greased and floured 2½-inch muffin tins; fill to ⅔ capacity,* ▲ *a greased and floured 10-by-4-inch bundt pan* and bake in the preheated oven until cake tester inserted in center comes out clean, about ● *20 minutes,* ▲ *1 hour.* Serve warm.

preparation time: ● 1 hour; ▲ 1½ hours
yield: ● 8 muffins; ▲ 10 to 12 portions

Special Notes
● If you do not have buttermilk, simply add ¼ teaspoon lemon juice to 1½ tablespoons milk and let stand 5 minutes.
● The flavor of the bread develops if wrapped and left unrefrigerated for 1 or 2 days. Serve at room temperature or reheated.
● Bread can be frozen for about 3 months. To serve, defrost, wrap bread in aluminum foil and warm in a preheated 300-degree oven, about 15 minutes.

Carrot Bread

Ingredients

8 muffins

¾	cup flour
¾	cup sugar
1	tsp ground cinnamon
1	tsp baking soda
½	tsp salt
2	eggs
1¼	cups shredded carrots
½	cup vegetable oil
⅓	cup chopped walnuts

9-by-5-by-3-inch loaf

1⅓	cups flour
1⅓	cups sugar
1½	tsps ground cinnamon
1½	tsps baking soda
¾	tsp salt
3	eggs
2	cups shredded carrots
⅔	cup vegetable oil
½	cup chopped walnuts

※ ALEXANDER HAMILTON INN, 21 West Park Row, Clinton, New York

Instructions

1) Preheat oven to 375 degrees.
2) Sift together flour, sugar, cinnamon, baking soda and salt onto a piece of wax paper
3) Beat eggs well in a ● *small bowl,* ▲ *medium bowl.*
4) Stir the carrots and oil into the eggs.
5) Add the flour mixture and nuts.
6) Pour batter into ● *8 greased and floured 2½-inch muffin tins; fill to ⅔ capacity,* ▲ *a greased and floured 9-by-5-by-3-inch loaf pan.*
7) Bake in the preheated oven until cake tester inserted in center comes out clean, about ● *20 to 25 minutes,* ▲ *1 hour.*

preparation time: ● 1 hour; ▲ 1½ hours
yield: ● 8 muffins; ▲ 8 to 10 portions

Special Notes
- Bread flavor mellows if allowed to stand 1 day, wrapped, unrefrigerated, before slicing.
- Bread keeps 2 weeks in refrigerator.
- Bread can be frozen from 2 to 3 months, but may be a little moist when thawed. Wrap in aluminum foil and warm in a preheated 300-degree oven for about 15 minutes.

Cape Cod Cranberry Bread

Ingredients

8 muffins

½	orange, unpeeled
	water
¾	cup coarsely chopped cranberries
½	cup sugar
½	beaten egg
1	cup flour
¾	tsp baking powder
½	tsp salt
¼	tsp baking soda
2	Tbs vegetable shortening
¼	cup chopped walnuts

9-by-5-by-3-inch loaf

1	orange, unpeeled
	water
1½	cups coarsely chopped cranberries
1	cup sugar
1	beaten egg
2	cups flour
1½	tsps baking powder
1	tsp salt
½	tsp baking soda
¼	cup vegetable shortening
½	cup chopped walnuts

✻ CAPTAIN WILLIAM'S HOUSE, 106 Depot Street, Dennis Port, Massachusetts.

Instructions

1) Cut orange into small pieces and remove seeds.
2) Work pieces through the fine blade of a meat grinder.
3) Place orange pulp and juice in a measuring cup and add enough boiling water to make ● *½ cup,* ▲ *1 cup.*
4) Combine cranberries, sugar, orange mixture and egg in a ● *small bowl,* ▲ *medium bowl.* Beat well and let stand at room temperature until needed.
5) Sift together into a medium bowl flour, baking powder, salt and baking soda.
6) Cut in shortening with a pastry blender or two knives until mixture resembles coarse meal.
7) Pour in the cranberry mixture and stir just to blend. Do not beat.
8) Fold in walnuts.
9) Pour mixture into ● *8 greased and floured 2½-inch muffin tins; fill to ⅔ capacity,* ▲ *a greased and floured 9-by-5-by-3-inch loaf pan.*
10) Let stand ● *10 minutes,* ▲ *20 minutes.*
11) Preheat oven to 350 degrees.
12) Bake in the preheated oven until cake tester inserted in the center comes out clean, about ● *15 to 20 minutes,* ▲ *60 to 70 minutes.*
13) Cool on wire rack 5 minutes, remove from pan and let cool completely on rack.

preparation time: ● 1 hour; ▲ 2 hours
yield: ● 8 muffins; ▲ 8 to 10 portions

Special Notes
● Flavor improves on standing. Wrap in aluminum foil and store at room temperature 1 day before slicing.
● Bread will keep 1 to 2 weeks in the refrigerator and frozen 2 to 3 months. To reheat, wrap in aluminum foil and place in a 300-degree oven, about 15 minutes.

Double Dillie Bread

Ingredients

1	package active dry yeast
¼	cup lukewarm water
1¼	cups small-curd cottage cheese
1	Tb butter
2	Tbs vegetable shortening
2	eggs
1	Tb minced onion
1	tsp dried dill weed
½	tsp dill seed
2¼	cups flour
3	Tbs sugar
¼	tsp baking soda
1	tsp salt
1	Tb milk

✳ FARAWAY HILLS COUNTRY INN, Beverly, West Virginia

Instructions

1) Sprinkle yeast over lukewarm water and stir until dissolved.
2) Combine cottage cheese, butter and vegtable shortening in a 1-quart saucepan and cook over low heat until warm.
3) Stir in 1 egg, onion, dill weed and dill seed.
4) In a large bowl, combine 1 cup flour, sugar, baking soda and salt; blend well.
5) Make a well in flour mixture, and add cheese mixture, and yeast; blend well.
6) Beat well, about 10 minutes, adding enough of the remaining flour to make a soft dough.
7) Cover bowl with a towel and let rise in a warm place until double in bulk (about 1 hour).
8) Stir dough until it collapses; put in a greased 2-quart soufflé dish.
9) Once again, cover with a towel and let rise until double in bulk (about 1 hour).
10) Preheat oven to 350 degrees.
11) Mix the other egg and milk in a small dish, and brush top of bread with it.
12) Bake in the preheated oven 50 to 60 minutes, or until golden and top sounds hollow when tapped with finger.
13) Cool before slicing.

preparation time (including standing time):   3½ hours
yield: 8 portions

Special Notes
- Bread freezes very well for 2 to 3 months. Cool completely before freezing.
- Bread can be refrigerated, wrapped in aluminum foil, for 1 week. Let it come to room temperature before serving.

Garlic Toast

Ingredients

½ 14-inch loaf French bread
1 garlic clove
4 Tbs butter, melted
2 Tbs freshly grated Parmesan cheese
1 Tb chopped parsley
½ tsp paprika

1 14-inch loaf French bread
2 garlic cloves
8 Tbs (1 stick) butter, melted
¼ cup grated Parmesan cheese
2 Tbs chopped parsley
1 tsp paprika

✻ BRENNAN'S RESTAURANT, 417 Royal Street, New Orleans, Louisiana

Instructions

1) Preheat oven to 350 degrees.
2) Cut bread in half lengthwise.
3) Slightly crush the garlic and rub the crust of bread with it.
4) Press garlic through a garlic press into the melted butter.
5) Brush the cut surfaces of bread generously with melted butter.
6) In a small bowl, combine Parmesan cheese, parsley and paprika.
7) Sprinkle mixture over butter-coated surface of bread. ⑤
8) Place bread on a cookie sheet, cutside up, and bake in the preheated oven 5 to 10 minutes or until lightly browned.

    preparation time: ● 20 minutes; ▲ 25 minutes

    yield: ● 7 2-inch slices; ▲ 14 2-inch slices

Special Notes
● Bread can be reheated if wrapped in aluminum foil and warmed in a pre-heated 325-degree oven for 10 minutes.
● Freeze the bread before baking (up to 3 months). Thaw and bake as directed.
● For other quantities of bread, you can safely multiply this recipe.

Hush Puppies

Ingredients

small

2	small celery stalks with leaves
½	medium green pepper
1	medium onion
½	cup yellow cornmeal
¼	cup flour
½	tsp salt
1½	Tbs sugar
1½	Tbs beaten egg
1½	Tbs baking powder
	vegetable oil for deep frying

medium

4	celery stalks with leaves
1½	medium green peppers
2	large onions
1¼	cups yellow cornmeal
⅔	cup flour
1¼	tsps salt
3½	Tbs sugar
1	egg
3½	Tbs baking powder
	vegetable oil for deep frying

large

12	celery stalks with leaves
3	medium green peppers
6	medium onions
3	cups yellow cornmeal
1½	cups flour
2	Tbs salt
½	cup sugar
3	eggs
½	cup baking powder
	vegetable oil for deep frying

✳ OLD FORT INN, Keith Street, Cleveland, Tennessee

Instructions

1) Put celery, green peppers and onions through the fine blade of a meat grinder into a ● *small bowl,* ▲ *medium bowl,* ■ *large bowl.*
2) Add cornmeal, flour, salt, sugar and egg; blend well.
3) Add baking powder just before frying.
4) Heat 2 inches of oil in a heavy saucepan or deep fryer to 360 degrees.
5) Drop a teaspoon of batter into fat for each hush puppy. Fry only 5 or 6 hush puppies at a time. Cook until golden brown. Drain on paper towels; serve immediately.

preparation time: ● 30 minutes; ▲ 45 minutes; ■ 1½ hours
yield: ● 20 hush puppies; ▲ 50 hush puppies; ■ 120 hush puppies

Special Notes
- If you do not have a meat grinder, mince the vegetables, being careful to retain the liquid exuded by the vegetables.
- Test a hush puppy before you start frying. If it breaks apart, reduce heat slightly. Retest until hush puppy holds its spherical shape.
- Hush puppies can be frozen successfully for 2 to 3 months. Thaw and reheat, uncovered, in a preheated 400-degree oven until crisp and heated through, about 5 minutes.
- Hush puppies cannot be reheated successfully after refrigeration. If you have leftovers, freeze them.

Nut Bread

Ingredients

6 muffins

1	Tb butter, softened
1½	tsps vegetable shortening
3	Tbs sugar
2	Tbs beaten egg
1½	Tbs orange marmalade
1	Tb cooked mashed potato
1	cup sifted flour
¾	tsp baking powder
¼	tsp baking soda
¼	tsp salt
3	Tbs orange juice
3	Tbs chopped pecans

9-by-5-by-3¼-inch loaf

4	Tbs butter, softened
1	Tb vegetable shortening
½	cup sugar
1	egg
¼	cup orange marmalade
2	Tbs cooked mashed potato
2¼	cups sifted flour
2	tsps baking powder
½	tsp baking soda
½	tsp salt
½	cup orange juice
½	cup chopped pecans

❋ RANCH KITCHEN, Route 66, Gallup, New Mexico

Instructions

1) Preheat oven to 350 degrees.
2) Combine butter and shortening in a ● *small bowl,* ▲ *medium bowl;* beat until creamy.
3) Add sugar gradually, beating until light and fluffy.
4) Add egg, marmalade and mashed potato; beat until blended.
5) Sift together flour, baking powder, baking soda and salt in a ● *small bowl,* ▲ *medium bowl.*
6) Set aside 1 tablespoon of the flour mixture.
7) Add remaining flour mixture to creamed mixture alternating with orange juice.
8) Toss nuts with the reserved flour, coating well.
9) Fold floured nuts gently into batter.
10) Pour batter into ● *6 greased and floured 2½-inch muffin tins; fill to ⅔ capacity,* ▲ *9-by-5-by-3-inch loaf pan.*
11) Bake in the preheated oven ● *15 to 20 minutes,* ▲ *50 to 60 minutes* or until cake tester inserted in center comes out clean.
12) Remove from pan and cool on wire rack.

preparation time: ● 1 hour; ▲ 1½ hours
yield: ● 6 muffins; ▲ 8–10 portions

Special Notes
● Bread and muffins are better if allowed to stand at room temperature, well wrapped, for 1 day before serving.
● Bread freezes for 2 to 3 months. After defrosting, wrap in aluminum foil and warm in a preheated 300-degree oven, about 15 minutes.

Pumpkin Muffins

Ingredients

12 muffins

1⅓	cups flour
½	cup sugar
2	tsps baking powder
¾	tsp salt
½	tsp ground cinnamon
½	tsp ground nutmeg
4	Tbs butter
½	cup raisins
½	cup canned pumpkin
½	cup milk
1	egg, lightly beaten

18 muffins

2	cups flour
¾	cup sugar
1	Tb baking powder
1	tsp salt
¾	tsp ground cinnamon
¾	tsp ground nutmeg
6	Tbs butter
¾	cup raisins
¾	cup canned pumpkin
¾	cup milk
2	eggs, lightly beaten

36 muffins

4	cups flour
1½	cups sugar
2	Tbs baking powder
2	tsps salt
1½	tsps ground cinnamon
1½	tsps ground nutmeg
12	Tbs (1½ sticks) butter
1½	cups raisins
1½	cups canned pumpkin
1½	cups milk
4	eggs, lightly beaten

✳ THE HEIDEL HOUSE, Illinois Avenue, Green Lake, Wisconsin

Instructions

1) Preheat oven to 400 degrees.
2) Sift together flour, sugar, baking powder, salt, cinnamon and nutmeg into a ● ▲ *medium bowl,* ■ *large bowl.*
3) Cut butter in with a pastry blender until mixture resembles coarse meal.
4) Add raisins, pumpkin and milk; stir until blended.
5) Add eggs and stir only enough to blend.
6) Fill ● *12,* ▲ *18,* ■ *36* greased and floured 2½-inch muffin tins ⅔ full.
7) Bake in the preheated oven 18 to 20 minutes, or until toothpick inserted in center comes out clean.
8) Remove muffins from tins and cool on wire racks.

preparation time: ● 45 minutes; ▲ 1 hour; ■ 1¼ hours

Special Note
● Muffins will freeze very well for 3 months. Just defrost, or warm, wrapped in aluminum foil, in a preheated 300-degree oven for about 12 minutes.

DESSERTS

Bread Pudding with Brandy Sauce

Ingredients

PUDDING

3	slices day-old white bread
1	cup milk
3	Tbs heavy cream
1	egg
3	Tbs sugar
¼	tsp vanilla extract
¼	tsp ground cinnamon
¼	tsp ground nutmeg
1	Tb butter, melted
2	Tbs seedless raisins

SAUCE

¼	cup sugar
1	tsp cornstarch
½	cup milk
1	egg yolk
¼	tsp vanilla extract
1	Tb brandy

PUDDING

8	slices day-old white bread
3	cups milk
¾	cup heavy cream
3	eggs
¾	cup sugar
1	tsp vanilla extract
¾	tsp ground cinnamon
¾	tsp ground nutmeg
3	Tbs butter, melted
⅓	cup seedless raisins

6-8

SAUCE

1	cup sugar
1	Tb cornstarch
1½	cups milk
3	egg yolks
1	tsp vanilla extract
3	Tbs brandy

✳ BRENNAN'S RESTAURANT, 417 Royal Street, New Orleans, Louisiana

Instructions

1) Preheat oven to 350 degrees.
2) Tear bread into small pieces and put into a ● *small bowl,* ▲ *medium bowl.*
3) Add milk and cream; stir to soak all the bread pieces. Reserve.
4) In a small bowl beat eggs and sugar until thick.
5) Add vanilla, cinnamon, nutmeg and butter.
6) Pour egg mixture over bread; stir gently to blend.
7) Add raisins.
8) Pour into a ● *20-ounce casserole,* ▲ *2-quart shallow baking dish.*
9) Set dish in a ● *1½-quart shallow baking dish,* ▲ *3-quart shallow baking dish* and fill larger dish with 1 inch of boiling water.
10) Bake in the preheated oven until set and golden brown, ● *25 to 30 minutes,* ▲ *45 to 50 minutes.* Remove from water bath.
11) While pudding is baking, prepare sauce: combine sugar and cornstarch in a ● *2-cup saucepan,* ▲ *1-quart saucepan;* blend well.
12) Gradually add milk, stirring until smooth.
13) Cook over moderate heat, stirring constantly, until mixture thickens and comes to a boil. Remove from heat.
14) Beat egg yolks in a small bowl with wire whisk.
15) Add some of the hot sauce to egg yolks, stirring constantly.
16) Slowly add egg yolks to saucepan, beating constantly.
17) Cook over low heat until hot, but do not allow mixture to boil.
18) Add vanilla and brandy.
19) Serve bread pudding warm with hot brandy sauce poured over each portion or served separately.

preparation time: ● 45 minutes; ▲ 1¼ hours

Special Notes
- The bread pudding can be baked ahead and warmed, covered, in a preheated 325-degree oven for about 15 to 20 minutes. Sauce is heated over low heat on top of the stove. Do not combine pudding and sauce until ready to serve.
- Bread pudding and the sauce can be frozen separately for 2 to 3 months. Thaw and reheat as above.

Date and Nut Pudding

Ingredients

PUDDING

1	cup boiling water
½	lb pitted dates
½	cup shortening
½	cup granulated sugar
2	eggs
½	cup dark molasses
1	tsp baking soda
2	cups flour
1	tsp baking powder
½	tsp salt
¼	tsp ground cloves
¼	tsp ground ginger
¼	tsp ground nutmeg
¼	tsp ground cinnamon
½	cup chopped walnuts

HARD SAUCE

8	Tbs (1 stick) butter, softened
3½	cups confectioners' sugar
3	egg yolks
¼	tsp ground nutmeg
½	tsp vanilla extract or 1–2 Tbs brandy or rum
3	egg whites, at room temperature

✳ THE OLD FORT, 81 Huguenot Street, New Paltz, New York

Instructions

1) In a small bowl, pour boiling water over dates and let stand 20 minutes.
2) Drain dates, reserving the liquid
3) In the large bowl of an electric mixer, beat shortening until creamy.
4) Add sugar gradually; beat until fluffy.
5) Add eggs, one at a time, and beat well after each addition.
6) Stir in molasses.
7) Add baking soda to reserved date liquid.
8) In a medium bowl, sift together flour, baking powder, salt, cloves, ginger, nutmeg and cinnamon. Reserve ¼ cup of flour mixture.
9) Gradually add flour mixture alternately with date liquid to shortening mixture; blend well.
10) In a small bowl, toss dates and nuts with the reserved flour to coat evenly.
11) Stir into batter.
12) Pour batter into a buttered 2-quart pudding mold. Butter inside of lid; fasten mold tightly.
13) Put mold on a rack in a deep 8-quart stock pot or Dutch oven.
14) Pour in enough boiling water to reach ⅔ up the outside of the mold.
15) Cover pot and steam pudding on top of the stove 1½ hours, adding more boiling water if necessary. Test pudding with a cake tester to see if it is done.
16) While pudding is steaming, make hard sauce: in a medium bowl beat butter until creamy.
17) Gradually add confectioners' sugar and beat until fluffy.
18) Beat in egg yolks, one at a time, until well blended.
19) Stir in nutmeg and either vanilla, brandy or rum.
20) Beat egg whites in a medium bowl until stiff peaks form.
21) Fold gently into sauce.
22) Chill in freezer at least 1½ to 2 hours before serving.
23) To unmold pudding, loosen edges with a metal spatula and invert onto a serving platter. Serve warm with the cold hard sauce.

preparation time (excluding chilling time): 2 hours

Special Notes
- Hard sauce is better if made a day in advance. Be sure it is well chilled before serving.
- Pudding can be made ahead, removed from mold and warmed by wrapping in aluminum foil and heating in a preheated 300-degree oven 10 to 15 minutes. However, it will not be as light as when it first comes out of steamer.
- Pudding and sauce can be frozen, separately, 2 to 3 months. You can serve the sauce straight from the freezer.

Crêpes Ambrosia

Ingredients

2

CRÊPES

1 egg
2 tsps flour
1 tsp milk
1 tsp water
pinch of salt
2 tsps butter, melted

SAUCE

1 cup hulled strawberries
(½ pint)
1 tsp sugar
1½ Tbs kirsch
1½ Tbs Cointreau

2 scoops ice cream

CRÊPES

1½ eggs
1 Tb flour
1½ tsps milk
1½ tsps water
pinch of salt
1 Tb butter, melted

6

SAUCE

3 cups hulled strawberries (1½ pints)
1 Tb sugar
¼ cup kirsch
¼ cup Cointreau
6 scoops ice cream

24

CRÊPES

6 eggs
½ cup flour
¼ cup milk
¼ cup water
⅛ tsp salt
4 Tbs butter, melted

SAUCE

12 cups hulled strawberries
(6 pints)
¼ cup sugar
1 cup kirsch
1 cup Cointreau

24 scoops ice cream

 ERNIE'S RESTAURANT, 847 Montgomery Street, San Francisco, California

Instructions

1) To prepare crêpes: combine eggs and flour in a ● ▲ *small bowl,* ■ *large bowl.* Beat with a wire whisk until smooth.
2) Add milk, water and salt; beat until smooth.
3) Refrigerate, covered, 3 hours.
4) With a pastry brush dipped in the melted butter, very lightly coat the bottom of a hot 5-inch crêpe pan or skillet.
5) Pour in about 1½ tablespoons of batter and quickly rotate the pan to coat it with a thin film of batter.
6) Cook over moderately high heat until underside is lightly brown.
7) Turn crêpe with a spatula; lightly brown other side.
8) Remove crêpe to a plate and reserve.
9) Repeat with remaining batter. Pile crêpes on top of each other.
10) Mash ⅓ of the strawberries in ● *an 8-inch skillet,* ▲ *a 10-inch skillet,* ■ *a 12-inch skillet.*
11) Add sugar, kirsch and Cointreau; cook only until liqueurs are heated.
12) Flame with a match and set aside.
13) Separate crêpes and coat in sauce; reheat together for 2 to 3 minutes.
14) Place a scoop of ice cream on each dessert dish.
15) Surround ice cream with the remaining whole strawberries.
16) Place one crêpe over each ice cream scoop.
17) Pour a little of the sauce over crêpe. Serve immediately.

preparation time (including 3-hour chilling period): ● 3½ hours ▲ 4 hours; ■ 5 hours

Special Notes
- Extra crêpes can be refrigerated for 1 or 2 days—or frozen for 2 to 3 months. Place a small piece of wax paper between crêpes before storing.
- The sauce will keep about a week in the refrigerator.
- Raw batter will keep, covered, in refrigerator for 2 to 3 days. Test 1 crêpe; if too thick add a bit of milk.

Curried Baked Pears

Ingredients

3	Tbs sugar
¼	tsp salt
¾	tsp curry powder
1½	tsps cornstarch
½	cup unsweetened pineapple juice
2	tsps lemon juice
2	fresh pears, pared, halved, and cored, or 4 canned pear halves
1	Tb butter, melted

½	cup sugar
½	tsp salt
2	tsps curry powder
2	Tbs cornstarch
2	cups unsweetened pineapple juice
2	Tbs lemon juice
6	fresh pears, pared, halved, and cored, or 12 canned pear halves
4	Tbs butter, melted

6

2	cups sugar
2	tsps salt
2	Tbs + 2 tsps curry powder
½	cup cornstarch
8	cups unsweetened pineapple juice
½	cup lemon juice
24	whole fresh pears, pared, halved, and cored, or 48 canned pear halves
1	cup (2 sticks) butter, melted

✳ BIT-O-SWEDEN, Route 2, Eureka Springs, Arkansas

Instructions

1) Preheat oven to 350 degrees.
2) Combine sugar, salt, curry powder and cornstarch in a ● *1-quart saucepan,* ▲ *1½-quart saucepan,* ■ *3-quart saucepan.*
3) Gradually stir in pineapple juice, blending well to keep mixture smooth.
4) Stir in lemon juice.
5) Cook over moderate heat, stirring constantly, until mixture thickens and comes to a boil. Remove from heat.
6) Place pear halves, cutside up, in ● *a 1½ quart shallow baking dish,* ▲ *a 3-quart shallow baking dish,* ■ *4 3-quart shallow baking dishes.*
7) Pour sauce over pears.
8) Pour butter over top.
9) Bake in the preheated oven 20 to 30 minutes, or until pears are tender and heated through.
10) Serve 2 pear halves with sauce to each person.

preparation time: ● 35 to 40 minutes; ▲ 50 minutes; ■ 1 hour

Special Notes
- Curry flavor gets stronger on standing, and therefore the finished pears should be served soon after baking.
- If they cannot be served immediately, do not pour sauce over pears until ready to bake.

Fried Strawberries

Ingredients

1 egg
¼ cup vegetable oil
½ cup milk
½ cup sifted flour
  peanut oil for deep frying
2 pints strawberries, hulled and dried
  confectioners' sugar

4-6

Instructions

1) In a small bowl beat egg, oil and milk until blended.
2) Gradually add flour and beat with a wire whisk until smooth.
3) Heat 2 inches of oil in a heavy 1-quart saucepan to 375 degrees.
4) Dip 3 or 4 strawberries in batter and drop in oil.
5) Fry 1 to 2 minutes or until puffed and golden brown.
6) Drain on paper towel.
7) Repeat with remaining berries.
8) Sprinkle with confectioners' sugar and serve immediately.

preparation time: 30 minutes

Special Notes
- This unusual dish is difficult to make, but worth the trouble if you love strawberries. The perfect way to prepare the strawberries is at the table; as with fondue, let each make his own.
- There are several precautions: do not fry too many at a time, to avoid lowering the temperature of the oil. The 375-degree temperature is crucial for strawberries to puff and brown. Also, make sure strawberries are dried well with paper towels; water will cause the oil to splatter.

Macadamia Nut Balls

Ingredients

2-3

SAUCE

- ¼ cup sugar
- 2 egg yolks
- ½ cup dry white wine
- ¼ cup ground macadamia nuts (about 2 ozs)

NUT BALLS

- ⅓ cup water
- 2½ Tbs butter
- ¼ tsp sugar
- pinch of salt
- ⅓ cup flour
- 1½ eggs
- 2½ Tbs ground macadamia nuts (about 1 oz)
- 1 tsp Cognac
- vegetable oil for deep frying
- confectioners' sugar

SAUCE

- ¾ cup sugar
- 6 egg yolks
- 1½ cups dry white wine
- ¾ cup ground macadamia nuts (about 6 ozs)

6-8

NUT BALLS

- 1 cup water
- 8 Tbs (1 stick) butter
- ½ tsp sugar
- ¼ tsp salt
- 1 cup flour
- 4 eggs
- ½ cup ground macadamia nuts (about 4 ozs)
- 1 Tb Cognac
- vegetable oil for deep frying
- confectioners' sugar

✳ ROYAL HAWAIIAN HOTEL, 2259 Kalakaua Avenue, Honolulu, Hawaii

Instructions

1) To make sauce: beat sugar and egg yolks in a 1-quart saucepan until thick.
2) Add wine gradually; blend well.
3) Cook over low heat, stirring constantly, until mixture thickens and coats a metal spoon; do not boil.
4) Remove from heat; stir in ground nuts. Reserve.
5) For the nut balls: heat water, butter, sugar and salt to the boiling point in a heavy ● *1-quart saucepan,* ▲ *1½-quart saucepan.*
6) Add flour all at once, beating vigorously with a wooden spoon.
7) Cook over low heat, beating constantly, until mixture pulls away from the sides of the pan and forms a ball in the center.
8) Transfer paste into a medium bowl and add eggs, one at a time, beating well after each addition with an electric mixer. Mixture should be stiff and glossy.
9) Add ground nuts and Cognac; blend well.
10) Heat 2 inches of oil in a heavy saucepan or deep fryer to 375 degrees.
11) Drop 1 heaping teaspoon of paste into the hot fat. Cut ball in half to see if it is done in the center. If not, reduce heat slightly and continue frying.
12) Fry 5 or 6 balls at a time until golden brown, about 2 to 3 minutes.
13) Drain balls on paper towels.
14) Dust balls lightly with confectioners' sugar.
15) Either heat sauce over low heat until warm—do not allow to boil—or serve cold.

preparation time: ● 45 minutes; ▲ 1¼ hours
yield: ● 18 1-inch balls; ▲ 48 1-inch balls

Special Notes
- You can freeze balls and sauce separately. Thaw, and reheat balls, uncovered, on a tray in a preheated 350-degree oven for 10 to 15 minutes or until crisp.
- The balls can be refrigerated, and then reheated as above, but they will be less crisp than the frozen, reheated nut balls.

Coffee Cream Mousse

Ingredients

¾	tsp gelatin
1½	tsps cold water
2	egg yolks
¼	cup confectioners' sugar
	pinch of salt
½	cup milk
½	tsp vanilla extract
½	cup heavy cream
1½	tsps powdered instant coffee
2	tsps confectioners' sugar

1½	tsps gelatin
1	Tb cold water
4	egg yolks
½	cup confectioners' sugar
⅛	tsp salt
1	cup milk
1	tsp vanilla extract
1	cup heavy cream
1	Tb powdered instant coffee
4½	tsps confectioners' sugar

6

2	packages gelatin
5	Tbs cold water
12	egg yolks
2	cups confectioners' sugar
½	tsp salt
4	cups milk
1	Tb vanilla extract
4	cups heavy cream
¼	cup powdered instant coffee
1	cup confectioners' sugar

Instructions

1) In a small dish sprinkle gelatin over cold water to soften.
2) Beat egg yolks, ● ¼ *cup sugar,* ▲ ½ *cup sugar,* ■ *2 cups sugar,* and salt until thick in a heavy ● ▲ *1-quart saucepan,* ■ *3-quart saucepan.*
3) Bring milk to a boil in a ● ▲ *small saucepan,* ■ *2-quart saucepan.* Stir in vanilla. Remove from heat.
4) Gradually add hot milk to the egg mixture, beating constantly with a wire whisk. Stir in gelatin and blend well.
5) Cook over low heat, stirring constantly, until mixture thickens and coats a metal spoon. Do not allow to boil.
6) Remove from heat and pour into a ● ▲ *medium bowl,* ■ *large bowl.* Cool to room temperature. Chill.
7) ● ▲ Combine cream and powdered instant coffee in ● ▲ *another medium bowl.* ■ Divide cream and powdered instant coffee between 2 large bowls.
8) Beat until soft peaks form. Fold in remaining sugar.
9) When custard mixture begins to set slightly, gently fold in whipped cream until completely incorporated.
10) Pour into dessert dishes or a serving bowl and chill until set, about 3 hours. If desired, decorate with whipped cream.

preparation time (excluding final chilling): ● 1 hour; ▲ 1½ hours; ■ 2 hours

yield: ● 1¾ cups; ▲ 3½ cups; ■ 14 cups

Special Notes
- Do not use freeze-dried or nugget coffee; only powdered coffee will dissolve properly.
- Coffee cream mousse will keep for 3 or 4 days in the refrigerator.

Mousse à l'Orange

Ingredients

2	eggs yolks
¼	cup sugar
2	Tbs cold water
1	tsp gelatin
1½	tsps cornstarch
½	cup fresh orange juice
½	tsp freshly grated orange peel
1	egg white, at room temperature
¼	cup heavy cream
2	Tbs whipped cream
½	tsp orange liqueur

3	egg yolks
½	cup sugar
¼	cup cold water
1	package gelatin
1	Tb cornstarch
1	cup fresh orange juice
1	tsp freshly grated orange peel
3	egg whites, at room temperature
½	cup heavy cream
½	cup whipped cream
1	tsp orange liqueur

6

12	egg yolks
2	cups sugar
1	cup cold water
4	packages gelatin
4	Tbs cornstarch
4	cups fresh orange juice
4	tsps freshly grated orange peel
12	egg whites, at room temperature
1½	cups heavy cream
1½	cups whipped cream
1	Tb orange liqueur

✳ CHEZ BRUCHEZ, 304 Seabreeze, Daytona Beach, Florida

Instructions

1) Beat egg yolks until thick in ● *small bowl,* ▲ *medium bowl,* ■ *large bowl.*
2) Add sugar, beating constantly, until yolks turn pale yellow. Set aside.
3) Pour cold water into a ● ▲ *small bowl,* ■ *medium bowl.* Sprinkle gelatin over top and let stand 5 minutes.
4) Put cornstarch in a ● *1-quart saucepan,* ▲ *1½-quart saucepan,* ■ *4-quart saucepan or Dutch oven.*
5) Gradually add orange juice; blend until smooth.
6) Add softened gelatin and orange peel.
7) Cook over low heat, stirring constantly, until mixture just reaches the boiling point.
8) Stir some of the hot liquid into the egg yolks and sugar, beating constantly with wire whisk.
9) Return mixture to the saucepan, stirring constantly, until blended.
10) Cook, stirring constantly, over low heat until mixture thickens. Do not allow to boil.
11) Remove from heat; pour into ● *medium bowl,* ▲ ■ *large bowl,* and let cool to room temperature.
12) Beat egg whites, until stiff peaks form, in ● ▲ *a medium bowl,* ■ *2 large bowls.*
13) Beat heavy cream until soft peaks form in a ● ▲ *small deep bowl;* ■ *large bowl.*
14) Transfer both egg whites and cream to the top of the cooled custard and gently but thoroughly fold them into it.
15) Pour mixture into ● *2 individual dessert dishes,* ▲ *3-cup soufflé dish or 6 individual dessert dishes,* ■ *3-quart soufflé dish or 24 individual dessert dishes.*
16) Chill until set, about 2 to 3 hours.
17) Combine whipped cream and orange liqueur and before serving decorate top of the mousse.

preparation time (excluding chilling time): ● 45 minutes; ▲ 1¼ hours; ■ 3 hours
yield: ● 1 cup; ▲ 3 cups; ■ 12 cups

Special Note
● Orange mousse will keep its light texture for only about 3 days in the refrigerator.

Velvet Hammer Dessert

Ingredients

1 qt rich coffee ice cream
3 Tbs crème de cacao
6 Tbs Scotch whisky
½ cup canned chestnuts, drained and chopped

6-8

※ LOVETT'S BY LAFAYETTE BROOK, junction Route 18 and Route 141, Franconia, New Hampshire

Instructions

1) Let ice cream soften but not melt.
2) Place in a blender; add crème de cacao and Scotch. Blend at high speed 15 seconds or until smooth.
3) Stir in chopped chestnuts.
4) Pour into individual dishes or an ice cube tray.
5) Freeze until ice crystals form around edge; beat ice cream mixture until smooth again. Cover with aluminum foil.
6) Refreeze overnight.

preparation time (excluding freezing time):   40 minutes
yield: 3 cups

Special Notes

- If a softer ice cream is desired, let tray stand at room temperature 5 minutes before serving.
- To prepare this dessert for more people, simply repeat the procedure. Do not place more than quantity for 1 recipe in blender container at one time.
- Will store in freezer for months as long as it is tightly covered (to prevent crystals from forming).

Sabayon

Ingredients

2-3

- 2 egg yolks
- 1/4 cup sugar
- 1/4 cup dry sherry
- 1/4 tsp vanilla extract
- 1/4 cup heavy cream
- 2 egg whites, at room temperature

6

- 6 egg yolks
- 3/4 cup sugar
- 3/4 cup dry sherry
- 1 tsp vanilla extract
- 3/4 cup heavy cream
- 6 egg whites, at room temperature

24

- 24 egg yolks
- 3 cups sugar
- 3 cups dry sherry
- 4 tsps vanilla extract
- 3 cups heavy cream
- 24 egg whites, at room temperature

❄ MASSON'S RESTAURANT FRANÇAIS, 7200 Pontchartrain Boulevard, New Orleans, Louisiana

Instructions

1) Beat egg yolks until thick in a heavy ● ▲ *1-quart saucepan,* ■ *3-quart saucepan.*
2) Gradually add sugar; beat until creamy.
3) Add sherry slowly; blend well.
4) Cook over low heat, stirring constantly, until mixture thickens and coats a metal spoon. Do not let mixture boil. Stir in vanilla.
5) Cool to room temperature.
6) Beat ● ▲ *cream* ■ *half the cream* in a chilled ● ▲ *small bowl,* ■ *large bowl* until soft peaks form. ■ Reserve and repeat with remaining cream.
7) Fold heavy cream gently into custard.
8 In a ● *small bowl,* ▲ *medium bowl,* ■ *large bowl* beat ● ▲ *egg whites,* ■ *8 egg whites* until stiff peaks form. ■ Reserve and repeat twice with remaining egg whites. Fold into custard-cream mixture.
9) Pour into individual ½-cup ramekins or a serving dish.
10) Chill 2 to 3 hours.

preparation time (excluding final chilling): ● 30 minutes;
▲ 45 minutes; ■ 1¼ hours
yield: ● 1½ cups; ▲ 1 quart; ■ 6 quarts

Special Notes
- An unusual feature of this delicious sabayon, is its longevity: it will keep at least 1 or 2 days. If on standing it appears lumpy, don't disturb any part that has settled out, scoop up the froth and beat it with a wire whisk.
- Sabayon can be made in advance through step 5. Two hours before serving, beat and fold in cream and egg whites and chill.

Chocolate Soufflé

Ingredients

1½	tsps powdered instant coffee
2½	Tbs hot water
1	1-oz square unsweetened chocolate
2½	Tbs confectioners' sugar
2	Tbs unsalted butter
1	Tb flour

½	cup hot milk
2	egg yolks
1½	tsps vanilla extract
3	egg whites, at room temperature
1	Tb granulated sugar
½	cup heavy cream
1	Tb confectioners' sugar
½	tsp vanilla extract

4

2	tsps powdered instant coffee
¼	cup hot water
1½	1-oz squares unsweetened chocolate
¼	cup confectioners' sugar
3	Tbs unsalted butter
1½	Tbs flour
¾	cup hot milk
3	egg yolks
2	tsps vanilla extract
5	egg whites, at room temperature
1	Tb granulated sugar
¾	cup heavy cream
1½	Tbs confectioners' sugar
¾	tsp vanilla extract

6

1	Tb powdered instant coffee
⅓	cup hot water
2	1-oz squares unsweetened chocolate
⅓	cup confectioners' sugar
4	Tbs unsalted butter
2	Tbs flour

1	cup hot milk
4	egg yolks
1	Tb vanilla extract
7	egg whites, at room temperature
2	Tbs granulated sugar
1	cup heavy cream.
2	Tbs confectioners' sugar
1	tsp vanilla extract

✳ CHARLES VIRION'S MONBLASON, Willowvale Road, Pine Plains, New York

❄ Charles Virion's Monblason

Instructions

1) In a cup, dissolve instant coffee in the hot water.
2) Melt chocolate in the top of a double boiler over simmering water.
3) Stir ● *2½ tablespoons confectioners' sugar,* ▲ *¼ cup confectioners' sugar,* ■ *⅓ cup confectioners' sugar* into the chocolate until well blended; then stir in coffee and blend until smooth.
4) Remove from heat.
5) In a 1-quart saucepan, melt butter over low heat.
6) Add flour and blend well with a wire whisk. Continue cooking 1 minute, stirring constantly.
7) Add hot milk, stirring constantly until mixture thickens. Remove from heat.
8) Stir in chocolate mixture and blend; let cool silghtly.
9) Carefully stir in 1 egg yolk at a time.
10) Stir in vanilla.
11) Preheat oven to 375 degrees.
12) Beat egg whites until soft peaks form in a ● *medium bowl,* ▲ ■ *large bowl.*
13) Add remaining confectioners' sugar gradually and beat until stiff peaks form.
14) Pour chocolate mixture into a large bowl. Stir rather thoroughly ⅓ of egg whites into chocolate mixture to aerate batter. Gently, but quickly, fold in remaining egg whites; no trace of whites should remain.
15) Pour mixture into a well-buttered ● *3-cup soufflé dish,* ▲ *6-cup soufflé dish,* ■ *2-quart soufflé dish.*
16) Bake in the preheated oven 5 minutes, reduce heat to 350 degrees and bake until soufflé is puffed and set, ● *20 to 25 minutes,* ▲ ■ *25 to 30 minutes.*
17) Meanwhile, prepare whipped cream accompaniment: beat cream until soft peaks form in a chilled ● *small bowl,* ▲ ■ *medium bowl.* Gradually add granulated sugar and beat until stiff. Stir in vanilla.
18) Serve soufflé immediately with whipped cream on the side.

preparation time: ● 1¼ hours; ▲ ■ 1½ hours

Special Notes
- Soufflé base can be prepared 1 hour ahead, through step 10. When ready to bake, beat egg whites and continue with directions.
- After 25 minutes in the oven, it is safe to open the door and gently shake to see if the soufflé is firm; if not close the door quietly and give it more time.
- If the soufflé is ready before your guests finish their entrée or salad, simply turn off the oven and leave it there for 10 minutes; the soufflé will remain upright.

Strawberry Soufflé

Ingredients

2

2	Tbs butter
3	Tbs flour
½	cup half-and-half or light cream
2	egg yolks
¼	cup granulated sugar
1	Tb strawberry preserve
3	egg whites, at room temperature
½	cup sliced fresh strawberries confectioners' sugar
1	sugared strawberry

CREME CHANTILLY

¼	cup heavy cream
1½	tsps confectioners' sugar
¼	tsp vanilla extract

4

4	Tbs butter
6	Tbs flour
1	cup half-and-half or light cream
4	egg yolks
½	cup granulated sugar
2	Tbs strawberry preserve
6	egg whites, at room temperature
1½	cups sliced fresh strawberries confectioners' sugar
1	sugared strawberry

CREME CHANTILLY

½	cup heavy cream
1	Tb confectioners' sugar
½	tsp vanilla extract

6-8

5	Tbs butter
½	cup flour
1⅓	cups half-and-half or light cream
5	egg yolks
⅔	cup granulated sugar
3	Tbs strawberry preserve
8	egg whites, at room temperature
1¾	cups sliced fresh strawberries confectioners' sugar
1	sugared strawberry

CREME CHANTILLY

1	cup heavy cream
3	Tbs confectioners' sugar
1	tsp vanilla extract

❄ MERIDIAN HILLS COUNTRY CLUB, 7099 Spring Mill Road, Indianapolis, Indiana

270

Instructions

1) Preheat oven to 350 degrees.
2) Melt butter in a 1-quart saucepan over low heat.
3) Add flour and blend well with a wire whisk.
4) Add half-and-half; cook, stirring constantly, until thickened and smooth. Remove from heat.
5) Beat egg yolks in a small bowl with half the granulated sugar.
6) Stir egg yolk mixture into milk mixture, stirring constantly until blended.
7) Add strawberry preserve and blend well. Pour into a large bowl.
8) Beat egg whites until soft peaks form in a ● *medium bowl,* ▲ ■ *large bowl.*
9) Gradually add remaining granulated sugar; beat until stiff peaks form.
10) Stir ⅓ of egg whites into strawberry mixture and blend well.
11) Gently fold in remaining egg whites with a spatula.
12) Pour ⅔ of the soufflé mixture into a buttered and sugared ● *2½-cup soufflé dish,* ▲ *6-cup soufflé dish,* ■ *2-quart soufflé dish* fitted with a collar.
13) Place sliced strawberries over batter.
14) Cover with remaining batter.
15) Bake in the preheated oven until puffed, brown and set, about ● *30 to 35 minutes,* ▲ *45 minutes,* ■ *60 to 70 minutes.*
16) Meanwhile make crème Chantilly: beat heavy cream in a chilled bowl until soft peaks form.
17) Gently fold in confectioners' sugar and vanilla.
18) When soufflé is done, sprinkle top with confectioners' sugar and place sugared strawberry in center. Serve immediately with crème Chantilly.

preparation time: ● 1¼ hours; ▲ 1¾ hours; ■ 2 hours

Special Notes
- To make a sugared strawberry: brush a strawberry with egg white and roll in granulated sugar until well-coated.
- To make a collar: use a strip of heavy-duty foil 4 inches longer than the diameter of the dish. Fold in half and wrap around dish, with foil extending 3 inches above dish. Secure with straight pins or string. Butter inside of foil.

CAKES AND PIES

Lindy's Cheesecake

Ingredients

3-by-8½-by-3-inch cake

CRUST
⅓	cup sifted flour
1	Tb sugar
¼	tsp freshly grated lemon peel
1	egg yolk
⅛	tsp vanilla extract
2	Tbs butter, softened

FILLING
8	ozs cream cheese, softened
½	cup sugar
1	Tb flour
½	tsp freshly grated orange peel
½	tsp freshly grated lemon peel
2	eggs
1	egg yolk
¼	tsp vanilla extract
1	Tb heavy cream

9-inch cake

CRUST
1	cup sifted flour
¼	cup sugar
1	tsp freshly grated lemon peel
1	egg yolk
¼	tsp vanilla extract
8	Tbs (1 stick) butter, softened

FILLING
2½	lbs cream cheese, softened
1¾	cups sugar
3	Tbs flour
1½	tsps freshly grated orange peel
1½	tsps freshly grated lemon peel
5	eggs
2	egg yolks
½	tsp vanilla extract
¼	cup heavy cream

❄ The former LINDY'S RESTAURANT, New York, New York

Instructions

1) Preheat oven to 400 degrees.
2) Combine flour, sugar and lemon peel in a small bowl; blend well.
3) Add egg yolk and vanilla.
4) Add softened butter; work mixture with your fingers to form a smooth dough.
5) Pat dough onto the bottom and slightly up the sides (to seal crack) of a ▲ *3-by-8½-by-3-inch pâté or loaf pan with removable sides,* ■ *9-inch springform pan.*
6) Bake in the preheated oven for 10 minutes, until lightly browned. Remove and let cool. Keep oven set at 400 degrees.
7) Beat cream cheese until smooth in a ▲ *medium bowl,* ■ *large bowl.*
8) Gradually add sugar, beating constantly, until mixture is light and fluffy.
9) Add flour, blend well.
10) Stir in orange and lemon peel.
11) Add eggs, one at a time, beating well after each addition.
12) Add yolks and blend well.
13) Add vanilla and heavy cream.
14) Pour into dough-lined pan.
15) Bake in the preheated oven ▲ *5 minutes,* ■ *10 minutes;* reduce heat to 250 degrees and bake until cake tester comes out clean, about ▲ *45 to 50 minutes,* ■ *1½ hours.*
16) Cool to room temperature; chill 2 to 3 hours before slicing.

preparation time: ▲ 1½ hours; ■ 2¼ hours
yield: ▲ 6 to 8 portions; ■ 12 to 14 portions

Special Note
• Cake will keep in the refrigerator 1 to 2 weeks.

Maxim's Cheesecake

Ingredients

3-by-8½-by-3-inch cake

CRUST

¼	cup graham cracker crumbs
1	tsp sugar
1	Tb butter, melted

FILLING

8	ozs cream cheese, softened
¼	cup sugar
1	egg yolk
2	tsps vanilla extract
1	egg white, at room temperature
⅓	cup sour cream
2	Tbs sugar

9-inch cake

CRUST

¾	cup graham cracker crumbs
2	tsps sugar
2	Tbs butter, melted

FILLING

1½	lbs cream cheese, softened
¾	cup sugar
4	egg yolks
4	tsps vanilla extract
4	egg whites, at room temperature
2	cups sour cream
⅓	cup sugar

Instructions

1) Preheat oven to ● *325 degrees,* ▲ *350 degrees.*
2) In a small bowl, combine crumbs, sugar and butter; blend well.
3) Butter sides of a ● *3-by-8½-by-3-inch loaf or pâté pan with removable sides,* ▲ *9-inch springform pan.*
4) Press crumb mixture into bottom of pan.
5) In a large bowl beat cream cheese with an electric beater until light.
6) Gradually add the ● *¼ cup sugar,* ▲ *¾ cup sugar* and beat until fluffy.
7) Add egg yolks one at a time, beating well after each addition.
8) Stir in half the vanilla.
9) Beat egg whites until stiff peaks form in a ● *small bowl,* ▲ *medium bowl.*
10) Gently fold egg whites into cream cheese mixture.
11) Pour mixture over crumbs.
12) Bake in the preheated oven until set and lightly browned on top, ● *30 to 35 minutes,* ▲ *1 hour.*
13) Let cool on wire rack 15 minutes.
14) Turn oven up to 400 degrees.
15) Blend sour cream, the remaining sugar and the remaining vanilla in a ● *small bowl,* ▲ *medium bowl.*
16) Gently spread over top of cheesecake and bake until set, ● *5 to 7 minutes,* ▲ *10 minutes.*
17) Cool to room temperature on wire rack; chill 3 hours in refrigerator before serving.

preparation time (excluding final chilling): ● 1 hour; ▲ 1½ hours
yield: ● 6 portions; ▲ 12 to 14 portions

Special Notes
- When cake is taken from the oven it is puffy; as it cools, it settles down and loses some of its volume.
- Cake will store in refrigerator for at least 1 week.

Cheddar Cheese Cake

Ingredients

3-by-8½-by-3-inch cake

CRUST
- ⅓ cup sifted flour
- 2 Tbs sugar
- ¼ tsp freshly grated lemon peel
- 2 Tbs butter, softened
- 1 egg yolk
- ⅛ tsp vanilla extract

FILLING
- 8 ozs cream cheese, softened
- 6 Tbs sugar
- 6 Tbs coarsely grated sharp Cheddar cheese
- 1 egg
- 1 egg yolk
- 1 Tb beer
- 1 Tb heavy cream
- ⅛ tsp vanilla extract
- ¼ tsp freshly grated orange peel
- ¼ tsp freshly grated lemon peel

9-inch cake

CRUST
- 1 cup sifted flour
- ¼ cup sugar
- 1 tsp freshly grated lemon peel
- 8 Tbs butter, softened
- 1 egg yolk
- ¼ tsp vanilla extract

FILLING
- 1½ lbs cream cheese, softened
- 1⅓ cups sugar
- ¾ cup coarsely grated sharp Cheddar cheese (about 3 ozs)
- 3 eggs
- 2 egg yolks
- 3 Tbs beer
- 3 Tbs heavy cream
- ¼ tsp vanilla extract
- ½ tsp freshly grated orange peel
- ½ tsp freshly grated lemon peel

❀ CARRIAGE HOUSE RESTAURANT, 1196 Post Road, Westport, Connecticut

278

Instructions

1) Preheat oven to 400 degrees.
2) To make crust: combine flour, sugar and lemon peel in a ▲ *small bowl,* ■ *medium bowl.*
3) Add butter, egg yolk and vanilla; blend well.
4) Pat dough into bottom and sides of a ▲ *3-by-8½-by-3-inch loaf or pâté pan with removable sides,* ■ *9-inch springform pan.*
5) Bake in the preheated oven 10 minutes or until lightly browned. Cool. Reset oven to 500 degrees, for step 12.
6) To make filling: in a large bowl of electric mixer, beat softened cream cheese until fluffy.
7) Gradually add sugar and beat until well blended.
8) Add Cheddar cheese; blend well.
9) Add whole eggs and yolks, one at a time, beating well after each addition.
10) Stir in beer, heavy cream, vanilla, grated orange and lemon peel; blend well.
11) Pour into cooled crust.
12) Bake in the preheated oven ▲ *5 minutes,* ■ *10 minutes.* Reduce heat to 250 degrees and bake until cake tester comes out clean, about ▲ *40 to 45 minutes,* ■ *2 to 2¼ hours.*
13) Cool on wire rack.
14) Remove side of pan and chill in refrigerator 3 hours before serving.

preparation time (excluding final chilling): ▲ 1¾ hours; ■ 3 hours
yield: ▲ 6 to 8 portions; ■ 12 to 16 portions

Special Note
• Cake keeps in refrigerator 1 week.

Golden Nugget Cake

Ingredients

5   egg whites, at room temperature.
1   cup sugar
1   cup chopped pecans
1   cup Ritz cracker crumbs
½   lb dates, chopped
½   tsp vanilla extract
1   tsp baking powder
¼   tsp salt
    whipped cream

❄THE BUCCANEER INN, 595 Dream Island Road, Sarasota, Florida.

280

Instructions

1) Preheat oven to 300 degrees.
2) In a medium bowl beat egg whites until frothy.
3) Gradually add sugar, 1 tablespoon at a time, beating until stiff peaks form.
4) Fold in pecans and cracker crumbs.
5) Reserve 2 tablespoons chopped dates for top.
6) Fold in remaining dates, vanilla, baking powder and salt.
7) Spread mixture into a greased jelly-roll pan, 10 by 15 by 1½ inches.
8) Sprinkle reserved dates over top.
9) Bake in the preheated oven 25 to 30 minutes, or until lightly browned and firm.
10) Cool. Cut into 15 3-inch squares.
11) Serve with a dab of whipped cream on top.

preparation time: 1½ hours

Special Notes
- Cake squares store for weeks in a plastic container.
- They can be frozen and will keep for 2 to 3 months.

Orange Wine Cake

Ingredients

8 cupcakes

½	orange
½	cup chopped raisins
¼	cup chopped walnuts
4	Tbs butter, softened
½	cup granulated sugar
1	egg
1	cup sifted flour
½	tsp baking soda
¼	tsp salt
½	cup buttermilk
½	tsp vanilla extract

ICING

4½	Tbs butter, softened
1	Tb freshly grated orange peel
1½	cups confectioners' sugar
1	Tb dry sherry

9-inch square

1	orange
1	cup chopped raisins
½	cup chopped walnuts
8	Tbs (1 stick) butter, softened
1	cup granulated sugar
2	eggs
2	cups sifted flour
1	tsp baking soda
½	tsp salt
1	cup buttermilk
1	tsp vanilla extract

ICING

⅓	cup butter, softened
1	Tb freshly grated orange peel
2	cups confectioners' sugar
1	Tb dry sherry

13½-by-8¾-by-1¾-inch cake

2	oranges
1½	cups chopped raisins
¾	cup chopped walnuts
¾	cup butter, softened
1½	cups granulated sugar
3	eggs
3	cups sifted flour
1½	tsps baking soda
¾	tsp salt
1½	cups buttermilk
1½	tsps vanilla extract

ICING

⅔	cup butter, softened
2	Tbs freshly grated orange peel
4	cups confectioners' sugar
3	Tbs dry sherry

✳ WILLIAMSBURG LODGE, Williamsburg, Virginia

Instructions

1) Preheat oven to 350 degrees.
2) With a swivel-bladed vegetable peeler, remove peel (but not the bitter white pith), from the orange. Save the orange flesh for another use.
3) Combine raisins, walnuts and orange peel in a ● ▲ *small bowl,* ■ *medium bowl.* Set aside.
4) Cream butter until light in a ● ▲ *medium bowl,* ■ *large bowl.*
5) Gradually add granulated sugar and beat until fluffy.
6) Add eggs, one at a time, beating well after each addition.
7) Sift together flour, baking soda and salt. Toss ● *1 tablespoon flour mixture,* ▲ *2 tablespoons flour mixture,* ■ *¼ cup flour mixture* with fruit and nuts to coat well. Reserve.
8) Stir remaining flour and buttermilk alternately into butter mixture; blend well.
9) Add vanilla, fruit and nuts; blend.
10) Pour batter into ● *8 greased and floured 2½-inch muffin tins; fill to ⅔ capacity,* ▲ *a greased and floured 9-inch square cake pan,* ■ *a greased and floured 13½-by-8¾-by-1¾-inch pan.*
11) Bake in the preheated oven until cake tester comes out clean, ● *20 to 25 minutes,* ▲ *35 to 40 minutes,* ■ *50 to 60 minutes.*
12) Let cool in pan on wire rack ● *5 minutes,* ▲ ■ *10 minutes.* Remove from pan and cool on wire rack.
13) To make icing: beat butter in a medium bowl until creamy.
14) Gradually add orange peel; blend well.
15) Add confectioners' sugar slowly; blend well.
16) Add sherry; beat well.
17) If icing is too thick to spread, add more sherry. Spread icing on ● *tops of cupcakes,* ▲ ■ *sides and top of cake.*

preparation time: ● 45 minutes; ▲ 1½ hours; ■ 1½ hours
yield: ● 8 cupcakes; ▲ 18 3-by-1½-inch slices; ▲ 24 3-by-1½-inch slices

Special Note
● This cake will keep refrigerated for 1 week; or frozen for 2 to 3 months.

Bulgur Pecan Pie

Ingredients

2 5-inch pies

1	egg
1	egg yolk
3	Tbs dark brown sugar
1	Tb vegetable oil
6	Tbs maple syrup
5	Tbs milk
½	tsp vanilla extract
¼	tsp salt
2	Tbs bulgur (cracked wheat)
½	cup shelled pecan halves
2	unbaked 5-inch pastry shells

1 9-inch pie

3	eggs
½	cup dark brown sugar
¼	cup vegetable oil
1	cup maple syrup
¾	cup milk
1	tsp vanilla extract
½	tsp salt
¼	cup bulgur (cracked wheat)
1	cup shelled pecan halves
1	unbaked 9-inch pastry shell

RED ROOSTER RESTAURANT, 1808 North Plum, Hutchinson, Kansas

Instructions

1) Preheat oven to 350 degrees.
2) Beat ● *egg and egg yolk,* ▲ *eggs* and brown sugar until blended in a ● *small bowl,* ▲ *medium bowl.*
3) Stir in oil, maple syrup, milk, vanilla, salt and bulgur; beat with a wire whisk until smooth.
4) Stir in pecans.
5) Pour into pastry shell.
6) Bake in the preheated oven until pie is set, ● *20 to 25 minutes,* ▲ *30 to 35 minutes.*
7) Cool on a wire rack.

preparation time: ● 35 minutes; ▲ 45 minutes
yield: ● 2 portions each pie; ▲ 6 to 8 portions

Special Notes
● Refrigerate pie if not used within several hours. It will keep 1 week.
● Bulgur can be purchased in health food stores or Middle Eastern grocery shops.

Chocolate Velvet Banana Pie

Ingredients

2 5-inch pies

½	cup semisweet chocolate bits
2	Tbs dry sherry
1½	Tbs sugar
1	tsp powdered instant coffee
⅛	tsp salt
⅛	tsp ground cinnamon
2	egg yolks
2	egg whites, at room temperature
1	small banana
1	tsp dry sherry
2	baked 5-inch pastry shells, cooled

1 9-inch pie

6	ozs semisweet chocolate bits
¼	cup dry sherry
3	Tbs sugar
2	tsps powdered instant coffee
¼	tsp salt
¼	tsp ground cinnamon
4	egg yolks
4	egg whites, at room temperature
2	medium bananas
1	Tb dry sherry
1	baked 9-inch pastry shell, cooled

※ COUNTRY SQUIRE, Highway 80, Killingworth, Connecticut

Instructions

1) In a heavy 1-quart saucepan combine chocolate bits, ● *2 table-spoons dry sherry,* ▲ *¼ cup dry sherry,* sugar, instant coffee, salt and cinnamon; cook over low heat, stirring constantly, until chocolate is melted.
2) Remove from heat, transfer to a medium bowl and let cool.
3) Beat egg yolks into chocolate mixture, one at a time, blending well.
4) Beat egg whites until stiff peaks form in a ● *small bowl,* ▲ *medium bowl.*
5) Fold egg whites gently into cooled chocolate mixture.
6) Peel and cut bananas into ¼-inch slices. Sprinkle slices with the remaining sherry.
7) Arrange half the banana slices on bottom of cooled pastry shell.
8) Gently fill shell with chocolate mixture. Garnish with remaining banana slices.
9) Chill until set, about ● 1 hour, ▲ 2 hours.

preparation time (excluding final chilling): ● ▲ 45 minutes
yield: ● 2 portions each; ▲ 6 to 8 portions

Special Notes
- Do not use freeze-dried or nugget instant coffee; it must be powdered.
- You will need the same amount of pastry for the 2 5-inch shells as for the 9-inch shell.
- Pie freezes very well. It can be served right from the freezer; for a softer filling allow to stand 10 minutes before serving.

Cider Apple Deep Dish Pie

Ingredients

2 5-inch pies

- 2 medium cooking apples, peeled, cored and thinly sliced
- 2 Tbs butter, melted
- 2 unbaked 5-inch pastry shells
- 6 Tbs coarsely grated sharp Cheddar cheese
- 6 Tbs flour
- ¼ tsp ground cinnamon
- 3 Tbs dark brown sugar
- 3 Tbs butter, softened

9-inch pie

- 4 large (about 2 lbs) cooking apples, peeled, cored and thinly sliced
- 4 Tbs butter, melted
- 1 unbaked 9-inch pastry shell
- ¾ cup coarsely grated sharp Cheddar cheese (about 3 ozs)
- ¾ cup flour
- ½ tsp ground cinnamon
- ⅓ cup dark brown sugar
- ⅓ cup butter, softened

❋ LAZY SUSAN INN, U.S. Route #1, Woodbridge, Virginia

Instructions

1) Preheat oven to 450 degrees.
2) In a ● *medium bowl,* ▲ *large bowl,* toss apples and melted butter to coat slices well.
3) Arrange apples in ● *2 5-inch pie shells,* ▲ *9-inch pie shell.*
4) Sprinkle Cheddar cheese over apples.
5) In a small bowl combine flour, cinnamon and brown sugar; blend well.
6) Work in softened butter with your fingers until mixture is crumbly.
7) Sprinkle flour mixture over apples.
8) Bake in the preheated oven ● *10 minutes,* ▲ *15 minutes;* reduce heat to 350 degrees and bake 15 to 20 minutes longer, or until apples are tender.

preparation time: ● ▲ 1 hour
yield: ● 2 portions each pie; ▲ 6 to 8 portions

Special Notes
- You will need about the same amount of pastry for 2 5-inch shells as for 1 9-inch shell.
- Pie can be served warm or at room temperature; but it is better warm. If prepared in advance, warm, uncovered, in a preheated 300-degree oven.
- I don't suggest freezing.

Sky-High Coconut Cream Pie

Ingredients

2 5-inch pies

¼	cup sugar
2	Tbs cornstarch
	pinch of salt
1	cup milk
2	egg yolks
1½	tsps butter
½	tsp vanilla extract
¼	cup shredded coconut
2	baked 5-inch pastry shells, cooled
2	egg whites, at room temperature
2	Tbs sugar
1	Tb shredded coconut

9-inch pie

½	cup sugar
¼	cup cornstarch
⅛	tsp salt
2	cups milk
4	egg yolks
1	Tb butter
1	tsp vanilla extract
½	cup shredded coconut
1	baked 9-inch pastry shell, cooled
6	egg whites, at room temperature
6	Tbs sugar
¼	cup shredded coconut

✳THE WILLOWS, 901 Hausten Street, Honolulu, Hawaii

290

Instructions

1) Combine ● *¼ cup sugar,* ▲ *½ cup sugar,* cornstarch and salt in a ● *1-quart saucepan,* ▲ *1½ quart saucepan;* blend well.
2) Gradually add the milk in a steady stream, stirring constantly, until mixture is smooth.
3) Cook over low heat, stirring constantly, until mixture is thickened and hot but not boiling. Remove from heat.
4) Beat egg yolks with a wire whisk in a small bowl until thick.
5) Beating constantly, gradually add half the hot liquid to egg yolks.
6) Return mixture to the pan and stirring constantly with the whisk, cook over low heat until mixture becomes very thick. Do not allow mixture to boil. While cooking, if mixture seems to be lumpy, beat vigorously with wire whisk until smooth.
7) Remove from heat, stir in butter, vanilla and ● *¼ cup coconut,* ▲ *½ cup coconut;* let mixture cool.
8) Preheat oven to 350 degrees.
9) Pour into cooled pastry shell(s).
10) Beat egg whites in a ● *medium bowl,* ▲ *large bowl* until they are frothy.
11) Gradually add remaining sugar and beat until stiff peaks form.
12) Spread meringue over entire shell, covering the filling completely. Swirl meringue in peaks.
13) Sprinkle remaining coconut over top.
14) Bake in the preheated oven 4 to 5 minutes or until lightly browned.
15) Cool ● *1 to 2 hours;* ▲ *2 to 3 hours* at room temperature before slicing.

preparation time (excluding final cooling period): ● 45 minutes; ▲ 1 hour

yield: ● 2 portions each pie; ▲ 6 to 8 portions

Special Note
● The pie will keep 3 to 4 days in the refrigerator, but the meringue will wrinkle and may weep a little. To avoid this, you can prepare all except the meringue in advance. Beat the egg whites and bake the pie on the day you plan to serve.

Coffee Mocha Pie

Ingredients

2 5-inch pies

2	1-oz squares unsweetened chocolate
8	Tbs (1 stick) butter, softened
2¼	tsps powdered instant coffee
½	cup confectioners' sugar
6	Tbs granulated sugar
2	eggs
2	baked 5-inch pastry shells, cooled

TOPPING

¼	cup heavy cream
1	Tb granulated sugar
¾	tsp powdered instant coffee

9-inch pie

4	1-oz squares unsweetened chocolate
1	cup (2 sticks) butter, softened
4½	tsps powdered instant coffee
1	cup confectioners' sugar
¾	cup granulated sugar
4	eggs
1	baked 9-inch pastry shell, cooled

TOPPING

1	cup heavy cream
¼	cup granulated sugar
2½	tsps powdered instant coffee

❄ PIERCE'S 1894 RESTAURANT, 228 Oakwood Avenue, Elmira Heights, New York

Instructions

1) Melt chocolate in the top of a double boiler over simmering water. Remove chocolate from heat and cool slightly.
2) Place butter in a medium mixing bowl and add melted chocolate.
3) Beat until light and fluffy.
4) Add instant coffee, confectioners' sugar and granulated sugar; beat until smooth.
5) Add eggs one at a time; beat 2 minutes after each addition.
6) Pour mixture into pastry shell.
7) Refrigerate overnight.
8) To make topping: whip cream in a chilled small narrow bowl until soft peaks form.
9) Add sugar and instant coffee gradually; beat a moment longer until stiffer peaks form.
10) Spoon whipped cream into a pastry bag with a star tip and decorate top of pie; or smooth cream over top with a spatula.
11) Serve immediately, refrigerate or freeze.

preparation time: ● 30 minutes; ▲ 45 minutes
yield: ● 2 portions each pie; ▲ 8 to 10 portions

Special Notes
- This pie is very rich and small slices are adequate.
- Pie will soften quickly if allowed to stand at room temperature. It is better to serve straight from the refrigerator.
- Pie freezes very well and can be served right from the freezer without defrosting. It can be frozen 2 to 3 months.

Grasshopper Pie

Ingredients

2 5-inch pies

CRUST

¾ cup chocolate wafer crumbs
3 Tbs butter, melted

FILLING

18 marshmallows
½ cup milk
¾ cup heavy cream
3 Tbs green crème de menthe
1½ Tbs white crème de cacao
¼ cup whipped cream
¼ cup strawberries

9-inch pie

CRUST

1¼ cups chocolate wafer crumbs
⅓ cup butter, melted

FILLING

48 marshmallows
1⅓ cups milk
2 cups heavy cream
½ cup green crème de menthe
¼ cup white crème de cacao
¼ cup heavy cream, whipped
½ cup strawberries

WIN SCHULER'S, 115 South Eagle Street, Marshall, Michigan

Instructions

1) In a small bowl, combine chocolate crumbs and butter; blend well.
2) Pat crumbs into bottom and sides of ● *2 5-inch pie plates,* ▲ *9-inch pie plate.* Chill until needed.
3) Combine marshmallows and milk in a ● *1-quart saucepan,* ▲ *3-quart saucepan;* cook over low heat, stirring constantly, until marshmallows are melted.
4) Cool to room temperature.
5) Whip cream until soft peaks form in a chilled ● *medium bowl,* ▲ *large bowl.* Fold in crème de menthe and crème de cacao.
6) If necessary, beat marshmallow mixture to make it smooth. Fold into the whipped cream.
7) Gently pour into the pie shell(s); freeze overnight before serving. S
8) Remove from freezer 5 minutes before serving.
9) Garnish with whipped cream and strawberries.

preparation time: ● 45 minutes; ▲ 1 hour
yield: ● 2 portions each; ▲ 6 to 8 portions

Special Notes
- Pie can be kept in freezer for 2 to 3 months (but I doubt if anyone could leave it alone that long).
- Pie can be served just chilled, instead of frozen. In that case, chill for 2 to 3 hours. Its texture then will be similar to that of a chiffon pie.

Key Lime Pie

Ingredients

2 5-inch pies

CRUST

½ cup graham cracker crumbs
2 Tbs butter, melted
1 Tb confectioners' sugar
½ tsp ground cinnamon

FILLING

2 egg yolks
⅔ cup sweetened condensed milk
½ cup fresh lime juice
   heavy cream, whipped and sweetened
   (optional)

9-inch pie

CRUST

1½ cups graham cracker crumbs
6 Tbs butter, melted
¼ cup confectioners' sugar
1 tsp ground cinnamon

FILLING

4 egg yolks
1 14-oz can sweetened condensed milk
1 cup fresh lime juice
   heavy cream, whipped and sweetened (optional)

Instructions

1) Preheat oven to 375 degrees.
2) Combine and blend well graham cracker crumbs, butter, sugar and cinnamon in a ● *small bowl,* ▲ *medium bowl.*
3) Pat crumbs into ● *2 5-inch pie plates,* ▲ *9-inch pie plate,* covering bottom and sides.
4) Bake shell in the preheated oven until golden, ● *3 to 4 minutes,* ▲ *5 to 8 minutes.* Let cool on a rack.
5) In a medium bowl, beat egg yolks until thick.
6) Gradually add condensed milk and lime juice, beating until mixture thickens.
7) Pour into cooled pie shell(s) and freeze until pie is firm, 3 to 4 hours.
8) Let stand at room temperature ● *5 minutes,* ▲ *10 minutes* before slicing. Serve with whipped cream, if desired.

preparation time: ● ▲ 30 minutes
yield: ● 2 portions each pie; ▲ 6 to 8 portions

Special Notes
- Key lime pie is also served chilled in refrigerator until set. This gives a custardlike filling instead of the hard texture of the frozen pie.
- Frozen pie will keep up to 3 months. You can cut off pieces without defrosting the whole pie. A delicious surprise for unexpected company.

Lemon Pie

Ingredients

pastry for 2 double-crust 5-inch pies
- 2 eggs
- 1¼ cups sugar
- 2 Tbs water
- 1 Tb butter, melted
- pinch of salt
- pinch of ground nutmeg
- ½ lemon, without skin or pith, very thinly sliced and quartered
- ½ lemon, with skin, very thinly sliced and quartered
- 1 Tb freshly grated lemon peel

pastry for double-crust 9-inch pie
- 4 eggs
- 2½ cups sugar
- ½ cup water
- 2 Tbs butter, melted
- ⅛ tsp salt
- ⅛ tsp ground nutmeg
- 2 lemons, without skin or pith, very thinly sliced
- 1 lemon, with skin, very thinly sliced
- 2 Tbs freshly grated lemon peel

❋ MRS. K's TOLL HOUSE, 9201 Colesville Road, Silver Spring, Maryland

Instructions

1) Preheat oven to 400 degrees.
2) Line the ● *2 5-inch pie plates,* ▲ *9-inch pie plate* with half the pastry.
3) In a medium bowl, beat eggs with sugar until thick.
4) Add water, butter, salt and nutmeg; blend well.
5) Stir in all the lemon slices and lemon peel.
6) Pour mixture into pie shell(s).
7) Cover with remaining pastry, seal edges and flute.
8) Bake in the preheated oven for ● *5 minutes,* ▲ *10 minutes.* Reduce heat to 350 degrees and bake ● *15 to 20 minutes* ▲ *30 minutes* longer.
9) Let cool completely. Chill 2 hours before serving.

preparation time (excluding final chilling): ● 45 minutes; ▲ 1 hour
yield: ● 2 portions each pie; ▲ 6 to 8 portions

Special Note
● Pie will keep in the refrigerator 1 week.

Hot Mince Pie with Rum Sauce

MINCEMEAT *for 2 9-inch pies*

1 lb boneless round steak, cubed
   water
3 ozs suet
2 lbs tart apples, peeled, cored and quartered
1 lb seeded raisins
¾ lb seedless raisins
½ cup minced citron
¼ cup dark Jamaican rum
2 cups sugar
¾ cup cider vinegar
¾ cup dark molasses
½ tsp ground nutmeg
1 tsp ground cloves
¼ tsp ground cinnamon
¼ tsp ground mace
1 tsp salt
½ cup beef broth

   pastry for double-crust 9-inch pie

SAUCE

2 eggs
1 cup sifted confectioners' sugar
6 Tbs dark Jamaican rum
½ cup heavy cream, whipped

❅ GREAT HOUSE RESTAURANT, 2245 Post Road, Warwick, Rhode Island

Instructions

1) To make mincemeat: place meat in a 4-quart Dutch oven and add water to cover.
2) Bring to a boil over moderate heat; reduce heat; simmer, covered, 1 hour or until tender. Drain.
3) Force meat, suet and apples through the coarse blade of a meat grinder.
4) Return mixture to the Dutch oven and add raisins, citron, rum, sugar, vinegar, molasses, spices and broth.
5) Simmer 15 to 20 minutes, stirring occasionally.
6) Pour 4 cups mincemeat into hot sterilized jar and seal or cool and store in refrigerator. Set other 4 cups aside for the pie.
7) Preheat oven to 400 degrees.
8) To make a pie: line a 9-inch pie plate with half the pastry.
9) Pour in mincemeat.
10) Cover with remaining pastry, sealing edges well with your fingers. Flute edges.
11) Cut 2 or 3 slashes in the top to allow steam to escape.
12) Bake in the preheated oven 15 minutes, reduce heat to 350 degrees and bake 20 minutes longer.
13) While the pie is baking, make rum sauce: beat eggs in a small bowl until thick.
14) Gradually add sugar, beating constantly, until light and fluffy.
15) Fold in rum and whipped cream; chill.
16) Serve pie warm with chilled sauce.

preparation time: 2¾ hours
yield: 6 to 8 portions and 4 extra cups mincemeat.

Special Notes
- Mincemeat does not freeze well but will keep in refrigerator 1 to 2 weeks.
- Pie, uncovered, can be reheated in a preheated 325-degree oven for 10 to 15 minutes.
- Rum sauce freezes very well and can be used on other pies, cakes or fruit.

Nut Meringue Pie

Ingredients

2 5-inch pies

2	egg whites, at room temperature
¾	cup granulated sugar
¾	cup crushed unsalted soda crackers
½	cup finely chopped pecans
1	cup sliced strawberries (about ½ pint)
1	Tb confectioners' sugar
½	cup heavy cream
1	Tb finely chopped pecans

9-inch pie

4	egg whites, at room temperature
1½	cups granulated sugar
1½	cups crushed unsalted soda crackers
1	cup finely chopped pecans
2	cups sliced strawberries (about 1 pint)
2	Tbs confectioners' sugar
1	cup heavy cream
¼	cup finely chopped pecans

❄ HICKORY HOUSE, 1625 East Central, Wichita, Kansas

Instructions

1) Preheat oven to 250 degrees.
2) In a medium bowl, beat egg whites until frothy and soft peaks begin to form.
3) Gradually add granulated sugar, 1 tablespoon at a time, beating constantly until stiff peaks form.
4) Carefully fold in cracker crumbs and ● *½ cup pecans,* ▲ *1 cup pecans.*
5) Spoon egg white mixture into ● *2 5-inch buttered pie plates,* ▲ *9-inch buttered pie plate.* With the back of a spoon spread mixture to cover the bottom and sides of plate.
6) Bake in the preheated oven until firm and lightly browned, ● *30 to 35 minutes,* ▲ *45 minutes.*
7) Cool completely on wire rack. ⬚S⬚
8) In a medium bowl combine strawberries and confectioners' sugar and toss lightly.
9) Spoon strawberry mixture into meringue shells.
10) Beat cream until soft peaks form in a ● *small bowl,* ▲ *medium bowl.*
11) Spoon whipped cream in a ring around strawberries.
12) Sprinkle remaining pecans over whipped cream.

preparation time: ● 1¼ hours; ▲ 1½ hours
yield: ● 2 portions each pie; ▲ 6 to 8 portions

Special Notes
- Unfilled meringue shells, protected by plastic bags, freeze beautifully. They will keep 2 to 3 months.
- Completed pie will keep in refrigerator 1 to 2 days, but the part of shell in contact with strawberries will become slightly soggy.

Shaker Sugar Pie

Ingredients

9-inch pie

1   cup light brown sugar
¼   cup flour
1   unbaked 9-inch pastry shell
2   cups light cream
1   tsp vanilla extract
8   Tbs (1 stick) butter
⅛   tsp ground nutmeg

✳GOLDEN LAMB INN, 27 South Broadway, Lebanon, Ohio

Instructions

1) Preheat oven to 350 degrees.
2) Mix brown sugar and flour in a small bowl.
3) Sprinkle mixture over bottom of the pastry shell.
4) Pour in cream; stir in vanilla.
5) Cut butter in small pieces and sprinkle over top.
6) Sprinkle top with nutmeg.
7) Bake in the preheated oven 40 to 50 minutes or until pie is set.
8) Cool.

preparation time: 1 hour
yield: 6 to 8 portions

Special Note
- Pie should be refrigerated after cooling, if not going to be eaten within a few hours, but restore to room temperature before serving.

Almond Tart

Ingredients

2 5-inch tarts

2	egg yolks
6	Tbs sugar
2½	Tbs water
¾	cup heavy cream
2	Tbs crumbled soft macaroons
½	cup ground, blanched almonds
1½	tsps freshly grated orange peel
¼	tsp almond extract
2	unbaked 5-inch pastry shells

9-inch tart

4	egg yolks
¾	cup sugar
⅓	cup water
1⅔	cups heavy cream
¼	cup crumbled soft macaroons
1	cup ground, blanched almonds
1	Tb freshly grated orange peel
½	tsp almond extract
1	unbaked 9-inch pastry shell

✻CLOUD CLUB, 405 Lexington Avenue, New York, New York

Instructions

1) Preheat oven to 350 degrees.
2) In a medium bowl, beat egg yolks until thick.
3) Gradually add sugar, beating until mixture is light and smooth.
4) Add water, cream and crumbled macaroons.
5) Let mixture stand 10 minutes. Break up macaroons finely with your fingers.
6) Stir in ground almonds, orange peel and almond extract.
7) Pour mixture into pastry shell(s) and bake in the preheated oven until filling is set and golden brown, ● *40 to 45 minutes,* ▲ *1 hour.*
8) Cool completely before slicing. If desired, decorate with sweetened whipped cream.

   preparation time: ● 1 hour; ▲ 1½ hours
   yield: ● 2 portions each pie; ▲ 6 to 8 portions

Special Notes
● Refrigerate pie after it has cooled completely, if not serving immediately.
● Pie will keep in refrigerator 1 week.

Chocolate Torte, Lili

Ingredients

9-by-5-by-3-inch loaf

½   cup strong, cold coffee
4   tsps sugar
2   Tbs Grand Marnier
½   lb unsalted butter, softened
2   eggs
12   ozs semisweet chocolate, melted
70   small vanilla wafers
½   cup heavy cream, whipped
2   tsps Grand Marnier

Instructions

1) In a small bowl, combine coffee, sugar and 2 tablespoons Grand Marnier.
2) In a medium bowl, cream butter until fluffy.
3) Add eggs one at a time and beat well after each addition.
4) Stir in cooled melted chocolate.
5) Line a 9-by-5-by-3-inch loaf pan with a sheet of aluminum foil large enough to cover the top; leave ends draped over edges.
6) Arrange a single layer of vanilla wafers on the bottom of the pan.
7) Sprinkle generously with coffee mixture.
8) Spread the chocolate mixture generously over cookies.
9) Continue layering until all the chocolate mixture is used, ending with a cookie layer.
10) Fold foil over top.
11) Chill in refrigerator at least 12 hours.
12) To serve: open the foil and, using foil as handles, pull torte from pan. Invert on serving platter and remove foil.
13) Combine whipped cream and remaining Grand Marnier.
14) Place cream in a pastry bag with a star tip and decorate top and sides as desired. Or, spread cream over cake with a spatula.

preparation time (excluding chilling period): 1 hour
yield: 10 to 12 portions

Special Note
- Torte will keep in refrigerator or freezer. If frozen, let stand at room temperature 30 minutes before slicing.

Honey Nut Torte

3	egg yolks
1½	cups sugar
1	tsp vanilla extract
1	cup zweiback crumbs
¼	tsp salt
1	Tb baking powder
½	tsp ground cinnamon
2	cups chopped walnuts
3	egg whites, at room temperature
⅓	cup honey
1½	cups water
½	cup heavy cream, whipped

✳The former KEYS, Indianapolis, Indiana

Instructions

1) Preheat oven to 350 degrees.
2) In a medium bowl, beat egg yolks with ½ cup of the sugar until light.
3) Stir in vanilla.
4) In a small bowl, combine zweiback crumbs with salt, baking powder, cinnamon and 1 cup of the nuts; blend well.
5) Stir into egg mixture.
6) In a medium bowl, beat egg whites until stiff peaks form.
7) To aerate, use a wooden spoon to stir half the egg whites into crumb mixture.
8) Gently fold in remaining egg whites with a spatula.
9) Pour into a well-buttered 3-quart shallow baking dish; bake in the preheated oven for 25 to 30 minutes, or until golden brown.
10) Meanwhile, combine remaining 1 cup sugar, honey and water in a 2-quart saucepan and let boil gently for 30 minutes.
11) Pour hot honey syrup over hot torte while still in pan and sprinkle remaining nuts over top.
12) Let cool before slicing, allowing all the syrup to be absorbed by torte. Cut into 8 3-inch squares. Serve with whipped cream.

preparation time: 1 hour
yield: 6 to 8 portions

Special Notes
- Torte squares, covered, keep for several weeks at room temperature; refrigerate in warm weather.
- Torte freezes for 2 to 3 months.

Venetian Creme Torte

Ingredients

9-by-5-by-3 inch loaf pan

CAKE

1½	cups sifted cake flour
6	Tbs cocoa
½	tsp baking soda
⅛	tsp salt
6	Tbs butter, softened
1¼	cups granulated sugar
2	eggs
¾	cup buttermilk
1	tsp vanilla extract

ICING

2½	Tbs flour
2½	Tbs granulated sugar
¼	tsp salt
⅔	cup milk
⅓	cup heavy cream
⅓	cup butter, softened
½	cup sifted confectioners' sugar
¼	tsp vanilla extract
¼	cup slivered, toasted almonds

9-inch cake

CAKE

2	cups sifted cake flour
½	cup unsweetened cocoa
½	tsp baking soda
	pinch of salt
8	Tbs (1 stick) butter, softened
1⅔	cups granulated sugar
3	eggs
1	cup buttermilk
1	tsp vanilla extract

ICING

⅓	cup flour
⅓	cup granulated sugar
½	tsp salt
1¼	cups milk
⅔	cup heavy cream
⅔	cup butter, softened
1	cup sifted confectioners' sugar
¾	tsp vanilla extract
½	cup slivered, toasted almonds

WOODBINE COTTAGE, River Road at the Harbor, Sunapee, New Hampshire

Instructions

1) Preheat oven to 350 degrees.
2) Sift together flour, cocoa, baking soda and salt onto a sheet of wax paper.
3) Cream butter in a medium bowl until smooth.
4) Gradually add granulated sugar and beat until fluffy.
5) Add eggs one at a time, beating well after each addition.
6) Add dry ingredients alternately with buttermilk, beating well until smooth.
7) Stir in vanilla.
8) Pour batter into ▲ *1 greased and floured 9-by-5-by-3-inch loaf pan,* ■ *2 greased and floured 9-inch cake pans.*
9) Bake in the preheated oven until cake tester inserted in center comes out clean, ▲ *60 to 70 minutes,* ■ *30 minutes.*
10) Cool in pans on racks 10 minutes. Remove from pans and cool completely.
11) Using a long thin bread knife, slice ▲ loaf into 4 layers, ■ each cake into 2 thin layers.
12) To prepare icing while cake is baking: combine flour, granulated sugar and salt in a ▲ *1-quart saucepan;* ■ 2-quart saucepan.
13) Gradually stir in milk, using a wire whisk to blend mixture until smooth.
14) Stir in cream.
15) Cook over low heat, stirring constantly, until mixture thickens and boils.
16) Boil for 1 minute.
17) Pour into a medium bowl and chill in refrigerator until cool, about 1 hour.
18) In a medium bowl beat butter until smooth.
19) Gradually add confectioners' sugar, beating until smooth and fluffy.
20) If lumps have formed in cream mixture while cooling, beat vigorously with a wire whisk to smooth.
21) Add cream mixture to butter mixture, beating until icing is smooth and fluffy. Stir in vanilla.
22) Spread icing between the cake layers; arrange the layers on top of each other to reform as one cake. Frost top and sides.
23) Sprinkle top with toasted almonds. Serve thin slices.

preparation time: ▲ 2½ hours; ■ 2½ hours
yield: ▲ 8 to 10 portions; ■ 12 to 16 portions

Special Note
• This cake's flavor is at its peak when served freshly made or straight from the freezer. Therefore, store it in the freezer, covered, rather than in the refrigerator.

Bourbon Cookies

Ingredients

2 cups vanilla wafer crumbs (6½-oz package)
1½ cups confectioners' sugar
1½ cups chopped walnuts
2 Tbs unsweetened cocoa
⅓ cup light corn syrup
3 Tbs bourbon whiskey
6 Tbs confectioners' sugar

medium

�֍ BALSAM EMBERS, 2350 Foothill Drive, Salt Lake City, Utah

Instructions

1) In a medium bowl combine wafer crumbs, 1½ cups confectioners' sugar, walnuts and cocoa; blend well.
2) Add corn syrup and bourbon; stir mixture with a rubber spatula or work with your hands until mixture is blended.
3) Chill in refrigerator 30 minutes.
4) Roll mixture into 1-inch balls.
5) Roll the cookies in the remaining sugar, adding more if necessary, to coat them well.
6) Refrigerate.

preparation time (including 30-minute chilling):   1 hour
yield: 3 dozen cookies

Special Notes
- Cookies are also good rolled in either flaked coconut or chopped walnuts instead of the confectioners' sugar:
  - ⅔   cup flaked coconut for 3 dozen
  - 1   cup finely chopped nuts for 3 dozen
- You can store these cookies in the refrigerator for weeks.
- You will find that as the cookies stand for 1 or 2 days, in or out of the refrigerator, the flavor improves.
- This recipe can be doubled successfully.

Nut Crisps

½   lb unsalted butter, softened
½   cup confectioners' sugar
2   cups sifted flour
2   tsps vanilla extract
    pinch of salt
2   cups chopped toasted almonds
    confectioners' sugar

medium

large

1   lb unsalted butter, softened
1   cup confectioners' sugar
4   cups sifted flour
4   tsps vanilla extract
½   tsp salt
4   cups chopped toasted almonds
    confectioners' sugar

❄ KEN'S STEAK HOUSE, 95 Worcester Road, Framingham, Massachusetts

Instructions

1) Preheat oven to 350 degrees.
2) Beat butter until creamy in a ▲ *medium bowl,* ■ *large bowl.*
3) Gradually add sugar and beat until fluffy.
4) Add flour, vanilla and salt; blend well.
5) Stir in almonds.
6) Shape mixture into logs 1½ inches long and about ½ inch thick and place on greased cookie sheets, 1½ inches apart.
7) Bake in the preheated oven 10 to 15 minutes or until lightly brown.
8) Carefully remove from cookie sheets and cool on wire racks. ⬚S
9) Sprinkle cookies with confectioners' sugar.

preparation time: ▲ 1 hour; ■ 1½ hours
yield: ▲ 50 cookies; ■ 100 cookies

Special Notes
- To toast almonds, spread them in a single layer on a jelly roll pan and bake in a preheated 350-degree oven, stirring occasionally, for 10 minutes, or until lightly browned.
- Cookies can be stored at room temperature for two weeks.
- Frozen cookies will keep 3 to 4 months. In stacking, separate layers with wax paper. After thawing, sprinkle with confectioners' sugar.

MISCELLANEOUS

Meat Sauce

Ingredients

1 medium onion, quartered
¼ lb mushrooms, sliced
3 medium garlic cloves, halved
1 lb ground lean beef
¼ lb ground lean veal
¼ tsp dried sage
¼ tsp dried oregano
1 Tb + ½ tsp salt
½ tsp coarsely ground black pepper
4 cups canned plum tomatoes (35-oz can), including liquid
1 cup canned tomato puree
½ cup tomato paste

medium

2 medium onions, quartered
½ lb mushrooms, sliced
5 large garlic cloves, halved
2 lbs ground lean beef
½ lb ground lean veal
½ tsp dried sage
½ tsp dried oregano
2 Tbs + 1 tsp salt
1 tsp coarsely ground black pepper
8 cups canned plum tomatoes (2 35-oz cans), including liquid
2 cups canned tomato puree
1 cup tomato paste

Instructions

1) Preheat oven to 350 degrees.
2) Grind onion, mushrooms and garlic in a meat grinder, using the finest blade. Reserve.
3) Mix beef and veal together in a ▲ *medium bowl,* ■ *large bowl.*
4) Spread meat on jelly-roll pan or other shallow ovenproof dish; cook in the preheated oven for 15 minutes.
5) Stir meat mixture to break up pieces and cook 5 minutes longer.
6) Meanwhile, in a 1-quart saucepan, combine sage, oregano, salt, pepper, ground onion, mushrooms and garlic. Cook over moderate heat until mixture is heated through.
7) Spread seasoning mixture over meat and cook 15 minutes longer in the oven.
8) Remove meat from the oven and transfer to a ▲ *4-quart Dutch oven,* ■ *8-quart Dutch oven.*
9) Add tomatoes, tomato puree and tomato paste. Blend well; over moderate heat bring mixture to a boil.
10) Reduce heat to low and simmer, partially covered, for ▲ *1¼ hours,* ■ *1½ hours.*
11) Taste for seasoning and adjust if necessary. Use wherever a spaghetti or tomato-meat sauce is called for.

preparation time: ▲ 2 hours; ■ 2½ hours
yield: ▲ 6 cups; ■ 12 cups

Special Notes
- Meat sauce can be stored in refrigerator for 1 week or frozen for 2 to 3 months.
- This sauce is the base for a special first course at Sardi's: Hot Shrimp à la Sardi. For each portion arrange 6 medium cooked shrimp in an individual au gratin dish. Remove crust from 1 slice of bread, and cut in half diagonally to make triangles. Fry bread in 1 tablespoon butter and ⅛ teaspoon minced garlic until golden on both sides. Reserve. Mix ½ cup of Sardi's meat sauce and 2 tablespoons to ¼ cup dry white wine, depending on your taste, together in a small saucepan. Cook over moderate heat until heated through. Stir in ¼ of a garlic clove, minced. Pour sauce over shrimp. Arrange the 2 triangles like butterfly wings in center of dish. Bake in a preheated 400-degree oven 10 minutes or until sauce is bubbly. Serve immediately.

Gran Fettucine Emilio

Ingredients

2-3

MEAT SAUCE

1	Tb butter
1	Tb olive oil
1	small onion, finely chopped
1	small carrot, finely chopped
1	small celery stalk, finely chopped
¼	lb ground lean beef
2	ozs ground lean pork
⅛	tsp freshly ground black pepper
½	cup tomato sauce
¾	cup dry white wine
½	cup beef broth
3	ozs prosciutto, sliced ⅛ inch thick
¼	lb mushrooms, sliced

BÉCHAMEL SAUCE

4	Tbs butter
¼	cup flour
2	cups milk
¼	tsp freshly ground black pepper
¼	tsp ground nutmeg

PASTA

8–12	ozs fettucine or other broad egg noodles
6	Tbs freshly grated Parmesan cheese
⅛	tsp freshly ground black pepper

MEAT SAUCE

2	Tbs butter
2	Tbs olive oil
1	medium onion, finely chopped
1	large carrot, finely chopped
1	large celery stalk, finely chopped
¾	lb ground lean beef
¼	lb ground lean pork
¼	tsp freshly ground black pepper
1	cup tomato sauce
1½	cups dry white wine
1¼	cups beef broth
6	ozs prosciutto, sliced ⅛ inch thick
½	lb mushrooms, sliced

BÉCHAMEL SAUCE

8	Tbs (1 stick) butter
½	cup flour
1	qt milk
½	tsp freshly ground black pepper
½	tsp ground nutmeg

6

PASTA

1½	lbs fettucine or other broad egg noodles
¾	cup freshly grated Parmesan cheese
¼	tsp freshly ground black pepper

❋ TOSI'S, 4337 Ridge Road, Stevensville, Michigan

Instructions

1) To make meat sauce: heat butter and oil in a ● *2-quart saucepan,* ▲ *4-quart Dutch oven.*
2) Add onion, carrot and celery; cook until tender.
3) Add meats. While cooking, break up meat with a fork; cook until brown.
4) Drain off fat.
5) Stir in pepper, tomato sauce, ● *¼ cup white wine,* ▲ *½ cup white wine* and beef broth; simmer, covered, ● *30 minutes,* ▲ *1 hour.*
6) Trim fat from prosciutto and place fat in ● *an 8-inch skillet,* ▲ *a 10-inch skillet.*
7) Cook over low heat until fat is rendered. Remove and discard any brown pieces.
8) Add mushrooms to fat in skillet; cook until just colored, adding a little butter if necessary.
9) Cut prosciutto into julienne strips. Add prosciutto and remaining wine to skillet; simmer 5 minutes.
10) Stir prosciutto mixture into meat sauce.
11) To prepare béchamel sauce: melt butter over low heat in a ● *1-quart saucepan;* ▲ *2-quart saucepan.*
12) Blend in flour with a wire whisk; cook 1 minute.
13) Add milk gradually, stirring constantly.
14) Once blended, cook, stirring occasionally, until mixture thickens and comes to a boil. Remove from heat.
15) Add pepper and nutmeg.
16) Blend béchamel sauce into meat sauce with a wire whisk. S
17) Cook fettucine according to package directions; drain. Reheat sauce.
18) For each serving use ⅔ cup sauce and toss fettucine and sauce in a large bowl or tureen to coat well.
19) Sprinkle 2 tablespoons cheese and a little freshly ground pepper over each serving.

    preparation time: ● 1¼ hours; ▲ 2 hours
    yield: ● 1 quart sauce; ▲ 2 quarts sauce

Special Notes
- Sauce will keep in refrigerator for 1 week; in the freezer, 2 to 3 months.
- The yield of sauce on both sizes is larger than needed in order to provide an extra quantity for freezing.

Orange Marmalade

Ingredients

2 cups coarsely ground orange peel (the whole skin from about 8 oranges)
2 cups coarsely ground canned, pitted apricots (1-lb-14-oz can plus 8-oz can), drained
4 cups sugar

※ PAUL SHANK'S GRACIOUS DINING at the SAFARI HOTEL, 4611 North Scottsdale Road, Scottsdale, Arizona

Instructions

1) Fill 8-quart Dutch oven with water and bring to a boil.
2) Add orange peel and boil 3 minutes. Drain.
3) Repeat steps 1 and 2 twice, discarding water after each blanching.
4) In the 8-quart Dutch oven combine orange peel, apricots and sugar.
5) Let mixture simmer slowly over low heat, stirring frequently, for 1½ to 2 hours or until mixture is thick. (It should drop in a thick sheet off a spoon.)
6) Pour into hot sterilized jars and seal.

preparation time: 3½ hours
yield: 4½ cups

Special Notes
• To avoid burning sugar, which is easy to do, make sure you stir frequently.
• You can double the recipe, but allow longer cooking time.

Café Brûlot

Ingredients

peel of 1 orange, cut in slivers
peel of ½ lemon, cut in slivers
1 cinnamon stick
4 whole cloves
5 ½-inch sugar cubes
1 oz curaçao
2 ozs Cognac
¾ cup strong coffee

peel of 2 oranges, cut in slivers
peel of 1 lemon, cut in slivers
2 cinnamon sticks
8 whole cloves
10 ½-inch sugar cubes
¼ cup curaçao
½ cup Cognac
2½ cups strong coffee

6

peel of 8 oranges, cut in slivers
peel of 4 lemons, cut in slivers
4 medium cinnamon sticks
1 tsp whole cloves
45 ½-inch sugar cubes
1 cup curaçao
2 cups Cognac
10 cups strong coffee

❄ CARIBBEAN ROOM at the PONTCHARTRAIN HOTEL, 2031 St. Charles Avenue, New Orleans, Louisiana

Instructions

1) Combine orange and lemon peel, cinnamon sticks, cloves and sugar cubes in a ● *chafing dish or 8-inch skillet,* ▲ *12-inch skillet,* ■ *6-quart Dutch oven.*

2) With the back of a ladle, crush cinnamon sticks, cloves and sugar cubes.

3) Add curaçao; heat until sugar is dissolved.

4) Add Cognac and warm slightly.

5) Ignite and let flame burn out.

6) Add coffee and heat thoroughly, but do not allow to boil. Serve in demitasse cups.

   preparation time: ● 20 minutes; ▲ 30 minutes; ■ 45 minutes
   yield: ● ¾ cup; ▲ 3 cups; ■ 12 cups

Special Note
● Café Brûlot keeps in the refrigerator 2 to 3 days. Reheat over low heat or in the top of double boiler over simmering water—do not let coffee boil.

Hot Buttered Rum

Ingredients

2-3

4	Tbs butter, softened
½	cup dark brown sugar, firmly packed
3	Tbs honey
1½	tsps rum extract
¾	tsp ground nutmeg
¼	tsp ground cinnamon
⅛	tsp ground cloves
	hot water
6–9	Tbs dark rum

8	Tbs (1 stick) butter, softened
1	cup dark brown sugar, firmly packed
6	Tbs honey
1	Tb rum extract
1½	tsps ground nutmeg
½	tsp ground cinnamon
¼	tsp ground cloves
	hot water
1	cup + 2 Tbs dark rum

6

24

2	cups (4 sticks) butter, softened
4	cups dark brown sugar, firmly packed
1½	cups honey
¼	cup (2 ozs) rum extract
2	Tbs ground nutmeg
2	tsps ground cinnamon
1	tsp ground cloves
	hot water
4½	cups dark rum

❄ THE VILLAGE GREEN RESORT MOTOR HOTEL, Interstate 5, at Cottage Grove, Oregon

❄The Village Green Resort Motor Hotel

Instructions

1) Cream butter until smooth in a ● *small bowl,* ▲ *medium bowl,* ■ *large bowl.*
2) Gradually beat in brown sugar; continue beating until fluffy.
3) Add honey, rum extract, nutmeg, cinnamon and cloves; beat until blended. ⒮
4) For each serving, place ¼ cup rum-butter mixture in a 12-ounce mug.
5) Stir in ¼ cup hot water; blend well.
6) Add 3 tablespoons dark rum and fill the mug with hot water.

preparation time: ● 20 minutes; ▲ 30 minutes; ■ 45 minutes
yield: ● ¾ cup rum butter, enough for 3 12-ounce drinks
　　　　▲ 1½ cups rum butter, enough for 6 12-ounce drinks
　　　　■ 6 cups rum butter, enough for 24 12-ounce drinks

Special Note
● Rum butter can be made ahead and stored in refrigerator for 2 weeks or frozen for 3 months.

Index of Restaurants By State

Index of Restaurants By State

333

Name of City	Name of State	Name of Restaurant	
	Philadelphia	Lickety Split	50
	Philadelphia	Middle East Restaurant	6
	Point Pleasant	Mountainside Inn	164
Rhode Island	Warwick	Great House Restaurant	300
Tennessee	Cleveland	Old Fort Inn	240
	Memphis	Dobbs Houses Luau	28, 98
Texas	Beaumont	Beaumont Country Club	72
	Dallas	Bakers Dozen at the Baker Hotel	174
	Dallas	Mario's	42
	Dallas	Zodiac Room Restaurant at Neiman-Marcus	124, 212
	Houston	Maxim's	276
Utah	Salt Lake City	Balsam Embers	314
Vermont	Chester	Chester Inn	66
Virginia	McLean	Evans Farm Inn	70
	Williamsburg	Williamsburg Lodge	282
	Woodbridge	Lazy Susan Inn	288
Washington	Seattle	Canlis' Restaurant	216
West Virginia	Beverly	Faraway Hills Country Inn	112
Wisconsin	Green Lake	The Heidel House	244
	Milwaukee	Frenchy's Restaurant	118
	Milwaukee	Karl Ratzsch's	122
	Oshkosh	Bellevue Restaurant at the Pioneer Inn	148, 200
Washington, D.C.		La Grande Seine at the John F. Kennedy Center for the Performing Arts	62

Index

Index